MCSE Lab Manual for Microsoft® Windows® XP Professional

Stanley Reimer and Martin Keding

COURSE
TECHNOLOGY
———————✳———————™
THOMSON LEARNING

Australia • Canada • Mexico • Singapore • Spain • United Kingdom • United States

COURSE TECHNOLOGY
™
THOMSON LEARNING

MCSE Lab Manual for Microsoft® Windows® XP Professional

by Stanley Reimer and Martin Keding

Managing Editor:
Stephen Solomon

Product Manager:
Charles Blum

Technical Editors:
Mike McClymont
Conan Kezema

Developmental Editor:
Moirag Haddad

Production Editor:
Elena Montillo

Quality Assurance Manager:
John Bosco

Associate Product Manager:
Tim Gleeson

Editorial Assistant:
Nick Lombardi

Marketing Manager:
Toby Shelton

Text Designer:
GEX Publishing Services

Compositor:
GEX Publishing Services

Cover Design:
Efrat Reis

TABLE OF
Contents

Introduction

The objective of this lab manual is to assist you in preparing for the Microsoft Certification Exam #70-270: Installing, Configuring, and Administering Microsoft Windows XP Professional by applying the Windows XP Professional exam objectives to relevant lab activities. This text is designed to be used in conjunction with MCSE Guide to Microsoft Windows XP Professional (0-619-12031-2); however, it also can be used to supplement any MCSE courseware. Although this manual is written with the intent of it being used in a classroom lab environment, it also may be used for self-study on a home network.

Features

In order to ensure a successful experience for instructors and students alike, this book includes the following features:

- **Microsoft Windows XP Professional MCSE Certification objectives** — For each chapter, the relevant objectives from MCSE Exam #70-270 are listed.
- **Lab Objectives** — Every lab has a brief description and list of learning objectives.
- **Completion Times** — Every lab has an estimated completion time so that you can plan your activities accurately.
- **Activity Sections** — Labs are presented in manageable sections.
- **Step-by-step instructions** — Students are given clear directions to promote technical proficiency.
- **Review questions** — Concepts presented in each lab are reinforced through review activity.

Hardware Requirements
- Pentium 233 MHz CPU or higher
- 128 MB of RAM
- 4 GB hard disk
- CD-ROM drive
- Network interface card connected to a cable system
- Modem (optional)
- Printer (optional)

Network Requirements

- A network configured in a workgroup environment
- At least one other computer configured with Windows XP Professional
- A network cross-over cable or a separate network hub for every two computers
- Optionally, for home use, a Small Office Home Office (SOHO) kit consisting of two Ethernet cards, an Ethernet hub or switch, and category 5 data cables
- Access to the Internet (optional but preferred)

Software/Setup Requirements

- Access to a Windows XP Professional CD
- Access to a Windows XP Professional Resource kit CD
- Windows 98 installed on a primary partition with at least 1.5 GB of storage space
- Windows XP Professional installed on an extended partition with at least 1.5 GB of storage space
- One blank floppy disk

A First Look at Windows XP Professional

Labs included in this chapter

➤ System Configuration for Labs

➤ Lab 1.1 Making a Windows XP Proposal

➤ Lab 1.2 Documenting a Windows XP System

➤ Lab 1.3 Working with Virtual Memory

➤ Lab 1.4 Monitoring Application and System Performance

➤ Lab 1.5 Using Event Viewer

➤ Lab 1.6 Documenting Your Windows XP Network Configuration

Microsoft MCSE Exam #70-270 Objectives	
Objective	Lab
Perform an attended installation of Windows XP Professional	1.1
Configure and troubleshoot desktop settings	1.2
Optimize and troubleshoot the following performance of the Windows XP Professional desktop:	
Memory performance	1.2, 1.3, 1.4
Processor utilization	1.4
Application performance	1.4, 1.5
Network performance	1.6
Configure and troubleshoot the TCP/IP protocol	1.6

 Student Answer Sheets to accompany the labs in this chapter are available for downloading from the Online Companion for this manual at *www.course.com*.

SYSTEM CONFIGURATION FOR LABS

Objective

As with all previous versions of Windows, there are usually two or three ways of accomplishing any single task with Windows XP Professional. For example, users can access the My Computer window by clicking **Start**, **My Computer**, or by typing **Windows Logo Key**, **E**. Windows XP Professional extends this concept by enabling users to customize the desktop and the Start menu to their preference. The following procedures will customize the Start menu and desktop to match the lab procedures.

Estimated completion time: **5 minutes**

ACTIVITY

1. Customize the Start Menu
   a. Right-click on an unused portion of the taskbar, and click **Properties** to display the Taskbar and Start Menu window.
   b. Click the **Start Menu** tab, and ensure the Start Menu option, is selected.
   c. Click **Customize** to the right of the Start menu option, and click the **Advanced** tab.
   d. Scroll through the Start menu items, and ensure that the **Run command** is selected.
   e. Scroll to System Administrative Tools, and click **Display on All Programs and the Start Menu.** This will provide quicker access to the Administrative Tools window.
   f. Click **OK** twice to return to the Windows Desktop.

2. Customize the Control Panel.
   a. Click **Start**, **Control Panel** to display the Control Panel window.
   b. Click **Switch to Classic View** under the Control Panel tasks. Note: You should become familiar with the Catalog View of the Control Panel. Changing to Classic View eliminates one extra layer of menus, making it easier to move around the control panel.
   c. Close Control Panel.

3. Optional Settings – Customize Desktop
   a. Right-click anywhere on the desktop, and click **Properties** to display the Display Properties window.
   b. Click the **Desktop** tab, and then click **Customize Desktop.**
   c. Click **My Computer** and **My Network Places** under Desktop Icons to place these icons on your desktop.
   d. Click **OK** twice to return to the Windows Desktop.

LAB 1.1 MAKING A WINDOWS XP PROPOSAL

Objective

The Animal Care Center is a veterinary clinic owned by Dennis Geisler that specializes in health-care services and products for small and large animals. In addition to Dennis, there are another veterinarian, an assistant, and three clerks. They have a small store and clinic that contains four Windows-based computers and a Novell NetWare 3.11 server networked to a 10-Megabit Ethernet hub. The Novell NetWare 3.11 server performs file and print services for the other computers. Two Windows 95 computers located at the main counter are used to process customer calls and checkouts. Two computers running Windows for Workgroups 3.11 are located in the veterinarians' offices. In addition to word-processing and spreadsheet software, all computers currently run a Windows 16-bit veterinary program for customer billing, inventory, and pet-treatment tracking. Dennis recently asked Computer Technology Services to provide him with information about the benefits and costs of Windows XP Professional. He wants to replace the Windows for Workgroups computer in his office with a fast Windows XP Professional computer that could act as a file and print server for the other computers. His plan is to replace the NetWare server after moving the files and programs to the new Windows XP system. He is also considering the purchase and installation of a new network-attached printer to replace the printer attached to the NetWare file server. After completing this lab, you will be able to:

➤ Identify Windows XP features and benefits

➤ Identify the hardware requirements for installing Windows XP Professional

➤ Use the HCL to determine hardware compatibility

➤ Identify the Windows XP network protocol options

➤ Identify the clients supported by Windows XP Professional

Estimated completion time: **30–60 minutes**

ACTIVITY

1. CTS wants you to write a proposal for Dennis that identifies the following features. Record your answers on the Lab 1.1 Student Answer Sheet.

    a. Windows XP features that would support a high-speed computer running Windows XP in his office. What type of system would you recommend for Dennis's office server?

    b. Windows XP features that would provide reliability by preventing a program from crashing the server.

    c. Windows XP security features that would help prevent an unauthorized user from gaining access to files and programs stored on the Windows XP computer.

2. In order to act as the file and print server, the computer in Dennis's office must be fast and reliable. On the Student Answer Sheet, identify the hardware requirements for such a computer.

3. Dennis needs to be able to share files and a printer with both Windows 95 and Windows 3.x computers. On the Student Answer Sheet, identify which client computer operating systems can be used to access data and printers on the Windows XP computer.

4. Dennis is concerned about his ability to run the veterinary software on the Windows XP computer in his office. On the Student Answer Sheet, discuss Windows XP support for 16-bit and 32-bit applications.

5. The Windows XP computer will need to communicate with the Windows 3.x and Windows 95 computers. In addition, Dennis has files on his Novell NetWare server that will need to be copied to the Windows XP computer. He also wants to obtain a network-attached printer to replace the one currently on the main counter. On the Student Answer Sheet, identify the communication protocols that Windows XP supports, along with which protocols you recommend to provide the connectivity necessary to communicate with the Novell server, the network-attached printer, and the Windows computers.

6. Dennis currently has some equipment that he would like to use with his Windows XP computer. Use the Windows XP Hardware Compatibility List (HCL) to see if the following components are compatible with Windows XP. On your Student Answer Sheet, identify the path leading to the HCL on the Microsoft Web site. Record the results of your search for each of the following components:

➤ Adaptec 1520A SCSI controller

➤ Lexmark Optra R Plus series printer

➤ NetGear FA310TX Fast Ethernet adapter

LAB 1.2 DOCUMENTING A WINDOWS XP SYSTEM

Objective

A month before you started working at Computer Technology Services, one of the employees at your company replaced all five of the Windows 95-based computers at the Melendres and Associates law firm with Windows XP Professional systems. Currently these computers are attached to a peer-to-peer network and are used to enter and access client case information. Although all of these computers are supposed to be the same, the legal assistants report that one of the system's performance is slower than the others. You have been asked to examine the settings on these computers to help determine what might be different. In Labs 1.2 through 1.5, you use Windows XP features and utilities to determine system configuration settings that could affect the performance of a computer system. After completing this lab, you will be able to:

➤ Access the Computer Management console

➤ Use the Computer Management console to record system hardware configuration information, including processor type and speed, amount of RAM, and video settings on your computer

➤ Use Device Manager to check for any device configuration errors

➤ Use the Disk Management tool to document drive capacity and format

Estimated completion time: **10 minutes**

ACTIVITY

1. Start your Windows XP computer, and log on as Administrator.

2. Click **Start**, **Run** to display the Run Window.

3. Type **msinfo32.exe**, and click **OK** to run the **System Information** program. The interface is shown in Figure 1-1.

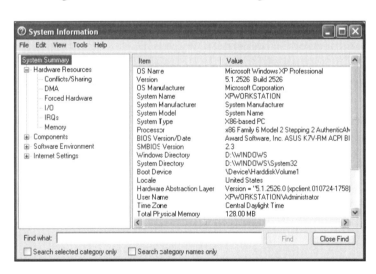

Figure 1-1   Accessing System Information in Windows XP

4. Using the **System Summary** on the results pane, record the system processor information on the Lab 1.2 Student Answer Sheet.

5. Expand the **Components** container in the tree pane.

6. Click **Display**, and, on your Student Answer Sheet, record the video system information shown in the results pane.

7. Expand the **Storage** container in the tree pane.

8. Click **Drives**, and then click **Disks**, and, on your Student Answer Sheet, record the required disk drive information shown in the results pane.

9. Click **CD-ROM**, and, on your Student Answer Sheet, record the required CD information from the results pane.

10. Click **Problem Devices** in the tree pane. Identify any problem devices, and record the message on the Student Answer Sheet.

LAB 1.3 WORKING WITH VIRTUAL MEMORY

Objective

Windows XP uses virtual memory to store and access software and data that would not otherwise fit in RAM. Virtual memory works by paging less frequently used information from RAM to a paging file on disk. The location and size of the paging file can affect the system performance. Therefore, when a system does not seem to be performing well, the performance can sometimes be improved by increasing the size of the paging file, or by relocating the paging file to a separate disk drive. After completing this lab, you will be able to:

➤ Use the System program from Control Panel to check system processing priority and record the size and location of page file

➤ Use Performance Monitor to view the number of page file accesses occurring every second

➤ Use Task Monitor to monitor processor performance

Estimated completion time: **10 minutes**

ACTIVITY

1. Click **Start**, **Control Panel**, and then double-click **System** to display the System Properties window.

2. Click the **Advanced** tab, and then click the **Settings** button in the Performance Section. Click the **Advanced** tab, and record the total page size on the Lab 1.3 Student Answer Sheet.

3. Click the **Change** button, and record the page file information for each drive.

4. Click **Cancel** three times, and close the Control Panel to return to the Windows desktop.

5. To record pages per second, you need to run the Performance Monitor utility, and select the pages/sec counter as described below:

   a. Click **Start**, **Administrative Tools**, **Performance** to display a Performance monitor window. The interface is shown in Figure 1-2.

   b. Ensure that the memory **Pages/Second** counter in the results pane is selected by clicking on it.

   c. Observe the graph, and note the yellow line illustrating the number of pages/second.

   d. Highlight the counter by clicking the **Light Bulb** on the toolbar.

   e. On the Student Answer Sheet, record the current maximum number of pages per second.

   f. Start **WordPad** (**Start**, **All Programs**, **Accessories**, **WordPad**).

   g. On the Student Answer Sheet, record the pages per second for loading WordPad. Leave WordPad open.

   h. Start **Notepad** (**Start**, **All Programs**, **Accessories**, **Notepad**), and, on the Student Answer Sheet, record the pages per second. Note that as more programs are loaded into memory, the pages per second increases.

   i. Close WordPad and Notepad.

   j. To end the Performance monitor, click **Exit** from the Console menu.

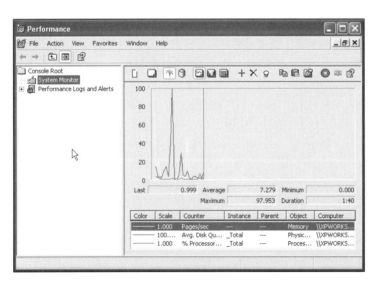

Figure 1-2 Viewing System Monitor

LAB **1.4** MONITORING APPLICATION AND SYSTEM PERFORMANCE

Objective

Application and system software running on a computer can affect the performance of the system. Windows XP Professional includes task and performance monitor tools that you can use to view applications and tasks currently in memory, and the processor usage percentage. After completing this lab, you will be able to:

➤ Use the System option from Control Panel to determine application priority settings

➤ Use Task Manager to determine what applications are loaded and how much memory and processor time they use

➤ Use Task Manager to track processor usage by the kernel and by applications

➤ Use Task Manager to unload applications

Estimated completion time: **15–20 minutes**

ACTIVITY 1

Windows XP can be configured to provide priority to either applications or background server tasks. Configuring the system for background tasks provides better performance for processing requests from client computers. However, this configuration slows down applications running on the system, and could also be the reason the computer seems to be running slower. Follow the steps below to document the performance settings on your computer.

1. Click **Start**, **Control Panel**, and double-click **System** to open the System Properties window.

2. Click the **Advanced** tab, the **Settings** button under the Performance section, and then the **Advanced** tab to display the Performance Options settings.

3. Record the Performance Options setting on the Lab 1.4 Student Answer Sheet.

4. Click **Cancel** twice to close all windows and return to the desktop.

ACTIVITY 2

Windows XP Professional can support up to two processors using Symmetric Multiprocessing (SMP). Knowing the performance of your processor is useful to help you determine whether adding a second processor is necessary. Follow the steps below to use the Task Manager to determine processor utilization time for running applications.

1. To determine what applications are automatically loading, click the **Start** menu, click **Turn Off Computer**, and then select the **Restart** option.

2. After the system restarts, log on using your assigned username and password.

3. Right-click over the taskbar to display the taskbar window.

4. Click **Task Manager** to display the Task Manager window shown in Figure 1-3.

Figure 1-3 Viewing the Applications tab in Task Manager

5. Click the **Applications** tab, if necessary, and, on the Lab 1.4 Student Answer Sheet, record any automatically loaded applications.

6. Click the **Processes** tab, and, on your Student Answer Sheet, record the three processes that use the most CPU time. (*Hint:* Click the CPU column to sort the processes by CPU time.)

7. Click the **Performance** tab to view the processor and memory usage graphs. To include the amount of processor time used by the Windows XP system kernel software, click the **View** menu, and then, if necessary, place a check mark in front of **Show Kernel Times** by clicking it. The amount of kernel time is shown in red on the graph. On your Student Answer Sheet, record the minimum and maximum CPU times, along with memory usage.

8. Start **Notepad**, and record the processor and memory utilization.

9. Start **WordPad**, and record the processor and memory utilization.

10. Click the **Applications** tab.

11. Click **Notepad**, and then click the **End Task** button to exit the application.

12. Click **WordPad**, and then click the **Switch To** button.

13. Enter some data in WordPad, and observe the processor utilization.

14. Save the document in a file named **Temp** in the My Documents folder on your C: drive.

15. Exit WordPad.

16. Switch to **Task Manager**, and use the **Performance** tab to view CPU usage history. Notice how kernel time increases in proportion to CPU usage. (The kernel time is shown in red.)

17. On your Student Answer Sheet, record the maximum kernel time and CPU usage.

18. Exit Task Manager.

ACTIVITY 3

The Performance Monitor tool you used in Lab 1.3 to track pages per second also can be used to obtain a more detailed view of processor time usage, as follows:

1. Use the procedure described in Step 5 of the Lab 1.3 Activity to start **Performance Monitor**.

2. Select the processor **% Processor Time** counter on the results pane.

3. Start **WordPad**, and record the maximum processor time utilization on the Lab 1.4 Student Answer Sheet.

4. Start **Task Manager**, and, on your Student Answer Sheet, record the maximum processor time utilization.

5. Exit WordPad and Task Manager.

6. Exit Performance Monitor, and close all windows.

LAB 1.5 USING EVENT VIEWER

Objective

Windows XP includes an Event Viewer utility that allows you to view any warnings and error messages issued by the operating system or application software. Warning and error messages may indicate failing or faulty components, or application configuration problems that could affect system performance. After completing this lab, you will be able to:

➤ Start Event Viewer from either the Computer Management console or from the Control Panel

➤ Use Event Viewer to view and record any system messages

➤ Use Event Viewer to view and record any application messages

Estimated completion time: **5–10 minutes**

ACTIVITY

1a. Start Event Viewer from the Control Panel.

    a. Click **Start**, **Control Panel**, and click **Administrative Tools** to open the Administrative Tools window.

    b. Double-click **Event Viewer**.

    c. On your Student Answer Sheet, record the three types of logs shown in the right console tree.

    d. Exit Event Viewer.

1b. Start Event Viewer from the Computer Management Console.

    a. Click **Start**, **Control Panel**, and click **Administrative Tools** to open the Administrative Tools window.

    b. Double-click **Computer Management**.

    c. Expand System Tools to see the Event Viewer object.

    d. Double-click **Event Viewer**.

2. Click **System** from the left console tree. The three types of messages that may be recorded in event logs are:

   ➤ *Informational* messages indicated by an "i" enclosed in a circle

   ➤ *Warning* messages indicated by an exclamation mark enclosed in a triangle

   ➤ *Error* messages indicated by an "x" enclosed in a red circle

3. From the System Log display, record any error messages on the Student Answer Sheet.

4. Double-click the most recent Informational message from the Browser, and record it on your Student Answer Sheet. (If you do not have any browser messages, record the first Informational message on the Student Answer Sheet.)

5. Click **Application** from the left console tree, and, on your Student Answer Sheet, record the most recent application message.

6. If auditing is enabled, the Security Log is used to record any events that you might be auditing, such as users logging on, or access attempts on secured files. Click the **Security** Log, and determine if there are any audit messages. If there are messages, record the most recent message on the Student Answer Sheet.

7. Exit the Computer Management console, and close all windows.

LAB 1.6 DOCUMENTING YOUR WINDOWS XP NETWORK CONFIGURATION

Objective

An important feature included with Windows XP is its ability to access the Internet and participate in a local area network as a member of either a domain or a workgroup. In order to access a local area network, a Windows XP computer needs a network interface card and appropriate driver, a network protocol, and identification information, including a unique computer name and membership in a domain or workgroup. A Windows XP domain requires the network to have one or more server computers running Windows XP Server and acting as domain controllers. After completing this lab, you will be able to:

> ➤ Determine if your computer is a member of a domain or workgroup

> ➤ Document your computer's name, along with its domain or workgroup name

> ➤ Determine your network card type and model

> ➤ Identify what protocol(s) are loaded

> ➤ Access information on another computer on the network

Estimated completion time: **10 minutes**

ACTIVITY

1. Identify your computer's name, along with your domain or workgroup membership.
   a. Click **Start**, **My Computer**, and then click **View System Information** under the System Tasks section to display the System Properties window.
   b. Click the **Computer Name** tab.
   c. Record your computer name and domain or workgroup membership on your Lab 1.6 Student Answer Sheet.
   d. Close all open windows.

2. Determine your network card type and model.
   a. Click **Start**, **My Computer**, **My Network Places**, and then click **View Network Connections** under the Network Tasks section to display the Network Connections window.
   b. Double-click **Local Area Connection** to display the Local Area Connection Status window.
   c. On your Student Answer Sheet, record the number of packets sent and received by your computer.

    d. Click the **Properties** button, and, on your Student Answer Sheet, record the network card type and protocol information.

    e. Click **Internet Protocol (TCP/IP)**, and then click the **Properties** button.

    f. Record your IP address information on your Student Answer Sheet.

    g. Click **Cancel** twice to return to the Local Area Connection Status window.

    h. Click **Close**.

    i. Close the Network Connections window.

3. Access computers in a workgroup.

    a. Click **Start**, **My Computer**, **My Network Places**, and then click **View Workgroup Computers** under Network Tasks.

    b. Click the **down-arrow** of the Address bar (near top of window) to display a list of available resources.

    c. Click **Entire Network**, and then double-click **Microsoft Windows Network** in the results pane.

    d. On your Student Answer Sheet, record the workgroups.

    e. Double-click your workgroup.

    f. Double-click the computer named **Instructor** (or your own if no others are present).

    g. On your Student Answer Sheet, record any shared folders.

    h. Close all windows.

CHAPTER TWO

INSTALLING WINDOWS XP PROFESSIONAL

Labs included in this chapter

➤ Lab 2.1 Removing Windows XP Professional

➤ Lab 2.2 Performing an Attended Installation from CD-ROM

➤ Lab 2.3 Activating and Updating Windows XP

➤ Lab 2.4 Installing the Windows XP Professional Support Tools and Setup Manager Wizard

➤ Lab 2.5 Creating an Unattended Installation File

➤ Lab 2.6 Modifying Unattended Installation Files

➤ Lab 2.7 Performing an Unattended Installation

Microsoft MCSE Exam #70-270 Objectives	
Objective	Lab
Perform an attended installation of Windows XP Professional	2.2, 2.3
Create unattended answer files by using Setup Manager to automate installation of Windows XP Professional	2.4, 2.5
Configure Windows XP Professional for multiple locations	2.5
Perform an unattended installation of Windows XP Professional	2.5, 2.6, 2.7

Student Answer Sheets to accompany the labs in this chapter are available for downloading from the Online Companion for this manual at *www.course.com*.

LAB 2.1 REMOVING WINDOWS XP PROFESSIONAL

Objective

Prior to practicing the Windows XP Professional installation on your computer, you need to remove the existing Windows XP Professional. After completing this lab, you will be able to:

➤ Remove Windows XP Professional from a dual-booting computer

➤ Verify that Windows XP has been removed

Requirements

➤ Your computer meets the requirements specified in Chapter 1 of this book

➤ Windows 98 is installed on drive C:

➤ Your existing Windows XP is installed on logical drive D:

➤ You have access to a Windows XP Professional CD-ROM

➤ You have one blank floppy disk for Lab 2.1

➤ In order to perform the unattended installation lab (Lab 2.4), you should have at least 760 MB of free space on your Windows 98 partition

Estimated completion time: **30-45 minutes**

ACTIVITY

1. Create a Windows 98 startup disk as follows:
   a. Start your computer with Windows 98.
   b. To open the Control Panel, click **Start**, point to **Settings**, and click **Control Panel**.
   c. Double-click **Add/Remove Programs**.
   d. Click the **Startup Disk** tab.
   e. Insert a blank disk in the drive, and click the **Create Disk** button.
   f. Click **OK** when you receive the Insert Disk message.
   g. Specify the path to your Windows 98 CD-ROM or .cab files, and click **OK**.
   h. Click **OK** when you receive the Insert Disk message.
   i. After you've created the disk, click **OK** to close the Add/Remove Programs window.

2. Remove Windows XP hidden and system files as follows:
   a. Use Windows Explorer or My Computer to open a window to your C: drive.
   b. Display hidden file types and file extensions as follows:
      - From the **Tools** menu, click **Folder Options**.
      - Use the **View** tab to select the **Show all files** option.
      - To view file extensions, remove the check from the **Hide file extensions for known file types** option.
      - Click **OK** to return to the C: drive window.
   c. Remove the Read-only and Hidden attributes from the following files:
      - Boot.ini
      - Ntdetect.com
      - Ntldr
      - Bootsect.dos
   d. Delete the following Windows XP startup files:
      - Boot.ini
      - Ntdetect.com
      - Ntldr
      - Bootsect.dos

3. Close all windows, and restart your computer from the Windows 98 startup disk. If necessary, select the option to start without CD-ROM support.

4. After the computer has started from the Windows 98 startup disk, you will be presented with an A:> command prompt. To replace the Windows XP loader files with the Windows 98 system files, type **SYS C:**, and press **Enter**.

5. Remove the Windows 98 startup disk, and use the **Ctrl+Alt+Del** key combination to restart your computer. Verify that the computer now starts Windows 98 without displaying the Windows XP startup options.

6. Remove the Windows XP partition.
   a. Click **Start**, **Run**, and type **fdisk**. Click **OK**, and then press **Enter** twice to accept large disk support.
   b. At this point, your instructor will give you specific instructions for deleting the Windows XP partition. Use caution: deleting the wrong partition will render your system useless!

7. Reboot your system and log on.

LAB 2.2 PERFORMING AN ATTENDED INSTALLATION FROM CD-ROM

Objective

The Animal Care Center recently purchased a computer from your company, Computer Technology Services (CTS). Dennis wants to have the computer installed in his office with Windows XP Professional. The computer currently has Windows 98 on the C drive, which Dennis wants to keep on his system. After completing this lab, you will be able to:

➤ Perform a new installation of Windows XP from a CD-ROM

➤ Allow dual booting of Windows 98 and Windows XP Professional

Estimated completion time: **50–60 minutes**

ACTIVITY

Before beginning this activity, you need to work with your instructor to fill out the Lab 2.2 Installation Planning Worksheet that follows this lab. It is recommended that your computer have Windows 98 installed on drive C: and Windows XP installed in a separate logical drive.

1. If necessary, start your computer in Windows 98 and log on.

2. Insert the Windows XP Professional CD-ROM. If your system does not auto detect the CD, click **Start**, **Run**, and type **<CD-ROM drive>:\setup.exe**. Click **OK** to start the setup program.

3. Click **Install Windows XP** to start the Windows XP install wizard.

4. For Installation Type, select **New Installation (Advanced)**, and then click **Next** to display the license agreement window.

5. Click **I accept this agreement**, and then click **Next** to display Your Product Key window.

6. Enter the product key found on the back of your CD package, or the one provided by your instructor. Click **Next** to display the setup options window.

7. In order to install Windows XP on a partition other than the existing primary partition, click **Advanced Options**. Place a check mark in the **I want to choose the install drive letter and partition during setup** box, and then click **OK**.

8. Change the language and region setting as necessary, and then click Next.

9. If you do not have access to the Internet, click **No, skip this step and continue installing Windows**.

10. Click **Next** to start the preparation phase of the install wizard. Your computer will automatically reboot.

11. Perform the text-based phase of Windows XP installation.

   a. If this is an evaluation copy of Windows XP, you will be presented with a setup notification screen. Press **Enter** to continue the setup.

   b. On the Welcome to Setup screen, press **Enter**.

   c. You will now be prompted for the destination drive for your XP installation. Highlight the **Unpartitioned space** option in the partition selection screen, and type **C** for Create.

   d. Enter the size of the Windows XP partition, or press **Enter** to accept the size shown. Record the partition size on the Student Answer Sheet. The partition list screen is shown again with the New (Raw) partition.

   e. Highlight the **New (Raw)** partition to select this as your destination partition, and press **Enter**. You see a setup screen that gives you the choice of formatting the new partition as NTFS or FAT.

   f. Select the format specified on your Lab 2.2 Installation Planning Worksheet, and press **Enter**. Wait while setup formats your partition. After the formatting process is completed, the setup process creates a list of files to be copied and begins copying files to the newly formatted partition. This whole process may take several minutes, so if you're a multitasking kind of person, it's a good time to take a short break or do some reading. However, if there is a floppy disk in your computer, you should remove it before you leave. The computer automatically reboots after completing the text-mode portion of the installation.

12. Perform the graphical user interface (GUI) portion of Windows XP installation as follows:

   a. After rebooting, the GUI portion of the installation begins, and the installation program automatically installs devices detected on your computer.

   b. After the detected devices have been installed, the GUI setup process displays the Regional Settings window. Click the **Customize** button to see the options you have in controlling how the system formats numbers, currency, and dates.

   c. Click **Customize**, and record the options requested on the Lab 2.2 Student Answer Sheet.

   d. Select the following options:

      ■ On the Numbers tab, click the down arrow on the **Negative number format** box, and click **[1.1]** as the option.

      ■ On the Numbers tab, click the down arrow on the **Display leading zeros** box, and click **.7** as the option.

      ■ On the Date tab, click the down arrow on the **Short date format** box, and click **mm/dd/yyyy** as the option.

   e. Click **OK** twice to return to the Regional Settings window.

   f. Click the **Details** button to display the Text Services and Input Languages window.

g. Record the keyboard layouts on your Student Answer Sheet.

h. Click **Cancel** to return to the Regional Settings window.

i. Click **Next** to continue the installation with the Personalize your Software window.

j. Enter the user name, as well as the organization specified on the Lab 2.2 Installation Planning Worksheet.

k. Click **Next** to display the Computer Name and Administrator password window.

l. Enter the computer name you specified on the Lab 2.2 Installation Planning Worksheet, and type **password** for the administrator password. Type **password** again to confirm the password. (Remember that passwords are case-sensitive.)

m. Click **Next** to continue.

n. If the installation program detects a modem in your computer, the Modem Dialing Information window appears. If this happens, enter your area code, verify that Tone dialing is selected, and click **Next**.

o. The Date and Time Settings window should now be displayed.

p. If necessary, update the date and time, and select your correct time zone.

q. Verify that Automatically adjust clock for daylight saving time is checked, and click **Next** to configure the network settings.

r. If your instructor has specified static IP addresses, click the **Custom settings** button. (You can skip this step if DHCP automatic IP addressing is specified on the Lab 2.2 Installation Planning Worksheet instead of an IP address.)

  - Click **Internet Protocol (TCP/IP)**, and click the **Properties** button to display the Internet Protocol general properties tab.

  - Click the **Use the following IP address** option.

  - Enter the four octets of the IP address specified on the Lab 2.2 Installation Planning Worksheet, separated by periods.

  - Enter the four octets of the subnet mask specified on the Lab 2.2 Installation Planning Worksheet.

  - Click **OK** to return to the Networking Components window.

s. Click **Next** to display the Workgroup or Computer Domain window.

t. Verify that the computer is being installed in a workgroup and not a domain. Enter the workgroup name specified on your Lab 2.2 Installation Planning Worksheet, and click **Next** to install and configure the networking components.

u. Wait while the setup program copies the necessary files from your CD and performs final setup tasks. This will take a while, so it may be another good time to take a break or read.

v. Your system then automatically reboots.

2

13. Finalize the Windows XP installation as follows:

   a. After rebooting, XP may attempt to optimize your display setting. If a display setting message box opens, click **OK** to proceed. A test box will open with the new settings. If your display settings are correct, click **YES.** If there is a problem, click **NO** to use basic display settings. An animated Welcome to Windows XP window will open.

   b. Click **Next** to check Internet Connectivity. Ensure that Connect through a Network is selected, and click **Next** to display the Activate Windows window.

   c. Lab 2.3 demonstrates the Activation process, so click **No, remind me every few days**, and go to the Who will use this computer window.

   d. Add up to five users specified on the Lab 2.2 Installation Planning Worksheet. Note: Users added on this screen will be Computer Administrators with black passwords. Users can later be modified using the User Accounts applet. Click **Next.**

   e. The Thank You! Page appears. Click **Finish** to proceed to the Windows XP welcome screen. This screen displays a list of users created above. Click one of these names to log on.

14. Have your instructor verify your installation and sign off on the Lab 2.2 Student Answer Sheet.

   a. Verify the TCP/IP address as follows:

- Click **Start**, **My Computer**, **My Network Places**, **View Computer Connections**, and double-click **Local Area Connections**.
- Click **Properties**.
- Click **Internet Protocol (TCP/IP)**, and click the **Properties** button.
- Verify that the correct TCP/IP address and mask are entered.
- Click **Cancel** twice to return to the Local Area Connection Status window.
- Click **Close**, and then close the Network and Dial-up Connections window.

   b. Check the computer name and workgroup:

- Click **Start**, **My Computer**, and click **View System Information** under the System Tasks section.
- Click the **Computer Name** tab. Verify the computer and workgroup names.
- Click **Cancel**, and then close all windows.

   c. Remove the Windows XP Professional CD-ROM.

Lab 2.2 Installation Planning Worksheet

Name:
Computer ID:

Work with your instructor to identify the following installation information:

Computer name to be used for your installation:

User name: (example: your name)

Organization: (example: Animal Health Center)

Drive (partition) to contain Windows XP Professional:

Format:

NTFS
(Select this format if your computer already has a FAT partition on drive C:.Use quick format for the purpose of this lab.)

FAT
(Select this format if Windows XP is the only operating system; you will convert to NTFS later. Use quick format for the purpose of this lab.)

Product key:
(Enter the product key provided with your Windows XP CD-ROM.)

TCP/IP information:

IP address:

Subnet mask:

Workgroup name: (example: AHC)

LAB 2.3 ACTIVATING AND UPDATING WINDOWS XP

Objective

After Windows XP has been installed, the Activation procedure must be run within 30 days. Failure to do so renders XP inoperable except for the activation procedure. This lab will demonstrate the methods to use to activate Windows XP. Windows XP also has an enhanced Windows Update Tool to provide dynamic updates for users, as well as updates during the install process. You will be using this tool to download the latest updates to your computer, as well as creating a shared folder for the unattended install in Lab 2.7. After completing this lab, you will be able to:

➤ Activate Windows XP Professional

➤ Update Windows XP Professional

➤ Create a folder containing update information for later installs

Estimated completion time: **5–10 minutes**

ACTIVITY

Once Windows XP is activated, it cannot be reinstalled on another computer or changed in significant ways without deactivating or reactivating the product. You will be installing Windows XP a number of times throughout this course; therefore, it is important that you DO NOT complete the activation procedure. The procedures below will only demonstrate the activation procedure, not actually activate Windows XP.

1. If necessary, start your computer with Windows XP, and log on as the administrator.

2. Click **Start**, **All Programs**, **Accessories**, **Activate Windows** to display the Activate Windows window.

3. Click **Yes, let's activate Windows now over the Internet**, and click **Next** to display the Registration with Microsoft window.

4. Click **Yes, I want to register and activate Windows at the same time**, and click **Next** to display the Collecting Registration Data window.

5. DO NOT click **Next**. After you have completed the requested form, the activation wizard attempts to connect to Microsoft via the Internet. If this connection is unavailable, it will automatically dial a 1-800-number and activate. The procedure only takes a few seconds.

6. Click **Back** twice to display the Activate Windows window.

7. Click **Yes, I want to telephone a customer service representative to activate Windows**, and click **Next** to display the Activate Windows by Phone window.

8. Using the scroll button, select your country. A toll-free, 24-hour phone number will be displayed for you to call. You will be asked to provide the Installation ID Number that is displayed in step 3 on the screen. The service representative will provide you with a confirmation ID that you will need to type in at step 4 on the screen. You will then click **Next** to complete the activation procedure.

9. This completes the two methods of activation demonstration. Close the Activation Window.

10. Windows XP Professional, by default, uses an automated update procedure to check and install updates and fixes. To configure the way that Windows XP carries out this procedure, do the following:

   a. Click **Start**, **Control Panel**, and click **Switch to Classic Mode** under the Control Panel tasks. Then, double-click **System** to display the System Properties window.

   b. Click the **Automatic Updates** tab.

   c. Click **Turn off automatic updating. I want to update my computer manually** to turn off automatic updates.

   d. Click **OK**, close the Control Panel window, and return to the desktop.

11. To manually update Windows, do the following:

   a. Click **Start**, **Help and Support** to display the Help and Support Center.

   b. Under Pick a Task, click **Keep your computer up-to-date with Windows Update** to display the Windows Update window. Windows XP will automatically connect to Microsoft Update Web Site.

   c. Click **Scan for Updates** to check for new updates. Windows XP will review your system and list critical fixes, updates, and drives under the Pick Updates to Install section. Click the updates that you want to install, and click **Add.**

   d. Click **Review and Update** to see your selected updates, and then click **Install Now** to begin the installation process.

   e. You may be required to reboot your system after the updates. If not, close the Help and Support Center window to return to the desktop.

12. To download current updates to a folder for future use, do the following:

   a. Click **Start**, **My Computer**, and double-click **C**: drive.

   b. Click **Make new folder** under file and folder tasks.

   c. Name the folder **xpupdatefiles**, and close My Computer.

   d. Click **Start**, **Run**, and type **<*CD-ROM drive*>:\winnt32 /duprepare:c:\xpupdatefiles.** The Windows install screen will start briefly and download any updates to your C: drive.

   e. Click **Start**, **My Computer**, and double-click C: drive. Scroll down to the xpupdatefiles folder and open it. Depending on updates currently available at the Microsoft Update Web site, a number of files may or may not be listed.

   f. Close My Computer.

2

LAB 2.4 INSTALLING THE WINDOWS XP SUPPORT TOOLS AND SETUP MANAGER WIZARD

Objective

The Windows XP Support Tools contains many utilities to assist you in installing, configuring, and troubleshooting Windows XP systems. Note: The support tools provided on the Windows XP Professional CD-ROM are a subset of the tools available on the Windows XP Resource Kit. The resource kit is purchased as a separate item. You will also need to use the Setup Manager Wizard that is included in the Windows XP Professional CD. The Setup Manager Wizard helps automate the installation of Windows XP Professional on multiple computers. After completing this lab, you will be able to:

➤ Install the Windows XP Professional Support Tools on your workstation

➤ Start the Setup Manager Wizard

Estimated completion time: **5–10 minutes**

ACTIVITY

1. If necessary, start your computer with Windows XP, and log on as the administrator.

2. Place a copy of the Windows XP Professional in the CD-ROM drive. (If the CD self-starts, click **Perform additional Tasks** and **Browse this CD.** Skip to Step 4.)

3. Click **Start**, **My Computer**, and then double-click your CD-ROM drive. Click **Explore** to list the CD content.

4. Double-click the **Support** folder, and then double-click the **Tools** folder.

5. Double-click the **Setup.exe** icon to display the Windows Support Tools setup wizard.

6. Click **Next**, and then select **Agree** in the license agreement.

7. Click **Next**, and then specify your name and organization.

8. Click **Next**, and then select **Complete** for installation type.

9. Click **Next**, and ensure that the installation will be on **D:\Program Files\Support Tools**.

10. Click **Install Now** to begin the installation. Click **Finish** to complete the Support Tools Installation.

11. To install the Setup Manager Wizard, double-click **Deploy.cab** to display the contents of this compressed file.

12. Double-click **setupmgr.exe** to display a file extraction window.

13. Click **Browse**, navigate to the **<XP drive>:\Windows** folder, and click **Extract**.

14. Double-click **setupmgr.chm** to display a file extraction window.

15. Click **Browse**, navigate to the **<XP drive>:\Windows** folder, and click **Extract**.

16. Close all windows and return to the desktop.

17. Create a shortcut to start the Setup Manager wizard.
    a. Click **Start**, **My Computer**, and then open your Windows XP drive by double-clicking it.
    b. Double-click the **Windows** folder.
    c. If necessary, click **Show the contents of this folder**.
    d. Scroll down, and right-click the **setupmgr** program.
    e. Select the **Send to** option, and then click the **Desktop (create shortcut)** option.
    f. Close all windows.
    g. Notice that a Shortcut to the setupmgr icon has been added to your desktop.

17. Start Setup Manager from the desktop shortcut.

18. After verifying that the Welcome to Setup Manager wizard window appears, click **Cancel** and close the Setup Wizard window.

Lab 2.5 Creating an Unattended Installation File

Objective

The Universal Aerospace Corporation has purchased five new workstations from your company for use in their Accounting Department. Kellie Thiele, the network administrator, is upgrading their NetWare server, so they have contracted with you to install Windows XP on the new computers. Rather than install each computer separately, you decide to create and use an unattended installation file to automate the Windows XP installation. To create an unattended installation file for Universal Aerospace, you first need to identify how Kellie wants the systems to be configured. Use the Lab 2.5 Installation Planning Worksheet to gather the information you need to build the unattended installation file. After completing this lab, you will be able to:

➤ Identify the information needed to create an unattended answer file

➤ Use the Setup Manager Wizard to create both an unattended answer file and a uniqueness database file

➤ View and print the contents of the unattended installation files, and identify the purpose of each file

Estimated completion time: **25 minutes**

ACTIVITY

Before beginning this activity, fill in the Lab 2.5 Installation Planning Worksheet that follows this lab. Your instructor will provide you with any additional information you may need. If manual IP addressing is used, be sure that the IP address and subnet mask are compatible with other computers on your network.

1. If necessary, start your computer with Windows XP, and log on as the administrator.

2. Start Setup Manager Wizard from the desktop shortcut you created in Lab 2.4. When the Welcome screen appears, click **Next**.

3. Select the **Create a new answer file** option, and click **Next** to display the Product to Install window. Record the product options on the Lab 2.5 Installation Planning Worksheet.

4. Verify that the Windows Unattended Installation option is selected, and then click **Next** to display the Platform window.

5. Verify that the Windows XP Professional platform is selected, and then click **Next** to display the User Interaction Level window.

6. The User Interaction Level lets you control what choices the operator on the computer being set up will have. Identify the default option on the Lab 2.5 Student Answer Sheet and describe its use. Because you want the installation to proceed without your involvement, click the **Fully automated** option, and then click **Next** to display the Distribution Folder window.

7. The Distribution Folder windows are used to create a network share that contains the files needed to perform the unattended installation. Because you will test the unattended installation by installing from a CD, click **No, this answer file will be used to install from a CD**, and click **Next** to display the License Agreement window.

8. Click the **I accept the terms of the License Agreement** check box, and then click **Next** to display the Customize the Software window.

9. In the Customize the Software window, enter the user and organization information specified on your Lab 2.5 Installation Planning Worksheet, and click **Next** to display the Display Settings Window.

10. Enter the Colors, Screen area, and Refresh frequency specified on your Lab 2.5 Installation Planning Worksheet, and click **Next** to display the Time Zone window.

11. Use the scroll button to select your time zone and click **Next** to display the Providing the Product Key window.

12. Enter the Product Key found on your CD or the one provided by the instructor. Click **Next** to display the Computer Names window.

13. The Computer Names window provides the Windows XP installation program with a unique name for the computer being installed. Enter the name of a computer specified on the Lab 2.5 Installation Planning Worksheet in the Computer Name field, and then click the **Add** button. Repeat this process for each computer specified on your worksheet. When all computer names have been added, click **Next** to continue. Note: For the purpose of this lab, at least two computer names must be added.

14. Enter the initial password for the administrator you specified on the Lab 2.5 Installation Planning Worksheet. This password should be changed after the system is operational. (Because passwords are case-sensitive, be sure to check your Caps Lock key.) After entering the password in both the Password and Confirm password fields, click **Encrypt Administrator password in answer file**. Click **Next** to display the Networking components window.

15. To manually specify an IP address and subnet mask for each computer:
    a. Click **Customize Settings**.
    b. Click **Internet Protocol (TCP/IP)**, and then click **Properties** to display the Internet Protocol (TCP/IP) Properties window.
    c. Click the **Use the following IP address** option, and then enter the IP address and subnet mask specified on your Lab 2.5 Installation Planning Worksheet.
    d. Click **OK** to return to the Networking Components window.

16. Click **Next** to display the Workgroup or Domain window.

17. Enter the Workgroup name specified on your Lab 2.5 Installation Planning Worksheet, and click **Next** to display the Telephony window.

18. Use the scroll button to select your country and enter your area code. Click **Next** to display the Regional Settings window.

19. On your Lab 2.5 Installation Planning Worksheet, record the default Regional Settings.

20. Explore the Regional Settings window:
    a. Click the **Specify regional setting in the answer file** option, and, on your Student Answer Sheet, record the default language.
    b. Click the **Customize the default language settings** check box.
    c. Click the **Custom** button, and, on your Student Answer Sheet, record the three language options.
    d. Click **Cancel**, and then select the Regional Settings options you identified on your Lab 2.5 Installation Planning Worksheet.
    e. Click **Next** to display the Languages window.

21. Select any additional languages specified in your Lab 2.5 Installation Planning Worksheet, and click **Next** to display the Browser and Shell window.

22. Unless special proxy values are specified on your Lab 2.5 Installation Planning sheet (in which case you would enter them), click **Next** to use the default Internet Explorer settings and display the Installation Folder window.

23. Click **Next** to accept the default Windows folder name and open the Install Printers window.

24. If you have a network printer, enter the name of the printer specified on your Lab 2.5 Installation Planning Worksheet, using the format **\\servername\printer**. Click **Next** to display the Run Once window.

25. The Run Once window specifies the name of a script file or program you want to run when a user logs on to this workstation. Add any commands specified on your Lab 2.5 Installation Planning Worksheet, and click **Next** to display the Additional Commands window.

26. The Additional Commands window specifies the name of a script file or program you want to run at the end of the install procedure. Add any commands specified on your Lab 2.5 Installation Planning Worksheet, and click **Finish**.

27. An Answers File Name window will appear. Click the **Browse** button and perform the following steps to create an answer file named Unattend.txt in a folder named Install on your C: drive.
    a. Use the scroll button to select your C: drive in the "Save in" text box.
    b. Click the **Create New Folder** icon.
    c. Type **Install** for the folder name, and press **Enter**.
    d. Double-click the newly created **Install** folder, and enter **Unattend.txt** in the Filename field; then click **Save** and **OK** to continue.

28. Close the Setup Manager Wizard.

29. Click **Start**, **Accessories**, **Notepad**, and then retrieve the following files from your C:\Install folder.
    a. Unattend.txt
    b. Unattend.udb
    c. Unattend.bat

30. On your Student Answer Sheet, record the command that you would have to type at the command prompt in order to run an unattended install.

31. In the Unattend.bat file, identify the following commands:
    a. The command used to provide the path to your Windows XP Professional installation source files
    b. The commands used to specify the name of the unattend files

32. In the Unattend.txt file, identify the following information:
    a. Locate the workgroup name and verify that it is correct.
    b. If you manually assigned an IP Address, locate the IP Address and Subnet numbers.
    c. Locate and identify the DHCP setting.
    d. Locate the [UserData] heading, and record its contents on your Student Answer Sheet.
33. In the Unattend.udf file, identify the following information:
    a. Identify the Unattend.txt headings, and record them on your Student Answer Sheet.
    b. On your Student Answer Sheet, record the value that would be substituted into the Unattend.txt file when using the following command:

    Winnt32 /unattend:unattend.txt /udf:Acct2,unattend.udb

Lab 2.5 Installation Planning Worksheet

User Interaction Level:

Notes: When performing an unattended installation, you can identify a network share or local CD-ROM as the location for the Windows XP installation files. If you want the wizard to copy files to a share, record it below.

Network distribution folder or CD-ROM folder:

User:

Organization:

Color, screen area, resolution, and refresh frequency to be used:

Time Zone:

Product Key:

Notes: When using the unattended installation file to install multiple computers, the Setup Manager Wizard creates a uniqueness database that allows you to use the same unattended installation file for multiple computers. In the table below, enter the names of computers you plan to install with the unattended answer files. If assigning manual IP addresses, include each computer's IP address and subnet mask.

Computer Name	IP Address or DHCP	Subnet Mask

(Lab 2.5 Installation Planning Worksheet continues on next page)

2

(Lab 2.5 Installation Planning Worksheet continued)

Temporary administrator password:

Workgroup/domain name:

Telephony:

Regional Settings:

Default Regional Settings options for the Windows version you are installing:

Default language setting:

Languages:

Internet Explorer Proxy Settings (if any):

Address: ...Port:

Network printer name:

Run Once command:

Additional Commands:

LAB 2.6 MODIFYING UNATTENDED INSTALLATION FILES

Objective

After the unattended answer file and uniqueness database files have been created, the next step is to make any modifications needed to support or enhance the installation process. You may want to change the way a hard drive is formatted. By default, Windows XP will automatically select a partition in which to install. To manually select a partition, the AutoPartition setting must be removed. If you manually assign IP addresses to each computer, you need to create a section in the uniqueness database file that contains each computer's IP address and subnet mask. After completing this lab, you will be able to:

➤ Modify the AutoPartition settings in the unattended answer file

➤ Modify the uniqueness database to include product identification and an IP address

➤ Use the WINNT32 utility to start an unattended installation of Windows XP Professional

➤ Verify your installation

Estimated completion time: **5–10 minutes**

ACTIVITY

1. If necessary, start your computer and log on as administrator.

2. Click **Start**, **My Computer**, and navigate to the C:\Install folder.

3. Use Notepad to remove the AutoPartition setting in the Unattend.txt file as follows:

a. Double-click the **Unattend.txt** file to open it with Notepad.

b. To manually select a partition for the Windows XP installation, remove the AutoPartition setting line.

c. Save the Unattend.txt file, and then close the file.

4. Use Notepad to add IP Address settings to your Unattend.udf file.

a. Right-click the **Unattend.udf** file, and click **Open With** to display the Open With window. Double-click **Notepad** to edit the Unattend.udf file.

b. If you are manually assigning IP addresses, add the following section after each computer's UserData section:

[*computername*:params.MS_TCPIP.Adapter1]
   DHCP=NO
   IPAddress=192.168.1.5
   Subnetmask=255.255.255.0

c. Save the unattend.udf file, and then close the file.

5. Use Notepad to add the location of the update files created in Lab 2.3 and change the location of the Windows XP Professional source files in the unattend.bat file as follows:

a. Right-click the **Unattend.bat** file, and click **Edit**.

b. Under the last Set statement, add the following line:

Set Dushare=c:\xpupdatefiles

c. Modify the Winnt32 command line to include the following:

/dushare:%dushare%

d. If necessary, modify the letter corresponding to your CD-ROM drive, so it matches the drive letter used by Windows 98.

e. Save the **Unattend.bat** file.

6. Have your instructor check your file modifications.

LAB 2.7 PERFORMING AN UNATTENDED INSTALLATION

Objective

After the unattended answer file and uniqueness database files have been created and modified, your next step is to test the unattended installation process by using these files to install Windows XP Professional on your computer. After completing this lab, you will be able to:

➤ Use the WINNT32 utility to start an unattended installation of Windows XP Professional

➤ Verify your installation

2

Estimated completion time: **40–50 minutes**

ACTIVITY

1. Obtain your five Windows XP installation floppy disks and then perform the steps outlined in Lab 2.1 to remove the existing Windows XP partition and restart your computer with Windows 98.

2. Insert the Windows XP Professional CD-ROM.

3. Click **No** when asked if you want to upgrade to Windows XP.

4. Exit the Windows XP Professional CD window.

5. Start the unattended installation batch file.

   a. Click **Start**, **Run**, and enter the command **C:\Install\Unattend.bat** *your-computer-name* in the Run window (replace *your-computer-name* with the name of the computer you specified on the Lab 2.2 Installation Planning Worksheet) to install Windows XP using the computer information you saved in the unattended installation file in Lab 2.5.

   b. Click **OK** to start the unattended installation.

   c. If your system has virus protection software installed, you may receive a message indicating a suspected virus activity has occurred when the setup program writes to the boot sector of the C: drive. Click the option to ignore any virus activity and continue the unattended installation.

   d. The Windows XP setup will appear on the screen and proceed to copy the Initial setup files to your computer. After all the necessary files are copied, your computer will automatically restart with the Windows XP setup program.

6. Because you have removed the AutoPartition line in Unattend.txt, you will be presented with the Windows XP destination option. Perform the following process to create and format a new partition for Windows XP.

   a. Highlight the **Unpartitioned space** option from the partition window, and press **C** to create a new partition.

   b. Enter a partition size of approximately 1 GB (2000 MB), leaving at least 50-100 MB of unpartitioned space for use in later lab projects.

   c. Press **Enter** to create the new partition.

   d. Highlight the New (Unformatted) partition, and press **Enter** to display the format options.

   e. Be sure that **Format the partition using the NTFS file system** is highlighted, and press **Enter** to start the formatting process.

7. Sit back and relax while Windows XP Professional is installed on your system. If your system has virus protection software installed, you might receive a message indicating a suspected virus activity when the installation program writes to the boot sector of the C: drive. Ignore any virus message and continue the installation.

8. After installation is complete, restart your computer to Windows XP Professional, and log on as the Administrator. Click **Exit** when you see the Windows XP "Getting Started" window. Congratulations, your new Windows XP Professional system is now up and running!

9. Have your instructor verify your installation by checking the following:
   - Verify IP address settings.
   - Verify computer name and workgroup name.

Using MMC, Task Scheduler, and Control Panel

Labs included in this chapter

➤ Lab 3.1 Customizing a Microsoft Management Console

➤ Lab 3.2 Creating Local Users

➤ Lab 3.3 Configuring Accessibility Services

➤ Lab 3.4 Configuring Other Services

➤ Lab 3.5 Configuring Hardware Profiles and Power Management

Microsoft MCSE Exam #70-270 Objectives	
Objective	Lab
Configure and troubleshoot desktop settings	3.1
Implement, configure, manage, and troubleshoot a security configuration	3.1
Create and manage local users and groups	3.2, 3.5
Configure and troubleshoot accessibility services	3.3
Configure and troubleshoot fax support	3.4

Student Answer Sheets to accompany the labs in this chapter are available for downloading from the Online Companion for this manual at *www.course.com*.

LAB 3.1 CUSTOMIZING A MICROSOFT MANAGEMENT CONSOLE

Objective

Dennis Geisler, the owner of the Animal Care Center, wants one of the users to perform limited administrative functions on the Windows XP Professional system when he is out of the office. These clerical functions include viewing user connection information, defragmenting the hard drive, viewing event messages, and adding local users and groups. These functions can be performed using the Windows XP Administrative tools, but Dennis wants you to create a special console that allows only a specified user to perform these limited functions. The limited tools should then be added to the Start menu to make them easy for users to access. After completing this lab, you will be able to:

> ➤ Create a Microsoft Management Console (MMC) with specific snap-ins and extensions

> ➤ Create multiple windows containing specific functions

> ➤ Limit users to only the windows you have configured

> ➤ Save the console on the start menu

Requirements

> ➤ Windows XP Professional installed as per Lab 2.6

Estimated completion time: **15–20 minutes**

ACTIVITY

1. Start your computer with Windows XP Professional, and log on as an administrator.

2. Create a folder named **Consoles** off the root of your Windows XP drive. Use the folder to store your customized management console files.

3. Open a new Microsoft Management Console window.
   a. Click **Start**, **Run**.
   b. Enter **mmc** in the Open text box, and click **OK**.
   c. A new console window with only the Console Root will be visible, as shown in Figure 3-1.
   d. Maximize the MMC Console window.

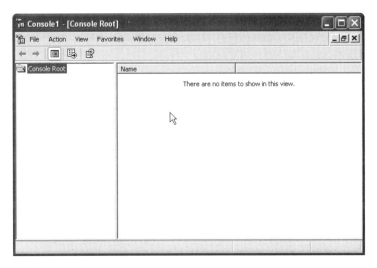

Figure 3-1   Creating a custom Microsoft Management Console

4. Add the Event Viewer snap-in.

   a. Click the **Add/Remove Snap-in** option from the File menu to display the Add/Remove Snap-in window.

   b. Click the **Add** button to display the Add Standalone Snap-in window, as shown in Figure 3-2.

   c. Double-click the **Event Viewer** snap-in to display the Select Computer window.

   d. Verify that the **Local computer** option is selected, and then click **Finish** to add the Event Viewer snap-in.

Figure 3-2   Adding a standalone snap-in to an MMC

5. Repeat steps 4c and 4d to add the following snap-ins:
   a. Computer Management
   b. Shared Folders
   c. Disk Defragmenter (When you select Disk Defragmenter, it will not display the Select Computer window. This is because the Disk Defragmenter program can be run only on the local computer.)

6. Verify that all four snap-ins have been added, and click **Close** to return to the Add/Remove Snap-in window.

7. Click **OK** to return to the Microsoft Management Console main window.

8. Create a separate Event Viewer window.
   a. Right-click the **Event Viewer** option from the console tree.
   b. Click the **New Window from Here** option.
   c. Remove the console tree from the Event Viewer window:
      ■ Click **Customize** from the View menu.
      ■ Remove the check mark from the **Console tree** option.
      ■ Click **OK**. Notice that the console tree has been removed from the Event Viewer window.

9. Create a separate Sessions window from the Shared Folders snap-in.
   a. Click **Console Root** from the Window menu.
   b. Expand the **Shared Folders** snap-in.
   c. Right-click the **Sessions** option from Shared Folders.
   d. Click the **New Window from Here** option.
   e. Remove the console tree from the Sessions window:
      ■ Click **Customize** from the **View** menu.
      ■ Remove the check mark from the **Console tree** option.
      ■ Click **OK**. Notice that the console tree has been removed from the Sessions window.

10. Create a separate Logical Drives window as follows:
    a. Click **1 Console Root** from the Window menu.
    b. **Expand the** Computer Management snap-in.
    c. Expand the **System Tools** extension.
    d. Right-click **Local Users and Groups**, and click the **New Window from Here** option.
    e. Remove the console tree from the Logical Drives window:
       ■ Click **Customize** from the **View** menu.
       ■ Remove the check mark from the **Console tree** option.
       ■ Click **OK** to close the Customize View window. Notice that the console tree has been removed from the Local Users and Groups window.

11. Create a separate Disk Defragmenter window.
    a. Click **1 Console Root** from the Window menu.
    b. Right-click **Disk Defragmenter**, and click the **New Window from Here** option.
    c. Click **Customize** from the **View** menu, and remove the check mark from the **Console tree** option.
    d. Click **OK** to close the Customize View window.

12. Click **1 Console Root** from the Window menu, and then close the Console Root window. (Do not close the entire MMC window.)

13. Tile the windows.
    a. Click the **Tile Horizontally** option from the **Window** menu.
    b. All four snap-in windows should now appear in the MMC main Console1 window similar to Figure 3-3.

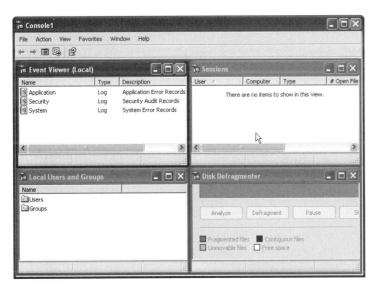

Figure 3-3   Configuring multiple snap-ins in an MMC

14. Save in Author mode as follows. Saving in Author mode allows you to make changes to this management console in the future.
    a. Click **Options** from the **File** menu.
    b. Verify that the Console mode is set to Author mode. On your Lab 3.1 Student Answer Sheet, record the description of the Author mode.
    c. Click **OK** to return to the management console.
    d. Click **Save As** from the **File** menu.
    e. Select your **Consoles** folder, and save the console using the name **Lab3-1**.

15. Select User limited mode.

    a. Click **Options** from the **File** menu.

    b. On the Student Answer Sheet, describe each user Console mode and its possible use.

    c. Select **User mode – limited access, multiple window** from the Console mode drop-down menu.

    d. Remove the check mark from the **Allow the user to customize views** option.

    e. Click **OK** to return to the main Console window.

16. Save the console on the Start menu.

    a. Click **Save As** from the **File** menu.

    b. Navigate to the root of the drive containing Windows XP Professional.

    c. Navigate to the \Documents and Settings\All Users\Start Menu\ Programs folder:

       - Double-click the **Documents and Settings** folder.

       - Double-click the **All Users** folder.

       - Double-click the **Start Menu** folder.

       - Double-click the **Programs** folder.

    d. Enter the name **Computer Management**, and click **Save**.

17. Test the console you created.

    a. Close the Computer Management console.

    b. Click **Start**, **All Programs**, **Computer Management** in the File name text box.

    c. The new Computer Management console you created should be shown along with the windows. Notice that the user is limited to the windows and snap-ins you assigned.

    d. Open the Author mode version of the console:

       - Click **Start**, **Run**.

       - Use the Browse button and select your **Lab3–1** console file from the Consoles folder.

       - If you receive an error message saying that Disk Defrag does not support more than one instance running at a time, click **OK** to continue.

       - Click **OK** to start your Author mode version of the console.

    e. Switch back and forth between the two consoles, and, on the Student Answer Sheet, identify at least two differences or limitations when running the user version of the management console, as compared to the author version.

18. Have your instructor or lab assistant check your console and sign off on your Student Answer Sheet.

19. Close all console windows and log off.

LAB 3.2 CREATING LOCAL USERS

Objective

To reduce operator errors affecting the operation of the Windows XP Professional computer at the Animal Care Center, Dennis wants you to create two user accounts to eliminate the need for users logging on as Administrator. You will set up one user account named AppUser that is limited to running applications, and another account named SysOp that can use the Management Console you created in Lab 3.1, but that does not have full administrative authority to the system. After completing this lab, you will be able to:

➤ Create a limited local user account

➤ Create a power-user account

➤ Verify user account restrictions

Estimated completion time: **20–30 minutes**

ACTIVITY

Windows XP has two main controls for adding and modifying users. The first is the User Accounts applet in Control panel, which has limited functionality. The second is Local Users and Groups under the Computer Management Console, which has full functionality. To demonstrate the functionality of each control, you will use the User Accounts applet to create the users and use Local Users and Groups to add extended security.

1. If necessary, start your computer with Windows XP Professional, and log on as an administrator.

2. Click **Start**, **Control Panel, User Accounts** to open the User Accounts window in Category view.

3. Create a limited user named AppUser.
   a. Click **Create a new account.**
   b. Type **AppUser** in the Name of the new account window, and click **Next.**
   c. Click **Limited** as the account type, and, on the Student Answer Sheet, record the access listed. Click **Create Account** when finished.
   d. Click the new **AppUser** account, and then click **Create a Password.**
   e. Type **password** as the new password, and retype **password** in the confirm password text box.
   f. Click **Create Password.**
   g. Click **Back** to return to the User Accounts window.

4. Create a Computer Administrator named SysOp. (To be changed later)
   a. Click **Create a new account.**
   b. Type **SysOp** in the Name of the new Account window, and click **Next.**

    c. Click **Computer administrator** as the account type, and click **Create Account**.

    d. Click the new **SysOp** account, and then click **Create a Password.**

    e. Type **password** as the new password, and retype **password** in the confirm password text box.

    f. Click **Create Password.**

    g. Click **Back** to return to the User Accounts window.

5. Add the requirement that users must type a user name and password to log on to this computer, as follows:

    a. Click **Change the way users log on or log off**.

    b. Ensure that the **Use the Welcome screen** box is cleared, and click **Apply Options.**

    c. Close the User Accounts window.

    d. Log off and log on to verify the User name and password requirement.

6. Windows XP contains a number of predefined system groups that are used to provide rights and permissions to multiple users. In this step you document default group membership for your newly created users.

    a. Click **Start**, **Control Panel** (in Classic view), **Administrative Tools**, and then **Computer Management**. Alternatively, you may use the Computer Management console you created in Lab 3.1.

    b. Expand **Local Users and Groups**.

    c. Double-click the **Groups** folder, and record the predefined groups on your Student Answer Sheet.

    d. Double-click the **Users** group, and list the members on your Student Answer Sheet. Click **Cancel** to close the Users Properties window.

    e. Double-click the **Administrators** group, and list the members on your Student Answer Sheet. Click **Cancel** to close the Administrators Properties window.

    f. Double-click the **Power Users** group, and list the members on your Student Answer Sheet. Click **Cancel** to close the Power Users Properties window.

    g. Close the Administrator Properties window.

7. The SysOp account currently has full Administrative Control but should be in the Power Users Group. To change membership, do the following:

    a. Double-click the **Administrators** group.

    b. Click **SysOp**, and then click **Remove.**

    c. Click **OK** to return to the Computer Management window.

    d. Double-click the **Power Users** group.

    e. Click **Add**, and type **SysOp** in the Select Users text box. Click **OK** to add.

    f. Click **OK**, and then close all windows.

    g. Click **Start**, **Help and Support**, and then search for Power Users. On your Student Answer Sheet, describe the differences between the Administrators group and the Power Users group.

8. Now you want to set the computer to launch the Management Console automatically at logon. Start by logging on as Administrator.

9. Use Scheduler to launch the Management Console automatically at logon.
    a. Open Control Panel.
    b. Double-click the **Scheduled Tasks** icon.
    c. Double-click the **Add Scheduled Task** icon, and click **Next** to start the Scheduled Task Wizard.
    d. Click **Browse**, and navigate to the \Documents and Settings\ All Users\Start Menu\Programs folder.
    e. Double-click **Computer Management**.
    f. Click the **When I log on** option, and click **Next**.
    g. In the Enter the user name: text box, replace Administrator with **SysOp**.
    h. Enter the password in both fields, and then click **Next**.
    i. Click **Finish** to save the task.

10. Test the AppUser account.
    a. Log off the Administrator user.
    b. Log on as **AppUser**.
    c. Verify that you can run applications such as Microsoft Office or WordPad.
    d. Start the Computer Management console.
    e. On the Student Answer Sheet, record any error messages you receive.
    f. On the Student Answer Sheet, record what Event Viewer logs you can view.
    g. On the Student Answer Sheet, record the results of viewing and modifying User information.
    h. On the Student Answer Sheet, record the results of clicking the Analyze button in the Disk Defragmenter window.
    i. Close the Computer Management console and log off.

11. Test the SysOp account.
    a. Log on as **SysOp**.
    b. Verify that you can run applications such as WordPad.
    c. Click the Computer Management console, which should have been opened automatically during log on.
    d. On the Student Answer Sheet, record what Event Viewer logs you can view.
    e. On the Student Answer Sheet, record the results of viewing and modifying User information.
    f. On the Student Answer Sheet, record the results of clicking the Analyze button in the Disk Defragmenter window.

12. Close all windows and log off.

Lab 3.3 Configuring Accessibility Services

Objective

You have just visited the Animal Care Center and learned that a new employee has a disability that often causes repeated keystrokes. This person also has a difficult time viewing smaller print on the screen. In this lab, you simulate making the system easier for this employee to use. You will configure and test the accessibility options available with Windows XP Professional. After completing this lab, you will be able to:

➤ Use the Control Panel to configure and troubleshoot accessibility services

Estimated completion time: **10–15 minutes**

Activity

1. If necessary, start your computer with Windows XP, and log on as an administrator.

2. Open Control Panel.

3. Follow Step 4 in Lab 3.2 to create a new restricted user named Special.

4. Log off, and then log on as the user named Special.

5. Open Control Panel, and then click **Switch to Classic View**. Double-click the **Accessibility Options** icon to display the window shown in Figure 3-4.

Figure 3-4   Configuring the Accessibility Options

3

6. In the FilterKeys area, check the **Use FilterKeys** box, and click the **Settings** button. On the Lab 3.3 Student Answer Sheet, record the keyboard shortcut for FilterKeys.

7. The user seems to be having a problem with a letter repeating when a key is accidentally pressed multiple times. Click the **Settings** button beside the Ignore quick keystrokes option, and on your Student Answer Sheet, record the default amount of time a key must be held down (repeat delay).

8. Try typing in the Test area. Notice how long you need to hold down a key before it repeats.

9. Using the Repeat delay scroll box, vary the time keys must be held down in order to repeat. Try typing in the Test area, and notice the difference between different time settings. On your Student Answer sheet, record the shortest (non-zero) repeat delay time a key must be held down.

10. Set the keyboard Repeat delay to **0.3** seconds, and click **OK**.

11. In the Keyboard shortcut box, remove the check mark from the Use shortcut option.

12. Click **OK** to save your settings.

13. Click the **Sound** tab, and, on your Student Answer Sheet, record the possible sound setting.

14. Click the **Use SoundSentry** option.

15. The High Contrast option is helpful for users who are visually challenged. To enable the High Contrast option, click the **Display** tab, and click the **Use High Contrast** check box.

16. Click the **Settings** button, and on your Student Answer Sheet, record the shortcut key sequence for the High Contrast option. Click **OK** or **Cancel** to return to Accessibility Options.

17. Click the **Mouse** tab, and then click **Settings.** Experiment with the various settings, and then return them to their original settings. Click **OK** or **Cancel** to return to Accessibility Options.

18. Click the **General** tab. On your Student Answer Sheet, record the default Notification settings.

19. Click **OK** to save the settings and exit.

20. Use the shortcut keys you recorded in Step 16 to test the High Contrast display option.

21. Use the same shortcut keys to turn off the high-contrast option.

22. Start Notepad, and notice how long you have to hold down each key to type.

23. Exit Notepad, and do not save any documents.

24. Log off, and then log on as **AppUser**.

25. On your Student Answer Sheet, record whether or not the accessibility options apply to other users.

26. Log off, and log on as Administrator. Remove all Accessibility Options and return to the desktop.

LAB 3.4 CONFIGURING OTHER SERVICES

Objective

The Windows XP Professional systems at the Melendres and Associates law firm are working well. However, Mr. Melendres wants you to stop by and do the following:

➤ Disable the modems on computers that are not connected to the phone line

➤ Change the screen resolution to support a new application

➤ Configure faxing from Mr. Melendres's computer

➤ Install an updated video driver and set video resolution

➤ Allow users to view hidden files on all folders

➤ Configure an Internet Explorer default home page

After completing this lab, you will be able to use the Control Panel to:

➤ Unplug hardware devices

➤ Configure and troubleshoot fax support

➤ Configure folder options

➤ Configure Internet Explorer

This lab involves changing system configuration settings that could affect system operation. You might need to obtain permission before proceeding. As an alternative, the objectives in this lab can be accomplished through participating in a classroom demonstration.

Estimated completion time: **30-45 minutes**

ACTIVITY 1

All of the new computers at the Melendres and Associates law firm came with built-in modems. However, only two computers are actually plugged into a phone. In this activity, you use the Add/Remove hardware feature to simulate how to disable the modems on the computers that are not attached to a phone line. If you do not have a modem attached to your computer, you can use the Printer port (LPT1) to simulate the process.

3

1. If necessary, start your computer and log on as Administrator.

2. Open the Control Panel.

3. Double-click **System**, and then click the **Hardware** tab.

4. Click **Device Manager** to display the devices configured on your system.

5. If you have a modem installed:
   a. Expand **Modems**, and right-click your modem.
   b. Click **Disable**, and click **Yes** to confirm the disable process.
   c. A red X should appear over your modem.
   d. Skip to Step 7.

6. To disable the printer port:
   a. Expand **Ports (COM & LPT)**, and right-click **Printer Port (LPT1).**
   b. Click **Disable**, and click **Yes** to confirm the disable process.
   c. A red X should appear over your Printer Port.

7. Close Device Manager, and click **OK** to close System Properties. Close Control Panel and return to the desktop.

ACTIVITY 2

Mr. Melendres has now added a phone line to his computer and wants you to configure faxing support. In this activity, you simulate this process by re-enabling either the modem device or printer port that you uninstalled in Activity 1. You would normally reverse the steps used in Activity 1; however, you will use the Add Hardware wizard for this procedure.

1. Open Control Panel.

2. Double-click **Add Hardware**, and click **Next** to start the Add Hardware wizard.

3. Since the Modem or Printer Port is already attached to your computer, click **Yes, I have already connected the hardware.**

4. Click **Next** to display a list of hardware found by Windows XP. Click the Modem or Printer Port with the red X, and click **Next.**

5. A message will be displayed listing the device as disabled. Click **Finish** to start the Device Problems Troubleshooting Wizard.

6. Click **Next** to re-enable your Modem or Printer Port.

7. Click **Finish** to close the troubleshooting window.

8. Close **Control Panel** to return to the desktop.

ACTIVITY 3

Configure fax services.

1. If necessary, start your computer with Windows XP Professional, and log on as an administrator.

2. Open Control Panel, and double-click **Add or Remove Programs**.

3. Click **Add/Remove Windows Components** to display the Windows Components wizard. This may take a few moments to display.

4. If Fax Services are checked, click **Cancel** and close all windows. Skip to Step 7.

5. Make sure that the Windows XP CD-ROM is in the CD drive, and place a check in the **Fax Services** box.

6. Click **Next** to install the Fax Services component, and then click **Finish.** Close all windows and return to the desktop.

7. Click **Start, All Programs, Accessories, Communications, Fax**, and then click **Fax Console** to start the Fax configuration wizard.

8. If you receive a message asking you to install a modem, follow these procedures to install a "fake" modem:

   a. Click **Yes** to start the modem install wizard.

   b. If a location Information window appears, fill in the necessary country and area code, and then click **OK** twice.

   c. Click **Don't detect my modem; I will select it from a list**, and then click **Next**.

   d. Select **Standard 56000 bps Modem**, and then click **Next**.

   e. Click **COM1** or **COM2**, and then click **Next**.

   f. Click **Finish** to exit the Wizard.

9. Click **Next** and fill in the Sender Information screen. On your Lab 3.4 Student Answer Sheet, record the information you enter.

10. Click **Next** to choose your modem and send / receive settings. Ensure that the enable send box is selected and the enable receive box is cleared. Click **Next** to continue.

11. Type **Melendres and Assoc** in the TSID dialog box, and click **Next.**

12. Click **Finish Fax Configuration** to close the wizard and display the Fax Console window.

13. Click **Fax Printer Configuration** from the Tools menu. You can also display this screen by right-clicking the fax printer in Printers and Faxes.

14. Click the **Devices** tab and click **Properties**. Record the default send settings on the Student Answer Sheet. Click **OK** to return to the Fax Properties page.

15. Click the **Archives** tab, and record the archive locations on the Student Answer Sheet.

16. Click **OK** twice, and then close all windows to return to the desktop.

ACTIVITY 4

Mr. Melendres wants to be able to view any hidden files, as well as see all file extensions when he opens a folder on his office computer. In this activity, you use the Folder Options of Control Panel to view hidden files and file extensions.

1. Open Control Panel.

2. Double-click the **Folder Options** icon.

3. Click the **View** tab.

4. Click the **Show hidden files and folders** option.

5. Click to remove the check mark from the **Hide file extensions for known file types** option.

6. Click **OK** to save your settings and return to Control Panel.

7. Close the Control Panel window.

8. Test folder options.
   a. Use My Computer to open the **Consoles** folder you created in Lab 3.1.
   b. Verify that you can view the .msc extension on the Lab3-1 console file.
   c. Right-click the **Lab3-1.msc** file, and click **Properties**.
   d. Click the **Hidden** attribute.
   e. Click **OK** to return to the Consoles folder.
   f. On the Lab 3.4 Student Answer Sheet, describe how hiding the Lab3-1.msc file changed your view.
   g. Close all windows and log off.

ACTIVITY 5

Mr. Melendres recently purchased a computer for his home from your company. He wants you to help him provide better Internet security and content control, along with a default home page. In this activity, you use the Control Panel to manage Internet security and provide some content control.

1. If necessary, log on using your administrator account.

2. Open Control Panel.

3. Double-click **Internet Options** to display the Internet Properties window.

4. On the General tab, change the Address to **http://www.lawyers.com**.

5. Mr. Melendres wants to know the amount of disk space used by temporary Internet files, as well as where the files are kept. To access this information:
   a. In the Temporary Internet files box, click the **Settings** button.
   b. On your Student Answer Sheet, record the path to the Internet temporary files, along with the default disk space.
   c. Reduce the amount of disk space to **15** MB.

   d. Click **OK** to return to the General tab.

   e. Reduce the Days to keep pages in history to **15**.

6. Mr. Melendres wants to apply the most restrictive Internet content setting to his computer because his children sometimes use the machine. To change these settings:

   a. Click the **Content** tab.

   b. In the Content Advisor box, click the **Enable** button to display the Content Advisor window shown in Figure 3-5.

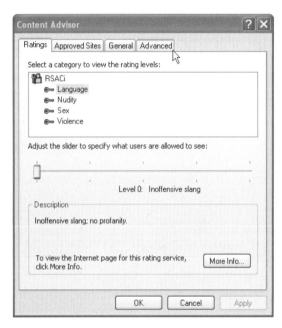

Figure 3-5   Configuring the Content Advisor in Internet Explorer

   c. On your Student Answer Sheet, record the four rating levels.

   d. Be sure the most restrictive setting is applied to each category.

   e. To change the password to "secret," click the **General** tab, and then click **Change Password**. Enter **secret** in both the "New password" and "Confirm new password" text boxes.

   f. Click **OK** to save your settings.

7. Mr. Melendres recently learned that certain Internet Web sites record information called cookies on local computers. He is concerned about these Internet cookies, and wants to be notified before a cookie is written to his system. Secure Socket Layers (SSL) provides a means to help secure data transmitted across the Internet. Because security is very important when transmitting legal documents, Mr. Melendres wants the highest level of SSL set on his system.

   a. Click the **Privacy** tab to display cookie settings.

   b. On your Student Answer Sheet, briefly record the levels of cookie settings that you can configure.

c. Click the **Advanced** tab, and scroll down to find the highest SSL level. On your Student Answer Sheet, record the highest SSL setting.

d. Click **OK** to return to the Internet Properties window.

8. Click **OK** to close the Internet Properties window and return to Control Panel.

9. Close the Control Panel window.

3

LAB 3.5 CONFIGURING HARDWARE PROFILES AND POWER MANAGEMENT

Objective

Mr. Melendres has recently purchased a notebook computer that he plans to use on the road or in the courtroom. He wants to be able to plug the notebook into his network when at the office, but does not want to receive network error messages when he is working offline. In addition, he wants to conserve battery power when using the notebook on the road. After completing this lab, you will be able to:

➤ Configure hardware profiles that allow a user to select either network or offline options

➤ Configure Windows XP Professional power management features

Estimated completion time: **20–25 minutes**

ACTIVITY

1. If necessary, start your computer with Windows XP, and log on as an administrator.

2. Open Control Panel.

3. Double-click the **System** icon to display the System Properties window.

4. Click the **Hardware** tab.

5. Click the **Hardware Profiles** button to display the Hardware Profiles window shown in Figure 3-6.

6. Configure a new hardware profile for office use.

   a. Highlight the current profile, and click the **Copy** button.

   b. Enter **Office** in the To: field, and click **OK**.

   c. Click the **Office** profile, and click the **Properties** button.

   d. Click the **Always include this profile as an option when Windows starts** option.

   e. Click **OK** to save.

Figure 3-6 Configuring hardware profiles

7. Configure a new hardware profile for on the road.
   a. Highlight the current profile, and click the **Copy** button.
   b. Enter **On the road** in the To: field, and click **OK**.
   c. Click the **On the road** profile, and click the **Properties** button.
   d. Click the **This is a portable computer** check box.
   e. Click the **The computer is undocked** option.
   f. Click the **Always include this profile as an option when Windows starts** option.
   g. Click **OK** to save.

8. Rename the current profile.
   a. Click the current profile, and click the **Rename** button.
   b. Enter **Original** in the To: field, and click **OK**.

9. Make Office the default profile, and the On the road profile the second choice.
   a. Click the **Office** profile.
   b. Click the **up arrow** until the Office profile is the first profile listed.
   c. Click **On the road**, and then click the **up arrow** until it is the second profile listed.

10. Click **OK** to save your profiles and return to the System Properties window.

11. Click **OK** to return to Control Panel.

12. Set the power options. Double-click the **Power Options** icon.

3

13. In the Power Schemes window, select **Portable/Laptop**.

14. Change the settings to turn off the monitor after **10** minutes, and turn off the hard disks after **20** minutes.

15. Click the **Hibernate** tab, and ensure that **Enable hibernate** is checked. On your Lab 3.5 Student Answer Sheet, record the description of the hibernate mode.

16. Click **OK** to save your power settings and return to Control Panel.

17. To disable the network adapter in your On the road profile:
    a. Restart the computer, log on as Administrator, and select the **On the road** profile from the startup hardware profiles you created in Step 7.
    b. Open Control Panel.
    c. Double-click the **System** icon, and click the **Hardware** tab.
    d. Click the **Device Manager** button.
    e. Expand the **Network adapters** category.
    f. Right-click your adapter, and click **Properties**.
    g. In the Device usage field, select the **Do not use this device in the current hardware profile (disable)** option, and click **OK** to return to the Device Manager window.
    h. Close all windows.

18. Test your profiles.
    a. Restart your computer.
    b. Select the **Office** profile, and press **Enter**.
    c. Log on as an administrator, and verify that you can access the network.
    d. Restart your computer.
    e. Select the **On the road** profile, and press **Enter**.
    f. Log on as an administrator and verify that the network is unavailable. On the Lab 3.5 Student Answer Sheet, record how you were able to determine that this profile disabled network access.
    g. Restart the computer, and select the **Office** profile.

19. Remove the Office and On the road profiles.
    a. Restart your computer, and log on as the administrator.
    b. Open Control Panel, and double-click the **System** icon.
    c. Click the **Hardware** tab, and then click the **Hardware Profiles** button.
    d. Click the **Office** profile to highlight it.
    e. Click the **Delete** button, and click **Yes** to confirm the deletion.
    f. If necessary, click the **On the road** profile to highlight it.
    g. Click the **Delete** button, and click **Yes** to confirm the deletion.
    h. Click **OK** twice to close the System window.
    i. Close the Control Panel window.
    j. Restart your computer, and verify that the extra profiles have been removed.

MANAGING WINDOWS XP FILE SYSTEMS AND STORAGE

Labs included in this chapter

➤ Lab 4.1 Creating and Managing Drives and Folders

➤ Lab 4.2 Managing Disk Storage and Mount Points

➤ Lab 4.3 Securing the File System

➤ Lab 4.4 Auditing File System Activity

➤ Lab 4.5 Sharing Folders

Microsoft MCSE Exam #70-270 Objectives	
Objective	**Lab**
Monitor and configure disks	4.1, 4.2
Configure and manage file systems	4.1
Convert from one file system to another	
Monitor, manage, and troubleshoot access to files and folders	
Control access to files and folders by using permissions	4.3, 4.4
Configure, manage, and troubleshoot file compression	4.2, 4.3
Manage and troubleshoot access to shared folders	
Create and remove shared folders	4.5
Control access to shared folders by using permissions	4.5

Student Answer Sheets to accompany the labs in this chapter are available for downloading from the Online Companion for this manual at *www.course.com*.

LAB 4.1 CREATING AND MANAGING DRIVES AND FOLDERS

Objective

Your company's policy when installing Windows XP is to separate the Windows XP operating system from application data and shared data by leaving some unallocated disk space. Keeping application data on a separate volume or volumes from the Windows XP operating system facilitates backup and recovery operations. In addition, leaving unallocated disk space allows the flexibility of assigning the extra space as one or more volumes when needed. The Animal Care Center wants to transfer shared data from the Novell server to the Windows XP Professional system. To do this, you need to establish another volume and create some shared folders. New volumes can be formatted using FAT16, FAT32, or the NTFS file system. Although any of these file systems can be used to store shared folders, NTFS volumes provide more security and reliability. FAT volumes have the advantage of being accessible from DOS or Windows 95 in the event Windows XP will not start. In this lab, you learn how to create FAT volumes and convert them to the NTFS file system. After completing this lab, you will be able to:

➤ Create and format a new disk partition

➤ Identify the limitations of Basic disk storage

➤ Change a drive letter on a volume or partition

➤ Convert a FAT file system to NTFS

 This lab involves working with disk partitions. Errors made in the lab could corrupt or delete the existing operating system or files. If the computer you use is used for other purposes or classes, you should have a removable disk or an image of the existing partitions, as described in the Introduction to this lab manual, before you continue.

Requirements

➤ At least 50 MB of unallocated space on your primary disk drive in an extended partition

Estimated completion time: **20–25 minutes**

ACTIVITY

1. If necessary, start your computer with Windows XP, and log on as an administrator.

2. Create a Microsoft Management Console (MMC) for disk management.

   a. Click **Start**, click **Run**, type **mmc** in the Open text box, and press **Enter**.

   b. From the **File** menu, click **Add/Remove Snap-in** to display the Add/Remove Snap-in window.

c. Click the **Add** button to display the Add Standalone Snap-in window.

d. Click **Disk Management**, and then click the **Add** button.

e. Verify that the **This computer** option button is selected, and then click **Finish** to return to the Add Standalone Snap-in window.

f. Click **Close**, and then click **OK** to return to the console window. Notice that the Console Root now includes the Disk Management tool.

g. Save this console to make it available in the Programs menu for all users:

- From the **File** menu, click **Save As**.

- Navigate to, and double-click, the **Documents and Settings** folder.

- Double-click **All Users**.

- Double-click **Start Menu**.

- Double-click **Programs**.

- Enter the name **Disk Management** in the File name text box.

- Click **Save**.

- Exit the Disk Management console.

3. Identify the disk type of your disk drive.

a. Start the Disk Management tool by clicking **Start**, pointing to **All Programs**, and clicking **Disk Management**.

b. Click **Disk Management (Local)** to display a Disk Management window similar to the one shown in Figure 4-1. (Depending upon your Windows 98 installation, the file system for your C: partition might be either FAT or FAT32.)

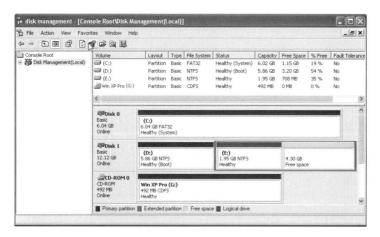

Figure 4-1   Managing hard disks in Windows XP

    c. Right-click **Disk 0**, and click the **Properties** option. Using the various tabs, record the requested information from the Student Answer Sheet.

4. Creating new partitions or logical drives changes letters assigned to existing drives, causing software problems. To prevent this, you can assign each volume or logical drive the letter you want it to have. In this step of the lab you will assign a drive letter to each drive, and to the CD-ROM. To assign a drive letter to each partition and to the CD-ROM drive:

    a. Right-click the drive containing your Windows XP operating system. If you are unsure which drive contains your operating system, do the following:

- Open **Control Panel**.
- Double-click the **System** icon.
- Click the **Advanced** tab.
- Click the **Environment Variables** button.
- The drive letter specified in the Path variable is the boot drive containing your Windows XP operating system.
- Close Control Panel.

    b. Click the **Change Drive Letter and Paths** option.

    c. Click the **Change** button, and, on your Student Answer Sheet, record the message you see.

    d. Right-click your **CD-ROM** drive.

    e. Click the **Change Drive Letter and Paths** option.

    f. Click the **Change** button to display the Change Drive Letter or Path window.

    g. Click the list arrow to display available drive letters.

    h. Click **R** (for ROM), and click **OK**. A warning message is shown.

    i. Click **Yes** to confirm the change.

    j. Notice that your CD-ROM drive has been changed to "R:".

5. Create a new logical drive consisting of half your existing free space.

    a. Right-click the free space.

    b. Click **New Logical Drive**, and click **Next** to launch the **New Partition Wizard**.

    c. Verify that the **Logical drive** option button is selected, and then click **Next** to display the Specify Partition Size window.

    d. Enter a partition size that will leave at least 25 MB of free space after the drive is created. (To format the new drive with the FAT32 file system, the drive must be at least 50 MB.)

    e. Click **Next** to accept the default drive letter and display the Format Partition window.

    f. If your new drive is at least 50 MB, use the scroll button in the "File system" text box to select the **FAT32** file system. If your drive is less than 50 MB, select the **FAT** file system.

g. Enter the name **SHARED DATA** in the Volume label text box, and click **Next** to display the summary window. On your Student Answer Sheet, record the summary information.

h. Click **Finish** to create and format the new logical drive. If you receive an error message indicating that the volume is in use, click **OK** to continue, right-click the new logical drive, and, click the **Format** option. Enter the volume name **SHARED DATA**, and depending upon the drive size, format the drive using FAT (less than 50 MB) or FAT32 (50 MB or larger).

i. Exit Disk Management.

6. Create the following folder structure on your new drive, using Windows Explorer and the File, New, Folder menu options. Select the drive and create the Forms, Projects, and Inventory folders; then select the Projects folder and create the Ads, Docs, Images, and Website folders.

7. To simulate storage use, copy to your Images folder three .bmp files from the WINDOWS folder located on your Windows XP drive. Copy all files that have the extension .txt from the WINDOWS folder to your Docs folder.

8. Find and record FAT or FAT32 folder information.

a. Click **Start**, **My Computer**.

b. Double-click your new drive to open the SHARED DATA window.

c. Right-click your **Projects** folder, and click **Properties** to display the General tab for your Projects folder.

d. On your Student Answer Sheet, record FAT or FAT32 folder information.

e. Click **Cancel** to return to the SHARED DATA window.

f. Close all windows.

9. To take advantage of the security and reliability features of Windows XP, you need to convert the drive to NTFS.

a. Make sure that all Windows Explorer windows to the drive you want to format are closed; otherwise the drive cannot be formatted or converted.

b. Windows XP does not contain a GUI function in Disk Manager to convert file system formats. As a result, to convert to NTFS, you need to open a Command Prompt window. Click **Start**, point to **All Programs**, point to **Accessories**, and then click **Command Prompt**.

c. From the Command Prompt window, enter the command:
   Convert *drive*: /fs:NTFS
   Replace *drive:* with the drive letter of the FAT32 drive you want converted to NTFS, and press **Enter**.

d. Enter **SHARED DATA** as the current volume label, and press **Enter** to perform the conversion.

e. Type **Exit**, and press **Enter** to exit the Command Prompt and return to the Windows XP desktop.

10. Record NTFS folder information.
    a. Click **Start**, **My Computer**.
    b. Double-click your new drive to open the SHARED DATA window.
    c. Right-click your **Projects** folder, and click **Properties** to display the General tab for your Projects folder.
    d. On your Student Answer Sheet, record the NTFS folder information.
    e. Click **Cancel** to return to the Shared Data window.
    f. Close the SHARED DATA window.
    g. Close My Computer.
    h. Log off.

LAB 4.2 MANAGING DISK STORAGE AND MOUNT POINTS

Objective

The number of scanned images stored on the shared Animal Care Center computer located in Dennis's office is filling up the Shared Data volume. Dennis has called you and wants you to make more disk space available to the Projects folder. He also wants to be able to use the extended features available when he opens the images folder. After completing this lab, you will be able to:

➤ Configure file compression

➤ Customize folder types

➤ Identify limitations of Basic disk storage

➤ Identify the steps necessary to extend a volume

➤ Identify the steps necessary to convert a Basic disk to Dynamic storage

➤ Mount a volume to an empty directory

Requirements

➤ At least 25 MB of unallocated space on your primary disk drive

This lab involves working with disk partitions. Errors made in the lab could corrupt or delete the existing operating system or files. If the computer you are using is used for other purposes or classes, before you continue, you should have a removable disk or an image of the existing partitions, as described in the Introduction to this lab manual.

Estimated completion time: **15–20 minutes**

ACTIVITY

1. If necessary, start your computer with Windows XP, and log on as an administrator.

2. One way to make more disk storage available is to compress the files. Because of the large number of repeated bit strings in scanned images, compressing scanned image files can free up a lot of disk space. In this step, you compress the Images folder and determine the amount of disk space saved.

   a. Click **Start**, **My Computer**, and navigate to your **Projects** folder.

   b. Right-click the **Images** folder, and click the **Properties** option.

   c. On your Lab 4.2 Student Answer Sheet, record the Size on disk value (folder size before compression).

   d. From the General tab, click the **Advanced** button.

   e. Click the **Compress contents to save disk space** check box, and then click **OK** to return to the Images Properties window.

   f. Click the **Apply** button.

   g. On the Confirm Attribute Changes window, ensure that the **Apply changes to this folder, subfolders and files** option is selected, and then click **OK**.

   h. On your Student Answer Sheet, record the Size on disk value (folder size after compression).

3. Windows XP provides additional features when viewing a folder based on the type of files. The default folder type is documents. In this step, you will change the folder type to images.

   a. Right-click the **Images** folder, and click the **Properties** option.

   b. Click the **Customize** tab to display the folder options window.

   c. Using the scroll button, choose **Photo Album** as the folder template.

   d. Click **OK** to close the Images Properties window.

   e. Double-click the **Images** folder and take note of the Picture tasks section.

   f. Close all windows.

4. Although compressing the files has provided temporary relief for the disk storage problem, to provide a longer-term solution, you may take some of the unallocated disk space and use it to extend the Projects folder. To attempt to extend the existing drive, do the following:

   a. In the Disk Management window, click the drive containing the Projects folder.

   b. Click the **Action** menu, and point to **All Tasks**.

   c. On your Student Answer Sheet, list the tasks you can perform on a Basic disk partition.

4

     d. On your Student Answer Sheet, record why the Extend a volume option is not available.

     e. Press **Esc** twice to return to the Disk Management console.

5. Dynamic storage drives support spanned, mirrored, striped, and RAID-5 volumes. As a result, a possible alternative to extending a drive is to convert the existing drive to Dynamic storage. To determine the feasibility of converting drive 0 to Dynamic storage, do the following:

     a. Right-click **Disk 0**. (Make sure that you right-click on Disk 0, not C: drive.)

     b. Click the **Convert to Dynamic Disk** option to display the Convert to Dynamic Disk window.

     c. Verify that Disk 0 is selected, and then click **OK** to display the Disks to Convert window.

     d. Click the **Convert** to confirm the upgrade.

     e. On your Student Answer Sheet, record the message you receive.

     f. Click **No** to abort the upgrade.

6. Another alternative to extending a partition is to create a new partition, and then mount that partition within an empty folder on the drive you want to extend. For example, in this step you provide more disk space for the Images folder by creating a new partition, moving the files from the Images folder to the new partition, and then mounting the new partition in the empty Folder directory.

     a. If necessary, start the Disk Management console.

     b. Follow the procedure in Lab 4.1, Step 5, to create another partition using the remainder of the unallocated disk space. On your Student Answer Sheet, record the drive letter of the new partition.

     c. Use My Computer to move all the files from the Images folder to the new drive.

     d. From the Disk Management console, right-click the new volume, and click the **Change Drive Letter and Paths** option to display the Change Drive Letter and Path window.

     e. To mount the drive in an NTFS folder, you first need to remove the drive letter. Click the **Remove** button, and then click **Yes** to confirm the action and return to the Disk Management console.

     f. From the Disk Management console, right-click the New Volume, and click the **Change Drive Letter and Paths** option to display the Change Drive Letter and Path window.

     g. Click the **Add** button to display the Add new Drive Letter or Path window.

     h. Click the **Mount in the following empty NTFS folder** option button.

     i. Click the **Browse** button, and navigate to your Images folder.

     j. Click your **Images** folder, and click **OK** to display the path to the mount point.

     k. Click **OK** to mount the drive in the Images folder.

7. View and record folder statistics.
    a. Click **Start**, **My Computer**.
    b. Open your SHARED DATA drive.
    c. Right-click your **Projects** folder, click **Properties**, and, on your Student Answer Sheet, record the storage space used.
    d. Open your **Projects** folder. On your Student Answer Sheet, describe the appearance of the Images folder.
    e. Right-click the **Images** volume, click **Properties**, and, on your Student Answer Sheet, record the NTFS mounted volume information.
    f. Click the **Properties** button, and, on your Student Answer Sheet, record the space utilization statistics.
    g. Click **Cancel** twice to close the Images windows.
    h. Double-click the **Images** volume object, and verify that all image files are accessible.

8. Close all windows and log off.

LAB 4.3 SECURING THE FILE SYSTEM

Objective

Mr. Melendres wants his legal assistants and secretaries to have access to case and client information on his computer, but he is concerned about securing information to prevent unauthorized access or changes to sensitive files. To provide access for the assistants and secretaries, you need to create user accounts and storage folders, and then use NTFS permissions to provide the required access permissions. After completing this lab, you will be able to:

➤ Create restricted user accounts and groups

➤ Secure the file system using NTFS permissions

➤ Use inheritable permissions to set default permissions to subfolders

➤ Predict NTFS permission changes when copying or moving an object

Estimated completion time: **30 minutes**

ACTIVITY

1. If necessary, start your computer with Windows XP, and log on as an administrator.

2. By default, XP has simple file sharing turned on. This allows all users full control of all shared folders. In order to grant access to specific users or groups, this feature must be turned off. To do so, do the following:
    a. Click **Start**, **My Computer**.

    b. Click **Tools** on the menu bar, and click **Folder Options.**

    c. Click the **View** tab, and scroll to the bottom of the Advanced settings box.

    d. Clear the **Use Simple File Sharing Recommended** box.

    e. Click **OK**, and then close all windows.

3. Create the following folder structure on your Windows XP boot partition:

    D:\Cases
        D:\Cases\In-Progress
        D:\Cases\In-Progress\JSmith
        D:\Cases\In-Progress\<YourName>
    D:\Cases\Completed
        D:\Cases\In-Progress\RRich
    D:\Clients

The Cases folder contains a subfolder for cases currently in progress. Within this folder Mr. Melendres creates an In-Progress folder for each case he is currently working on. When a case is completed, Mr. Melendres moves the folder to the Completed folder. The Clients folder contains a Microsoft Access database containing name, address, e-mail address, phone number, and notes for each client who has contacted the Melendres and Associates law firm.

4. Use Notepad to create the following files:

    a. A text file named **Claim1** in the Your-Name folder.

    b. A text file named **Lawsuit** in the JSmith folder.

    c. A text file named **Corp** in the RRich folder.

5. Create a user named LegalSec1 as follows:

    a. Open Control Panel.

    b. Double-click **Users Accounts**.

    c. Click **Create a new Account**, and enter the following user information: User name: **LegalSec1**

    d. Click **Next**.

    e. Click **Limited** as the account type, and click **Create Account.**

    f. Click the **LegalSec1**, and then click **Create Password.**

    g. Enter a new password, and retype the password in the confirm password dialog box.

    h. If you want, enter a Hint to remind you of the password, and click **Create Password.**

6. Create a group named Assistants.

    a. Click **Start**, **Control Panel**, **Administrative Tools**, and then double-click **Computer Management**. (If you have a My Computer icon on your desktop, you can right-click it and select **Manage**.)

    b. Open the Local Users and Groups, and click **Groups** to display the window shown in Figure 4-2.

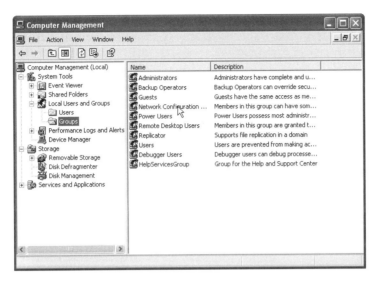

Figure 4-2   Managing groups in Windows XP

4

   c. From the **Action** menu, click the **New Group** option.

   d. Enter **Assistants** in the Group name text box, and **Legal Assistants** in the Description text box.

   e. Click the **Add** button to display the Select Users window.

   f. Type **LegalSec1** in the Enter the object names to select section, and click **OK**.

   g. Click the **Create** button to create the group and return to the New Group window.

   h. Click **Close** to return to the Local Users and Groups window. Verify that the new group Assistants is shown.

   i. Close all windows to return to the desktop.

7. Check default permissions.

   a. Click **Start**, **My Computer**.

   b. Right-click your **Windows XP boot drive**, and click the **Properties** option.

   c. Click the **Security** tab. On your Lab 4.3 Student Answer Sheet, record the default permissions.

   d. Click **Cancel** to close the Properties window.

   e. Double-click your Windows XP boot drive.

   f. Right-click the **Cases** folder, and click the **Properties** option.

   g. Click the **Security** tab. On your Student Answer Sheet, record the default permissions.

   h. Click **Advanced** to display the Advanced Security Settings for Cases window.

    i. By default, all permissions are inherited from the root of the drive. To stop the inheritance, remove the check mark from the **Inherit from parent the permission entries that apply to child objects** check box. On your Student Answer Sheet, record the two possible options for dealing with the inheritable permissions.

    j. Click the **Remove** button. On your Student Answer Sheet, describe the results of removing the inheritable permissions option.

    k. Click the **Inherit from parent the permission entries that apply to child objects** check box.

    l. Click the **Apply** button. On your Student Answer Sheet, record the results.

    m. Click **OK** twice, and then close the local drive window.

8. Provide the Assistants group with permissions to maintain the Clients database.

    a. Click **Start**, **My Computer**, and open your Windows XP boot drive.

    b. Right-click the **Clients** folder you created in Step 2, and click **Properties**.

    c. Click the **Security** tab. On your Student Answer Sheet, record the default user permissions assigned to the Clients folder.

    d. Click **Advanced**, and turn off inheritable permissions by clicking the **Inherit from parent the permission entries that apply to child objects** check box.

    e. Click the **Remove** option to remove inheritance from the security list.

    f. Click **OK**, and click **Yes** on the warning box.

    g. Click the **Add** button to display the Select Users or Groups window.

    h. Type **Administrators**; **Assistants** in the dialog box, and click **OK**. Verify that both the Administrators and Assistants groups have been added to the Security window, as shown in Figure 4-3.

    i. Grant the Administrators group Full Control:

      ■ Click the **Administrators** group in the upper Name window.

      ■ Click the **Allow** box for Full Control in the Permissions for Administrators window.

    j. To allow the legal assistants to update the client database files, grant the Assistants group the Modify right:

      ■ Click the **Assistants** group in the upper Name window.

      ■ Click the **Allow** box for Modify in the Permissions for Assistants window.

    k. Click **OK** to save your permission changes.

Figure 4-3 Adding members to local groups

9. Provide the Administrators group with Full Control to the Cases folder and all subfolders.

   a. Right-click the **Cases** folder, and click **Properties**.
   b. Click the **Security** tab.
   c. Click **Advanced**, and turn off inheritable permissions by clicking the **Inherit from parent the permission entries that apply to child objects** check box.
   d. Click the **Remove** option to remove inheritance from the security list.
   e. Click **OK**, and click **Yes** on the warning box.
   f. Click the **Add** button to display the Select Users or Groups window.
   g. Type **Administrators** in the dialog box, and click **OK**.
   h. Click the **Allow** box for Full Control in the Permissions for Administrators window.
   i. Click the **Advanced** button to display the Advanced Security Settings for Cases window.
   j. Click the **Replace permission entries on all child objects with entries shown here that apply to child objects** check box.
   k. Click **OK**. Describe the Security message on your Student Answer Sheet.
   l. Click **Yes** to return to the Cases Properties window.

m. To allow users to find the In-Progress and Completed folders, you need to provide the Assistants group with the List Folder Contents right to the Cases folder:

- Click the **Add** button, and type **Assistants** in the dialog box. Click **OK** to add Assistants to the Security window with default rights.
- Remove all rights except List Folder Contents.

n. Click **OK** to save your changes and return to My Computer.

10. Provide the Assistants group with the default of Read only access to the Completed folder and all its subfolders.

a. Open the **Cases** folder from My Computer.

b. Right-click the **Completed** folder, and click the **Properties** option.

c. Click the **Security** tab. On your Student Answer Sheet, record the default security settings.

d. Click **Assistants**, and then click **Read** in the Allow column.

e. Click **OK** to save the permissions.

11. Provide the Assistants group with the permissions needed to change documents in the In-Progress folder.

a. Right-click the **In-Progress** folder, and click the **Properties** option.

b. Click the **Security** tab. On your Student Answer Sheet, record the default security settings.

c. Click **Assistants**, and then click **Modify** in the Allow column.

d. Click **OK** to save the permissions.

12. Check subfolder permissions.

a. Double-click the **In-Progress** folder to display its subfolders.

b. Right-click the **JSmith** folder, and click the **Properties** option.

c. Click the **Security** tab. On your Student Answer Sheet, record the permissions for the JSmith folder.

d. Click **Cancel**, and then click the **Back** button.

e. Double-click the **Completed** folder to display its subfolders.

f. Right-click the **RRich** folder, and click the **Properties** button.

g. Click the **Security** tab. On your Student Answer Sheet, record the permissions for the RRich folder.

h. Click **Cancel**, and then click the **Back** button.

13. Move the JSmith folder from the In-Progress folder to the Completed folder, and check permissions.

a. Use My Computer to open the **Cases** folder.

b. Double-click the **In-Progress** folder to open it.

c. Right-click the **JSmith** folder, and click the **Cut** option.

d. Click the **Up** button to move back to the Cases folder window.

e. Double-click the **Completed** folder to open it.

f. From the **Edit** menu, click the **Paste** option.

g. Right-click the **JSmith** folder, and click **Properties**.

h. Click the **Security** tab. On your Student Answer Sheet, record the permissions for the Assistants group.

i. Remove the check marks from all permissions except Read, Execute, and List.

j. Click **OK** to save your changes.

k. Click the **Up** button to return to the Cases folder window.

14. Copy the **Your-name** folder from the In-Progress folder to the Completed folder and check its permissions.

a. Double-click the **In-Progress** folder to open it.

b. Right-click the **Your-name** folder, and click the **Copy** option.

c. Click the **Up** button to return to the Cases folder window.

d. Double-click the **Completed** folder to open it.

e. From the **Edit** menu, click the **Paste** option.

f. Right-click the **Your-name** folder, and click the **Properties** option.

g. Click the **Security** tab. On your Student Answer Sheet, record the rights for the Assistants group.

h. On your Student Answer Sheet, describe why the permissions obtained when copying the Your-name folder were different from the permissions obtained when moving the JSmith folder.

i. Click **Cancel** to return to the Completed folder window.

j. Close all windows and log off.

LAB 4.4 AUDITING FILE SYSTEM ACTIVITY

Objective

Windows XP provides the capability to audit resources and services for either successful or failed access attempts. Auditing is useful to monitor resource usage, locate intruder activity, or track changes made to files and folders. For example, assume that in order to track any changes made to the Cases/In-Progress folder, Mr. Melendres wants you to enable auditing on the In-Progress folder and all its subfolders. After completing this lab, you will be able to:

➤ Turn on a local audit policy

➤ Configure auditing for files and folders

Estimated completion time: **10 minutes**

ACTIVITY

1. The first step to configuring auditing for the Melendres and Associates firm is to enable the local audit policy on the computer. Follow the procedure described below:

   a. Click **Start**, **Control Panel**, and double-click the **Administrative Tools** icon.

   b. If necessary, double-click the **Local Security Policy** icon to expand the **Local Policies** folder.

   c. Click the **Audit Policy** folder to list all audit policy options, as shown in Figure 4-4.

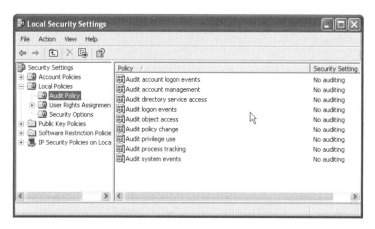

Figure 4-4   Configuring the Audit Policy

   d. To audit changes to files, double-click the **Audit object access** option to display the Local Security Settings—Audit object access window.

   e. Click both the **Success** and **Failure** check boxes.

   f. Click **OK** to enable object access auditing.

   g. Close the Local Security Setting window.

   h. Close the Administrative Tools window.

2. After enabling object access auditing, you need to specify which objects, such as files or folders, you want to audit. Follow the procedure listed below to audit any changes made to files in the In-Progress folder and in all its subfolders.

   a. If necessary, use My Computer to open the **Cases** folder.

   b. Right-click the **In-Progress** folder, and click the **Properties** button.

   c. Click the **Security** tab, and then click the **Advanced** button.

   d. Click the **Auditing** tab to display the Auditing Entries window.

   e. Click the **Add** button to display the Select User or Group search window.

   f. To search for a user, computer, or group, type in a full or partial name in the Enter the object names to select dialog box. Type **Everyone**, and click **OK**.

4

g. In the Object tab window, click the Successful box for successful completion of the following access events:

- Create Files / Write Data
- Create Folders / Append Data
- Delete Subfolders and Files
- Delete

h. Click **OK** to add this Auditing entry to the Audit tab.

i. Click **OK** to save your changes, and return to the In-Progress Properties window.

j. Click **OK** to return to My Computer.

k. Close all windows and log off.

3. Log on as LegalSec1 and modify the file in the JSmith folder to indicate that the case is completed. Close all windows and log off.

4. Log on as an administrator and check the audit file.

a. Launch the Computer Management console you created in Lab 3.1. Click **Start**, point to **All Programs**, and click **Computer Management**. (If you no longer have the Computer Management console, open Control Panel and double-click the **Administrative Tools** icon.)

b. Open Event Viewer, and double-click the **Security** log.

c. On your Lab 4.4 Student Answer Sheet, record the security message information.

d. Exit Event Viewer.

LAB 4.5 SHARING FOLDERS

Objective

The Animal Care Center wants to share and secure the Projects, Forms, Website, and Images folders you created in Lab 4.1. The owner, Dennis Geisler, wants users to be able to access files but have the ability to change only those files they have created in the Docs folder. The SysOp user should be able to update files in any of the shared folders. In addition, because users will be able to create files in the Docs subfolder, Dennis is concerned about the Docs subfolder taking up too much disk space. Dennis wants you to limit the amount of disk space that can be used by Docs. When the space in Docs is used, users will be encouraged to remove old and unwanted files. After completing this lab, you will be able to:

➤ Share folders

➤ Manage shared folder permissions

➤ Access shared folders

➤ Set disk quotas

Estimated completion time: **40–45 minutes**

ACTIVITY 1

Share the Forms folder, and set and test permissions for the folder.

1. If necessary, start your computer with Windows XP, and log on as an administrator.

2. If necessary, follow the procedure in Lab 3.2 to create users named **AppUser** and **SysOp**.

3. Share the Forms folder with the share name Office Forms. Provide all users with Read permission, Administrators with Full Control, and the SysOp user with Change permission.

   a. Click **Start**, **My Computer**, and open the drive containing your Projects, Forms, and Inventory folders.

   b. Right-click the **Forms** folder, and click **Properties**.

   c. Click the **Sharing** tab to display the window shown in Figure 4-5.

Figure 4-5   Configuring a network share

   d. Click the **Share this folder** option button.

   e. In the Share name text box, enter **Office Forms**.

   f. Verify that the User limit is set to **Maximum allowed**.

   g. Click the **Permissions** button. On your Lab 4.5 Student Answer Sheet, record the default permissions.

h. If necessary, highlight the group **Everyone**, and then click the **Remove** button to remove the group Everyone from the Permissions window.

i. Click the **Add** button. In the Enter the object names to select dialog box, type **Administrators**, **Users**, and click **Check Names** to verify your spelling.

j. Click **OK** to return to the Permissions for Office Forms window.

k. On your Student Answer Sheet, record the default permissions for the Users group.

l. Highlight the **Administrators** group, and click the **Allow** box for Full Control permission.

m. Click the **Add** button, and type **SysOp** in the dialog box. Click **OK** to return to the Permission for Office Forms window.

n. Verify that the **SysOp** user is selected, and then click the **Allow** box for Change permission.

o. Click **OK** to save the permissions and return to the Forms folder Sharing tab.

p. Click **OK** to complete sharing your Forms folder.

q. Close all windows and log off.

4. Assume you are the SysOp user located on another computer and you need to edit the Office Forms shared folder. Proceed as follows:

a. Log on as the **SysOp** user.

b. Click **Start**, **My Network Places**, and double-click the **View Workgroup Computers** network task, to display all computers in your workgroup. Your computer name should appear on the screen.

c. Double-click your computer name to display a window showing shared folders and printers.

d. Double-click the **Office Forms** share.

e. Create two text document files, one named **Travel.txt** and the other named **PO.txt**.

f. Use Notepad to enter the line **Use this form to report travel expenses** in the Travel.txt file.

g. Save the Travel.txt file and exit Notepad.

h. Close all windows and log off.

5. Test the Office Forms share as a user.

a. Log on using your **AppUser** user name.

b. Use **My Network Places** to navigate to the Office Forms shared folder.

c. Double-click the **Travel.txt** form to open it, and verify its contents.

d. Add a line that says **$100.00 mileage expense for Joe Smith**.

e. Attempt to save the form. On the Student Answer Sheet, record what happens.

f. Exit Notepad without saving the document, and close all windows.

6. Try accessing and changing the file using My Computer.

   a. Click **Start**, **My Computer**, and open the drive containing your Forms folder.

   b. Open the **Forms** folder, and double-click the **Travel.txt** document to start Notepad.

   c. Add a line that says **$100.00 mileage expense for Joe Smith**.

   d. Attempt to save the Travel.txt document. On the Student Answer Sheet, record what happens.

   e. Exit Notepad and log off.

   f. On the Student Answer Sheet, explain why you were unable to save the Travel.txt file in both cases.

7. Repeat Steps 4 and 5 to test SysOp and AppUser permissions.

ACTIVITY 2

Share the Projects Folder, and provide, and then test the following access permissions.

➤ Administrator has Full Control permissions to all folders and subfolders.

➤ SysOp has Modify permissions to all folders and subfolders.

➤ Users have Read permissions to the Images and Website folders.

➤ Users have the ability to create and manage their own documents in the Docs folder, but can only read other user documents.

1. Log on as an administrator.

2. Share the Projects folder.

3. Provide Users with the Change permission, and Administrators with Full Control permissions. Provide Administrators with Full Control to all folders and subfolders, SysOp with Modify permissions to all folders and subfolders, and Users with Read permissions as follows:

   a. If necessary, use My Computer to navigate to the drive containing your Projects folder.

   b. Right-click the **Projects** folder, and click **Properties**.

   c. Click the **Security** tab, and then click **Advanced**. Remove the check from the **Inherit from parent the permissions entries that apply to child objects** check box. Click **Remove** to confirm the action.

   d. Click **OK** and **Yes** to the warning message.

   e. Click the **Add** button and type **Administrators; Users; SysOp**, and click **Check Names**.

   f. Click **OK** to return to the Properties window.

   g. Highlight **Administrators**, and click the **Allow** box for Full Control.

   h. Highlight **SysOp**, and click the **Allow** box for Modify.

i. Verify that Users have only Read, Execute, and List permissions.

j. Click the **Advanced** button, and check the **Replace permission entries on all child objects with entries shown here that apply to child objects** check box. Click **OK**, and then click **Yes** to confirm the action.

k. Click **OK** to return to the My Computer window.

4. Provide the Users group with permissions to create and manage only their own documents in the Docs folder.

a. Double-click the **Projects** folder to open it.

b. Right-click the **Docs** folder, and click the **Properties** option.

c. Click the **Security** tab. On your Lab 4.5 Student Answer Sheet, record the default permissions.

d. Click the **Advanced** button to display the Advanced Security Settings for Docs window.

e. Highlight the **Users** group, and click the **Edit** button.

f. Click the **Create Files / Write Data** permission, and then click **OK** to return to the Advanced Security Settings for Docs window. Notice that another entry has been added for the Users group.

g. Click **OK** twice to return to the Docs Properties window.

h. Click the **Add** button, and type **CREATOR OWNER** in the dialog box. Creator Owner is a special group whose rights apply only on a file-by-file basis to the creator or owner of that file. By assigning this group the Full Control permission, you allow the owner or creator of a file to manage that file, yet prevent them from modifying or deleting other files in the folder.

i. Click **OK**. If necessary, highlight the **CREATOR OWNER** object, and click the **Allow** box for Full Control.

j. Click **OK** to return to the My Computer window.

5. Close all windows and log off.

6. Test access to your Projects folder by logging on as the AppUser. Then create and access documents in the Docs folder using both My Network Places and My Computer. Record your results on the Student Answer Sheet.

7. From My Network Places, browse to the Website folder. Attempt to create a file in the Website folder. Record the results on your Student Answer Sheet.

8. From My Network Places, browse to the Images volume. Notice that while this folder is located on a different drive, it is still accessible from the Projects share. Attempt to create a file in the Images volume. Record the results on your Student Answer Sheet.

9. Log off.

ACTIVITY 3

Restrict users from the Images volume by setting the following NTFS permissions.

➤ Administrators have Full Control.

➤ Users have only Read, Execute, and List permissions.

➤ SysOp has Modify permission.

1. Log on as an administrator.

2. Launch your Disk Management console.

3. Right-click the **Images** volume named Legal Docs, and click **Properties**.

4. Click the **Security** tab, and click the **Remove** button to remove the group **Everyone**.

5. Click the **Add** button, and type **SysOp; Administrators; Users** in the dialog box.

6. Click **OK** to return to the Images Legal Docs Properties window.

7. Highlight **Administrators**, and click the **Allow** box for Full Control.

8. Highlight **SysOp**, and click the **Allow** box for Modify.

9. Verify that the Users group has only Read, Execute, and List permissions.

10. Click **OK** to save your changes.

11. Exit the Disk Management console.

12. Close all windows and log off.

13. Repeat Activity 2, Step 8, to test permissions to the Images volume.

ACTIVITY 4

Set disk quotas on the disk containing the Projects folder.

1. Log on as an administrator.

2. Open My Computer.

3. Right-click the drive containing your Projects folder, and click the **Properties** option.

4. Click the **Quota** tab, and click the **Enable quota management** and **Deny disk space to users exceeding quota limit** check boxes.

5. Set the disk limit to **10 KB** and the warning level to **8 KB**.

6. Click the **Log event when a user exceeds their quota limit** check box.

7. Click **OK** to save the quota configuration. Click **OK** again.

8. Log off.

9. Log on as the **AppUser**.

10. Use My Computer to navigate to the Docs folder.

11. Use Notepad to create documents until you receive a warning. Record the message on your Student Answer Sheet.

12. Create additional files until you have exceeded your quota.

13. Log off.

14. Log on as an administrator, and start **Event Viewer**.

15. On your Student Answer Sheet, record the security log quota message.

16. Close all windows and log off.

4

CHAPTER FIVE

USERS, GROUPS, PROFILES, AND POLICIES

Labs included in this chapter

➤ Lab 5.1 Creating Local Users and Groups

➤ Lab 5.2 Assigning Group and User Permissions

➤ Lab 5.3 Configuring and Managing User Profiles

➤ Lab 5.4 Applying Account Policies

➤ Lab 5.5 Applying Policies for Auditing and User Rights

Microsoft MCSE Exam #70-270 Objectives	
Objective	Lab
Implement, configure, manage, and troubleshoot local user accounts	
Create and manage local users and groups	5.1
Implement, configure, and troubleshoot account settings	5.4, 5.5
Implement, configure, and troubleshoot account policy	5.4, 5.5
Implement, configure, manage, and troubleshoot local user authentication	
Configure and troubleshoot local user accounts	5.2
Configure and manage user profiles	5.3

Student Answer Sheets to accompany the labs in this chapter are available for downloading from the Online Companion for this manual at *www.course.com*.

LAB 5.1 CREATING LOCAL USERS AND GROUPS

Objective

The Melendres and Associates law firm wants to set up a Windows XP Professional computer as a server for sharing case and billing information. Currently each attorney and a legal assistant share a Windows XP computer to enter ongoing legal information on current cases and to archive completed cases for future reference. The administrative assistant's computer is used to enter and print client bills. Mr. Melendres wants to combine each attorney's case information with the billing system on a single Windows XP Professional system. He then wants to create user and group accounts to allow the following access to the system:

➤ Allow only Mr. Melendres and his legal assistant, Meme Rodregus, to update the Melendres case information

➤ Allow only Ms. Damrau and her legal assistant, Rose Wiggerts, to update the Damrau case information

➤ Allow all employees to read the case information from any attorney

➤ Allow only the administrative assistant, Jan Cunningham, and Mr. Melendres to maintain the billing system files

➤ Allow Jan Cunningham to back up and restore network files

After completing this lab you will be able to:

➤ Define a naming convention and use it to name users and groups

➤ Identify default and system groups

➤ Create local groups

➤ Create local users and assign them to one or more groups

➤ Use default groups to provide backup rights

Estimated completion time: **30 minutes**

ACTIVITY 1

Create a MMC control for Local Users and Groups.

1. Start your computer with Windows XP Professional, and log on as an administrator.

2. Click **Start**, click **Run**, and type **mmc** in the Open text box, and press **Enter**.

3. From the **File** menu, click the **Add/Remove Snap-in** to display the Add/Remove Snap-in window.

4. Click the **Add** button to display the Add Standalone Snap-in window.

5. Double-click the **Local Users and Groups** Snap-in to display the Choose Target Machine window.

6. Verify that the **Local computer** option is selected, and then click **Finish**.

7. Click **Close**, and click **OK** to return to the Console window.

8. From the **File** menu, click **Save As**.

9. Navigate to the root of the drive containing Windows XP Professional.

10. Navigate to the \Documents and Settings\All Users\Start Menu\Programs folder:
    - Double-click the **Documents and Settings** folder.
    - Double-click the **All Users** folder.
    - Double-click the **Start Menu** folder.
    - Double-click the **Programs** folder.

11. Enter the name **Local Users and Groups** in the File name textbox, and click **Save**.

12. Close all windows.

ACTIVITY 2

Define a user naming convention and identify default Windows XP system and local groups.

1. If necessary, start your computer with Windows XP, and log on as an administrator.

2. On the Lab 5.1 User and Group Planning sheet that follows this lab, define a user naming convention and use it to define logon names for all users. (Refer to *MCSE Guide to Windows XP Professional*, Course Technology, Chapter 5, for information on defining a naming convention.) The attorneys should be set up as power users.

3. On your Student Answer Sheet, identify the Windows XP default groups.
   a. Click **Start**, **All Programs**, **Local Users and Groups** (created above), and expand **Local Users and Groups**.
   b. Click the **Groups** folder to display all group names.
   c. Record the default groups on your Lab 5.1 Student Answer Sheet. From your Student Answer Sheet, identify any of the default groups that can be used on your Lab 5.1 User and Group Planning Sheet.
   d. Resize the Local Users and Groups window so it uses about half the screen.
   e. Minimize the Local Users and Groups window.

4. Identify the Windows XP system groups.
   a. Click **Start**, **My Computer**, right-click the drive containing your Windows XP operating system, and click the **Properties** option.
   b. Click the **Security** tab, and then click the **Add** button to display the Select Users or Groups window.

    c. Click **Advanced**, **Find Now**, and compare the groups listed in the Select Users or Groups window to the groups in your Local Users and Groups window. The system groups are the groups listed in the Select Users or Groups window, and not listed in the Local Users and Groups windows.

    d. To list only the System Groups, click **Object Types** at the top of the window and clear the check marks from **Users** and **Groups.** Click **OK**, and then click **Find Now.**

    e. Record the system groups on your Student Answer Sheet. From a reference book (such as *MCSE Guide to Microsoft Windows XP Professional*, Course Technology) briefly record the purpose of each system group along with its default member(s).

    f. Close all windows.

ACTIVITY 3

Create the file system, create local users and groups, and add a user to a group.

1. Create the file system.

    a. Click **Start**, **My Computer**, and open the drive containing your Windows XP operating system.

    b. Create a folder named **Lab5**.

    c. Create the following folders and subfolders within the Lab5 folder.

        Melendres

            In-Progress

            Complete

        Damrau

            In-Progress

            Complete

        Billing

2. According to the recommended Microsoft procedure, you should assign folder permissions to local groups. Then, users who need access to the folders are made members of the appropriate local groups. On the User and Group Planning sheet, define the local groups you will need to assign permissions to the folders you created in Step 1.

3. Create local users.

    a. Open the **Local Users and Groups** control that you created in Lab 5.1.

    b. Click the **Users** folder in the left-side tree window to display all existing users in the right-side results window.

    c. On your Lab 5.1 Student Answer Sheet, record any user names that are marked as disabled.

    d. Click the **Action** menu, **New User** option to display the New User window.

    e. In the User name text box, enter the Logon name of a user from your Lab 5.1 User and Group Planning Sheet.

f. Enter the user's full name and description in the Full name and Description text boxes.

g. Enter an initial password, and remove the check mark from the **User must change password at next logon** option.

h. Click the **Create** button.

i. Repeat Steps (f) through (i) to create all the users on your Lab 5.1 User and Group Planning Sheet. Click **Close** to return to the Local Users and Groups window.

4. Create local groups and assign users.

a. Click the **Groups** folder in the left-side tree window to display all groups in the right-side results window.

b. From the **Action** menu, click **New Group** to display the New Group window.

c. Enter a Group name and Description from your Lab 5.1 User and Group Planning Sheet.

d. To add group members, click the **Add** button to display the Select Users window.

e. Click **Advanced**, and then click **Object Types** at the top of the window.

f. Remove the check from the **Built-in security principles**, and click **OK**.

g. Click **Find Now** to display a list of users.

h. Use the scroll bar to find the first user's name and click it.

i. Ctrl+click each additional user name until all users for the group are highlighted.

j. Click the **OK** button to insert the names in the bottom window.

k. After all group members are included, click the **OK** button to return to the New Group window.

l. Click the **Create** button.

m. Repeat Steps (b) through (l) until all four groups are created.

n. Click the **Close** button to return to the Local Users and Groups window.

5. Add Jan Cunningham to the Backup Operators group.

a. Click the **Users** folder to display the existing user accounts.

b. Double-click Jan Cunningham's account to display the Properties page.

c. Click the **Member Of** tab to display current group memberships.

d. Click the **Add** button, and type **Backup Operators** in the dialog box.

e. Click **OK** to add Backup Operators to the list of groups Jan belongs to.

f. Click **OK** to return to the Local Users and Groups window.

g. Close the Local Users and Groups window.

6. Close all windows and log off.

Lab 5.1 User and Group Planning Sheet

Name:

Computer ID:

User/Group Naming Convention:

User Names

Logon name	Full Name	Description	Password
	Sebastian Melendres	Head Attorney ❏ Power user ❏ Limited User ❏ Other	❏ Change at logon ❏ Cannot change ❏ Never expires
	Julie Damrau	Attorney ❏ Power user ❏ Limited User ❏ Other	❏ Change at logon ❏ Cannot change ❏ Never expires
	Meme Rodregus	Legal assistant for Mr. Melendres ❏ Power user ❏ Limited User ❏ Other	❏ Change at logon ❏ Cannot change ❏ Never expires
	Rosemary Wiggerts	Legal assistant for Ms. Damrau ❏ Power user ❏ Limited User ❏ Other	❏ Change at logon ❏ Cannot change ❏ Never expires
	Jan Cunningham	Administrative Assistant ❏ Power user ❏ Limited User ❏ Other	❏ Change at logon ❏ Cannot change ❏ Never expires

Local Groups

Group Name	Resource Managed	Description/Department	Members
	Sebastian Melendres cases		
	Julie Damrau cases		
	Client billing system		
	Read all case information		
	Back up/restore the system		

LAB 5.2 ASSIGNING GROUP AND USER PERMISSIONS

Objective

In this lab you complete the process of securing the Melendres and Associates server. You will assign permissions to the groups and users to accomplish the access needs defined in Lab 5.1. In addition, Mr. Melendres has a folder with certain files that he cannot let anyone access. Because support people, such as you, need to log on as administrator, he wants to secure the folder so that it cannot be accessed by anyone with administrator privileges. After completing this lab you will be able to:

➤ Provide NTFS permissions to groups and users

➤ Secure a folder from administrator access by taking ownership

➤ Test security permissions

5

Estimated completion time: **30 minutes**

ACTIVITY

1. On the Lab 5.2 Permissions Planning Sheet, determine the permissions to be granted to each group. Be sure to include the Administrators group with Full Control.

2. If necessary, start your computer with Windows XP, and log on as an administrator.

3. Secure the Billing folder.
   a. If necessary, click **Start**, **My Computer**, and navigate to your newly created Lab5 folder.
   b. Right-click the **Billing** folder, and click the **Properties** option.
   c. Click the **Security** tab to display the security window shown in Figure 5-1.

Figure 5-1   Configuring basic NTFS permissions

> d. Click **Advanced**, and remove the check mark from the **Inherit from parent the permission entries that apply to child objects** check box.
>
> e. Click **Remove** to remove all inheritance.
>
> f. Click **OK**, and then click **Yes** on the warning message.
>
> g. Add the groups and permissions identified on your Lab 5.2 Permissions Planning Sheet.
>
> h. Click **OK** to close the Billing Properties window.

4. Secure the Melendres folder.

> a. Right-click the **Melendres** folder, and click the **Properties** option.
>
> b. Click the **Security** tab, and then click **Advanced.**
>
> c. Remove the check mark from **the Inherit from parent the permission entries that apply to child objects** check box.
>
> d. Click **Remove** to remove all inheritance.
>
> e. Click **OK**, and then click **Yes** on the warning message.
>
> f. Add the groups and permissions identified on your Lab 5.2 Permissions Planning Sheet.
>
> g. Click **OK** to close the Melendres Properties window.

5. Secure the Damrau folder.

> a. Right-click the **Damrau** folder, and click the **Properties** option.
>
> b. Click the **Security** tab, and then click **Advanced**.
>
> c. Remove the check mark from the **Inherit from parent the permission entries that apply to child objects** check box.

d. Click **Remove** to remove all inheritance.

e. Click **OK**, and then click **Yes** on the warning message.

f. Add the groups and permissions identified on your Lab 5.2 Permissions Planning Sheet.

g. Click **OK** to close the **Damrau** Properties window.

h. Use the **UP** button to navigate back to your Lab5 folder.

6. If necessary, on your Lab 5.2 Permissions Planning Sheet, make any additional permission assignments indicated.

7. Each attorney needs a private area to which only that attorney has access. This can be accomplished by creating a "Private" subfolder for each attorney, and giving only the attorney full control of the folder. The attorney can then log on and take ownership of his or her Private folder. After this is done, all users are locked out, including the Administrator. The only way the Administrator can gain control is by taking ownership and adding the Administrators group to the security permissions list. Follow the procedure below to set up a Private folder for Mr. Melendres.

a. Double-click the **Melendres** folder to open it.

b. Create a subfolder named **Private**.

c. Right-click the **Private** folder, and click **Properties**.

d. Click the **Security** tab, and then click **Advanced**.

e. Remove the check mark from the **Inherit from parent the permission entries that apply to child objects** check box.

f. Click **Remove** to remove all inheritance.

g. Click **OK**, and then click **Yes** on the warning message.

h. Click the **Add** button, and type the user name you assigned to Mr. Melendres in the dialog box.

i. Click **OK** to return to the Private Properties window, and then click **Full Control** in the Allow column for the Melendres user.

j. Try to give ownership to Mr. Melendres:

- Click the **Advanced** button to display the Advanced Security Settings for Private window, as shown in Figure 5-2.

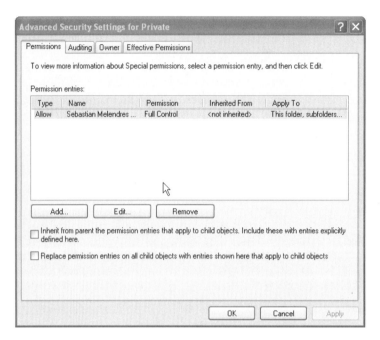

Figure 5-2 Configuring advanced NTFS permissions

- Click the **Owner** tab, and record the current owner of this folder.
- On your Lab 5.2 Student Answer Sheet, record the results of attempting to give ownership to Mr. Melendres.
- Click **OK** to return to the Private Properties window.

k. Click **OK** to save the permission changes and return to the My Computer window.

l. Close all windows and log off.

m. Log on as the Melendres user.

n. Use My Computer to navigate to the Lab5\Melendres folder.

o. Right-click the **Private** subfolder, and click the **Properties** option.

p. Click the **Security** tab, and then click the **Advanced** button to display the Access Control Settings for Private.

q. Click the **Owner** tab.

r. On your Student Answer Sheet, record the names of users you can select as owners.

s. Click the Melendres user, and then click **OK** to make Mr. Melendres the owner of the folder.

t. Click **OK** to save your changes and return to My Computer.

u. Close all windows and log off.

8. On your Lab 5.2 Permissions Planning Sheet, make an entry for each attorney's Private folder. Include path, whether to inherit parent permissions, owner, and permissions.

9. Repeat Step 7 to establish a Private folder for Ms. Damrau.

10. Share the Melendres, Damrau, and Billing folders.

    a. Share each of the following folders, and change the shared permissions by removing the group Everyone, and adding the group Users with Full Control:

      ■ Melendres

      ■ Damrau

      ■ Billing

    b. On your Student Answer Sheet, describe why it is not necessary to provide specific groups and users with shared permissions.

    c. Close all windows and log off.

11. Test and debug the system.

    a. Log on as the Melendres user.

    b. Use My Network Places to browse to the Melendres In-Progress folder.

    c. Create a subfolder named **BMeulner**.

    d. Within the BMeulner subfolder, use Notepad to create a text file named **CaseLog**. Place the following line in the CaseLog file: **Case opened on mm/dd/yyyy**.

    e. Close Notepad and navigate to the Melendres Private folder.

    f. Create two text files named **GoodGuys** and **BadGuys** in the Private folder.

    g. Close all windows and log off.

    h. Log on as Rosemary Wiggerts and use My Network Places to navigate to the Melendres In-Progress folder. Attempt to access the CaseLog file in the BMeulner folder.

    i. On your Student Answer Sheet, record the results of your attempt to access the file.

    j. On your Student Answer Sheet, record the results of your attempt to change the file and save it.

    k. Close all windows and log off.

    l. Log on as Administrator.

    m. Use My Computer to navigate to the Melendres folder.

    n. On your Student Answer Sheet, record the results of attempting to access the Private subfolder.

    o. To view the contents of the Private folder, the administrator must be an owner of the folder, and the Administrators local group must be given Full Control permissions to the Private folder. On your Student Answer Sheet, record the steps you take to make the administrator an owner of the Private folder with Full Control permissions.

    p. On your Student Answer Sheet, describe how Mr. Melendres could learn that you have accessed the Private folder.

12. Close all windows and log off.

Lab 5.2 Permissions Planning Sheet

Name:

Computer ID:

Notes: Use this table to identify each folder name in the "Folder Path" column, along with whether this folder is to inherit permissions from its parent. Record group and user names across the top row, and then place the permissions for each group or user in the corresponding folder's row.

Folder Path	Inherit	Owner	*Group1*	*Group2*	*Group3*	Group/User	Group/User
Group/User	**Parent Permissions**						
	❏ Yes						
	❏ No						
	❏ Yes						
	❏ No						
	❏ Yes						
	❏ No						
	❏ Yes						
	❏ No						
	❏ Yes						
	❏ No						
	❏ Yes						
	❏ No						
	❏ Yes						
	❏ No						
	❏ Yes						
	❏ No						
	❏ Yes						
	❏ No						

LAB 5.3 CONFIGURING AND MANAGING USER PROFILES

Objective

At the Animal Care Center, several people share the Windows XP Professional computer in Dennis's office by logging on with either the AppUser or SysOp user name. The problem is that sometimes a user accidentally deletes a program icon, or makes changes to the desktop wallpaper or color scheme. Dennis wants you to configure a standard desktop for the SysOp and AppUsers that cannot be changed. After completing this lab, you will be able to:

➤ Configure a desired user profile

➤ Access user profile information

➤ Create mandatory profiles

➤ Test user profile configurations

Requirements

➤ A Microsoft Management Console as created in Lab 3.1

➤ The following user accounts as created in Lab 3.2:

  ➤ AppUser (Restricted user)

  ➤ SysOp (Power user)

Estimated completion time: **15–20 minutes**

ACTIVITY

1. View default user profile information.
   a. Log on as AppUser.
   b. Click **Start**, **My Computer**, and open the drive containing your Windows XP boot files.
   c. Navigate to the Documents and Settings folder, and double-click the **AppUser** subfolder.
   d. Double-click the **Desktop** folder, and record its contents on your Lab 5.3 Student Answer Sheet.
   e. Close all windows.

2. Configure a profile for the AppUser.
   a. Create desktop shortcuts to the WordPad and Calculator programs.
   b. Set a unique desktop wallpaper and screen saver.
   c. View profile information:
      ■ Click **Start**, **My Computer**, and open the drive containing your Windows XP boot files.

- Navigate to the Documents and Settings folder, and double-click the **AppUser** subfolder.
- Double-click the **Desktop** folder, and record its contents on your Student Answer Sheet.
- Close all windows and log off.

3. Configure a profile for the SysOp user.
   a. Log on as the SysOp user.
   b. Create a desktop shortcut to the Microsoft Management console.
   c. Set the desktop background and the screen saver as follows:
      - Right-click on any unused area of the desktop, and click **Properties**. Click the **Desktop** tab.
      - Use the scroll bar to select the **Red moon desert** background.
      - Click the **Screen Saver** tab, and select the **Starfield** screen saver.
      - Click **OK** to save and apply your changes.
   d. Close all windows and log off.

4. Make the SysOp profile mandatory.
   a. Log on as Administrator.
   b. Click **Start**, **My Computer**, and navigate to the Documents and Settings folder.
   c. Right-click the **SysOp** folder, and click **Properties**.
   d. Click the **Security** tab, and click the **SysOp** user in the name list window.
   e. In the Permissions window, reduce SysOp to only Read & Execute, Read, and List Folder Contents permissions.
   f. Click **OK** to save changes, and return to the My Computer window.
   g. Double-click the **SysOp** folder, and change the name of the NTUSER.DAT file to **NTUSER.MAN**. (It may be necessary to perform the following to view protected system and hidden files: from the **View** menu, click **Folder Options**, then click the **View** tab. Click the **Show hidden files and folders** option. Remove the check from **Hide protected operating system files (Recommended)**. Click **OK**.)
   h. Close all windows and log off.
   i. To ensure that the settings are saved, log on as SysOp, and then log off again.

5. Repeat Step 4 to make the AppUser profile mandatory.

6. Test the user profiles.
   a. Log on as SysOp.
   b. Right-click on an empty spot on the desktop and click **New**, **Text Document** to attempt to create a Notepad document. Record the results on your Student Answer Sheet.

    c. Right-click your desktop and use the **Properties** option to change your background to **Autumn**. Record the results on your Student Answer Sheet.

    d. Log off.

    e. Log on as AppUser.

    f. Attempt to change the desktop or background settings. Record the results on your Student Answer Sheet.

    g. Log off.

5

LAB 5.4 APPLYING ACCOUNT POLICIES

Objective

Because of an increase in its number of cases, the Melendres and Associates law firm has added another attorney and plans to hire three temporary employees to help enter documents into a shared directory. With the three new employees in the office, Mr. Melendres wants to tighten up security to prevent unauthorized access to files. After completing this lab, you will be able to:

➤ Configure a password policy

➤ Configure an account lockout policy

➤ Configure an audit policy

➤ Configure user rights

➤ Identify common rights and their default users or groups

Estimated completion time: **15–20 minutes**

ACTIVITY

1. If necessary, start your computer with Windows XP, and log on as an administrator.

2. Using the following steps, create three new local user accounts named Temp1, Temp2, and Temp3. Set up the accounts so the users cannot change their password.

    a. Open the **Local Users and Groups** control that you created in Lab 5.1 and select **Users**.

    b. Click **New User** from the Action menu to open the New User window.

    c. Type **Temp1** for the User Name.

    d. Enter **password** in the password and the confirm password box.

    e. Clear the **User must change password at next logon box**.

    f. Place a check mark in the **User cannot change password** box.

    g. Click **Create** to add the new user.

    h. Repeat Steps c through e for Temp2 and Temp3.

3. Create a local group named Temps, and make the three new user accounts members.

   a. Click the **Groups** folder to display all existing groups.

   b. From the **Action** menu, click **New Group**, and enter the group name **Temps**.

   c. Click the **Add** button, and type **Temp1; Temp2; Temp3**. Click **OK** to add members.

   d. Click the **Create** button to create the Temps group.

   e. Click **Close** to return to the Local Users and Groups window.

4. Change the temporary user names to T_Assist1, T_Assist2, and T_Assist3.

   a. Click the **Users** folder to display all users.

   b. Right-click **Temp1**, and then click the **Rename** option.

   c. Type the new **T_Assist1** username, and press **Enter**.

   d. Repeat this process for the temporary users 2 and 3.

   e. Click the **Groups** tab, and double-click the **Temps** groups. Verify that the user names have been changed.

   f. Click **Cancel** and close all windows.

5. Within the Lab5 folder, create a subfolder named **Shared**.

6. Follow the procedure below to use the CREATOR OWNER system group to provide all users with permissions to create and manage their own files in the Shared folder, but to only read files created by other users.

   a. Right-click the **Shared** folder, and click the **Properties** option.

   b. Click the **Security** tab, and click **Advanced**. Remove the check from the **Inherit from parent the permission entries that apply to child objects** check box. Click the **Remove** button to complete the operation.

   c. Click **OK** and **Yes** to the security warning message.

   d. Click the **Add** button, and type **Creator Owner; Administrators; Power Users; Users** in the dialog box.

   e. Click **OK** to return to the Shared Properties window.

   f. Grant the following Allow permissions:

      ■ Administrators – Full Control

      ■ CREATOR OWNER – Full Control

      ■ Power Users – Full Control

      ■ Users – Read, Read & Execute, and List Folder Contents

   g. To allow users to create files, you need to perform the following substeps:

      ■ Click the **Advanced** button to display the Advanced Security Settings for Shared.

      ■ Highlight the **Users** group, and click the **Edit** button.

- Click to **Allow** the **Create Files / Write Data** permission, and click **OK**.
- Click **OK** to save the permissions and return to the Shared Properties window.

h. Click **OK** to close the Shared Properties window.

i. Close all windows.

7. Configure a password policy that forces users to enter a different password consisting of at least 6 characters every 90 days:

a. Open **Control Panel**, and double-click the **Administrative Tools** applet.

b. Double-click the **Local Security Policy** applet to display the Local Security Settings window shown in Figure 5-3.

5

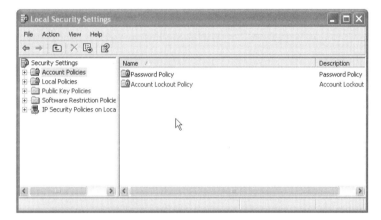

Figure 5-3   Configuring account policies

c. Expand the **Account Policies** folder, and click the **Password Policy** subfolder.

d. Double-click the **Enforce password history** policy, and set passwords remembered to **10**. Click **OK** to return to the Local Security Settings window.

e. Double-click **Maximum password age**, and set the days to **90**. Click **OK** to return to the Local Security Settings window.

f. To prevent users from rapidly making several password changes, double-click the **Minimum password age** policy, and set the days to **1**. Click **OK** to return to the Local Security Settings window.

g. Double-click the **Minimum password length** policy, and set the number of characters to **6**. Record the maximum password length on your Lab 5.4 Student Answer Sheet. Click **OK** to return to the Local Security Settings window.

h. Double-click the **Passwords must meet complexity requirements** policy, and record the default setting on your Student Answer Sheet. Click **Cancel** to return to the Local Security Settings window.

i. Double-click the **Store passwords using reversible encryption for all users in the domain** policy, and record the default setting on your Student Answer Sheet. Click **Cancel** to return to the Local Security Settings window.

j. Close all windows and log off.

8. Test the password policy.

a. Log on as the Meme Rodregus user.

b. Click **Start**, **Control Panel**, and then double-click **User Accounts**.

c. Click **Change My Password**.

d. Enter the old password in the Current password box, and enter a new password of **pass** in both the New password and Confirm new password text boxes, and then click **OK**.

e. Record the message you receive on your Student Answer Sheet.

f. Enter **password** for the password, and click **OK**.

g. Click the **Change Password** button again, and try to change the password to **theboss**.

h. Record the message you receive, along with the reason for the message, on your Student Answer Sheet.

i. Click **Cancel**, and close the Windows Security window.

j. Log off.

9. Configure a lockout policy that will lock a user's account for 20 minutes if five unsuccessful logon attempts are made within a 10-minute period.

a. Log on as an administrator.

b. Open **Control Panel**, and double-click the **Administrative Tools** applet.

c. Double-click the **Local Security Policy** applet to display the Local Security Settings window.

d. If necessary, expand the Account Policies folder, and then click the **Account Lockout Policy** in the left-side tree window.

e. Double-click the **Account lockout threshold** option, and record the default setting on your Student Answer Sheet. If necessary, change the value to **5**, and click **OK** to save your change.

f. A **Suggested Value Change** message box will appear with suggested values for Account Lockout Duration and Reset Account Lockout Counter After policies. Record the suggested values on your Student Answer Sheet, and click **OK** to accept.

g. Double-click the **Account lockout duration** policy, and change the minutes to **20**. Click **OK** to save the change. Click **OK** on the suggestion box to return to the Local Security Settings window.

h. Double-click the **Reset account lockout counter after** policy, and change the minutes to **10**. Click **OK** to save the change, and return to the Local Security Settings window.

i. Log off.

10. Test the lockout policy.

a. Attempt to log on as the Melendres user, and use incorrect passwords until the account is locked out.

b. Record the lockout error message, along with the number of logon attempts, on your Student Answer Sheet.

c. Log on as administrator.

d. Start the **Local Users and Groups** control created in Lab 5.1.

e. Click the **Users** folder.

f. Double-click the **Melendres** account.

g. On your Student Answer Sheet, describe the action you need to take to unlock the Melendres account.

h. Close all windows.

LAB 5.5 APPLYING POLICIES FOR AUDITING AND USER RIGHTS

Objective

In addition to securing existing accounts and providing access permissions, Mr. Melendres wants to monitor any changes made to the In-Progress case files, as well as learn of any failed attempts to access unauthorized files. Mr. Melendres wants to prevent the temporary employees from logging on locally to the shared Windows XP Professional system. Only valid users should be allowed to access the computer from the network. In addition, he currently cannot access the security log when logged in with his user name. He wants to be able to access the security log information, as well as have a list of rights he has as a power user. After completing this lab, you will be able to:

➤ Configure an audit policy

➤ Configure user rights

➤ Identify common rights and their default users or groups

Estimated completion time: **15–20 minutes**

ACTIVITY

1. If necessary, start your computer with Windows XP, and log on as an administrator.

2. If necessary, start the **Administrative Tools** applet from Control Panel, and double-click **Local Security Policy**.

3. Configure audit policies that will audit unsuccessful attempts to log on, changes to file system objects, and system events.

a. If necessary, expand the Local Policies folder.

b. Click the **Audit Policy**. Enable each of the following auditing policies:

- Audit **Failure** of **account logon events**.
- Audit **Success** or **Failure** of **object access**.
- Audit **Success** or **Failure** of **system events**.

4. Disable the ability to shut down the system without logging on.

a. Click the **Security Options** policy.

b. Review the enabled options.

c. To prevent the Windows XP system from being shut down before an authorized user logs on, double-click the **Shutdown: Allow system to be shut down without having to log on** policy, select **Disabled**, and then click **OK**.

5. Close the Local Security Settings window.

6. Close the Administrative Tools window.

7. Configure an audit policy that will record any failed attempts made by members of the Temps group to access information in either of the attorney folders.

a. Click **Start**, **My Computer**, and navigate to your **Lab5** folder.

b. Right-click the **Melendres** folder, and click the **Properties** option.

c. Click the **Security** tab, and then click the **Advanced** button to display the Access Control Settings for Melendres window.

d. Click the **Auditing** tab, and click **Add** to display the Select User or Group window.

e. Type **Temps** in the dialog box, and click **OK** to display the Auditing Entry for Melendres window shown in Figure 5-4.

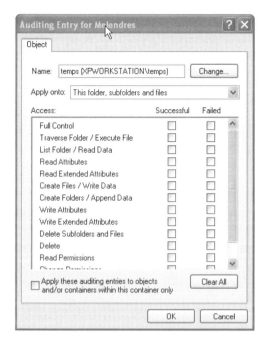

Figure 5-4   Configuring folder access auditing

    f. Click the **Failed** check box on List Folder / Read Data access.

    g. Click the **Apply these auditing entries to objects and/or containers within this container only** check box, and then click the **OK** button to save your entry in the auditing window.

    h. Click **OK** to return to the Melendres Properties window.

    i. Click **OK** to return to My Computer.

    j. Repeat steps (a) through (i) to audit failed attempts to access the Damrau folder.

8. Configure an audit policy that will record any successful update information to each attorney's In-Progress folder:

    a. Double-click the **Melendres** folder to display the In-Progress and Complete subfolders.

    b. Right-click the **In-Progress** folder, and click the **Properties** option.

    c. Click the **Security** tab, and click the **Advanced** button.

    d. Click the **Auditing** tab, and record any existing audit entries for the In-Progress folder on your Student Answer Sheet.

    e. Click the **Add** button, and type **Everyone** in the dialog box. Click **OK** to display the Auditing Entry for In-Progress window.

    f. In the Successful column, click the **Create Files / Write Data** and **Create Folders / Append Data** check boxes.

    g. Click the **Apply these auditing entries to objects and/or containers within this container only** check box.

h. Click **OK** to save your changes, and return to the Auditing window.

i. Click **OK** to return to the In-Progress Properties window.

j. Click **OK** to return to My Computer.

k. Close all windows.

9. Mr. Melendres does not want the temporary employees to have the right to log on locally to his computer; only valid users should be able to access the computer from the network. In addition, Mr. Melendres currently cannot access the security log when logged in with his user name. He wants to be able to access the security log information as well as have a list of rights he has as a power user. Follow the procedure described below to configure the user rights policy.

a. Double-click **Local Security Policy** from the Administrative Tools applet of Control Panel.

b. Expand the **Local Policies** folder, and double-click the **User Rights Assignment** subfolder to display User Rights in the results window.

c. Double-click the **Access this computer from the network** option, and click on the **Everyone** system group. Click **Remove**, and then click **OK** to return to the Local Security Settings window.

d. Double-click the **Deny logon locally** right, and click the **Add User or Group** button.

e. Type **Temps** in the dialog box, and click **OK** twice to save your change and return to the Local Security Settings window.

f. Double-click **Manage auditing and security log**, and click the **Add User or Group** button.

g. Type **Melendres** in the dialog box, and click **OK** twice to save your change and return to the Local Security Settings window.

h. Double-click each right, and on your Student Answer Sheet, record the rights that a power user has.

10. Close all windows and log off.

11. Test your audit policy by logging on as a temporary employee, and attempting to access the In-Progress folder. Record your results on the Student Answer Sheet.

12. Log on using the Melendres account, and start **Event Viewer**. Document the security messages on your Student Answer Sheet.

13. After recording any security messages, close Event Viewer and log off.

CHAPTER SIX

WINDOWS XP SECURITY AND ACCESS CONTROLS

Labs included in this chapter

➤ Lab 6.1 Working with Local Computer Policies

➤ Lab 6.2 Applying User Configuration Policies

➤ Lab 6.3 Customizing the Logon Process

➤ Lab 6.4 Working with Encryption

➤ Lab 6.5 Automating the Logon System

Microsoft MCSE Exam #70-270 Objectives	
Objective	Lab
Implement, configure, and troubleshoot local Group policy	6.1, 6.2, 6.5
Implement, configure, manage, and troubleshoot a security configuration	6.1
Configure and troubleshoot desktop settings	6.2
Implement, configure, manage, and troubleshoot a security configuration	6.3
Implement, configure, manage, and troubleshoot local user authentication Configure and troubleshoot local user accounts	6.3
Encrypt data on a hard disk by using the Encrypting File System (EPS)	6.4

 Student Answer Sheets to accompany the labs in this chapter are available for downloading from the Online Companion for this manual at *www.course.com*.

101

Lab 6.1 Working with Local Computer Policies

Objective

The Superior Technical College has recently upgraded all of its administrative computers to Windows XP Professional. The college has called Computer Technology Services, and you have been asked to assist Brenda Bohle, the network administrator, in securing these systems from intruders. Because some of the systems are used to access information on state servers across the Internet, the college wants to provide maximum security for data transmitted. In addition, to prevent excessive use of disk space, the management wants to place a limit of 200 MB on each user. After completing this lab, you will be able to:

➤ Create a Microsoft Management Console for the local computer policy

➤ Identify components of the Computer Configuration settings

➤ Configure an IP Security policy

➤ Configure Windows file protection scanning

➤ Configure a Disk Quota policy

Estimated completion time: **15–20 minutes**

Activity

1. If necessary, start your computer with Windows XP Professional , and log on as an administrator.

2. Create a Microsoft Management Console to manage the local group policy and users.

   a. Click **Start**, click **Run**, type **mmc** in the Open text box, and press **Enter**.

   b. From the **File** menu, click **Add/Remove Snap-in** to display the Add/Remove Snap-in window.

   c. Click the **Add** button to display the Add Standalone Snap-in window.

   d. Scroll down and double-click the **Group Policy** option.

   e. Verify that the **Local Computer** object is selected, and click **Finish** to return to the Add Standalone Snap-in window.

   f. Scroll down and double-click the **Local Users and Groups** snap-in.

   g. Verify that the **Local Computer** option is selected, and click **Finish** to return to the Add Standalone Snap-in window.

   h. Click **Close**. Verify that both Local Computer Policy and Local Users and Groups Snap-ins are shown in the Add/Remove Snap-in window.

   i. Click **OK** to close the Add/Remove Snap-in window, and return to the MMC Console Root.

j. Click the **File** menu, **Save as** option, and enter the name **Computer Policy Management** in the File name text box.

k. Click the **Save** button to save the console in the Administrative Tools folder.

3. In the left-side Tree window, expand the **Computer Configuration** folder of the Local Computer Policy, and record the three subfolders (Computer Configuration policies) on your Lab 6.1 Student Answer Sheet.

4. Expand each subfolder, and, on your Student Answer Sheet, record the path to the Password Policy subfolder.

5. On your Student Answer Sheet, record the path to the Audit Policy subfolder.

6. Click the **IP Security Policies** folder to view the security options shown in Figure 6-1.

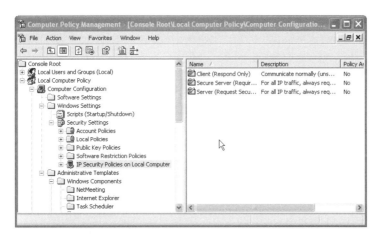

Figure 6-1   Configuring IP security policies

7. Turn on the IP Security policy that requires the use of Kerberos security, and that does not allow unsecured communication with clients who do not respond to the security request. Record the security policy you select on your Student Answer Sheet.

a. Double-click an IP Security option from the right-side results window.

b. Click the **General** tab, and read the description for this security setting.

c. If the description reads that it will not allow unsecured communications with clients, record that security policy name on your Student Answer Sheet.

d. If the description reads that it allows communications with clients, repeat Step 7, selecting a different IP Security policy. Click **Cancel** to return to the console window.

e. Right-click the IP Security Policy that does not allow unsecured communication and select **Assign**.

8. Click the **Administrative Templates** subfolder within the Computer Configuration branch of Local Computer Policy, and on your Student Answer Sheet, list the four subfolders contained within the Administrative Templates folder.

9. If necessary, expand each **Administrative Templates** subfolder. On your Student Answer Sheet, identify which of the four Administrative Template subfolders contains the Windows File Protection subfolder.

10. Within the Windows File Protection folder, double-click the **Set Windows File Protection scanning** option, and click the **Explain** tab. List the scanning frequency options on your Student Answer Sheet. Which scanning frequency is the default?

11. Click the **Setting** tab, and click **Enabled**. Select the option that will scan files at each startup. Click **OK**.

12. Click the **Disk Quotas** folder from the Tree window.

13. Assume you want to enable disk quotas on all NTFS volumes so that when a user reaches the default of 200 MB, the system responds as though the physical space on the volume is exhausted, and logs the event on the Application log. On your Student Answer Sheet, identify which Disk Quota policies you would enable.

14. Enable the 200 MB Disk Quota policies identified in Step 13.
    a. Double-click one of the policies you identified in Step 13.
    b. Click the **Enabled** option button from the Policy tab. If you are given the option to set the quota limit, set the limit to 200 MB.
    c. Click **OK** to save the setting.
    d. Repeat Steps 14a through 14c for the other quota policies that you identified in Step 13.

15. Close the Computer Policy Management console and log off.

LAB 6.2 APPLYING USER CONFIGURATION POLICIES

Objective

The Superior Technical College recently purchased several new Windows XP Professional-based systems from your company for use in its desktop publishing program. Brenda Bohle, the network administrator, wants you to help her secure these systems to prevent students from browsing the network or changing desktop settings. In addition, she wants to protect the Administrator account from unauthorized access by renaming the account to Admin, and then creating a dummy administrator account. After completing this lab, you will be able to:

➤ Configure local user configuration policies to restrict user functions on a Windows XP workstation

➤ Rename the Administrator account, create a fake administrator user, and audit any access to this account

Estimated completion time: **20 minutes**

ACTIVITY

1. If necessary, start your computer with Windows XP, and log on as an administrator.

2. Click the **Start** button, and record all of the menu options on your Student Answer Sheet.

3. Start the Computer Policy Management console from **Start**, **All Programs**, **Administrative Tools**.

4. Expand the **User Configuration** policy to display the three policy folders within the User Configuration policy.

5. List the contents of the **Software Settings** policy folder on your Student Answer Sheet.

6. List the contents of the **Windows Settings** policy on your Student Answer Sheet.

7. List the seven subfolders in the Administrative Templates policy on your Student Answer Sheet.

8. Click the **Start Menu and Taskbar** policy folder to display the options shown in Figure 6-2.

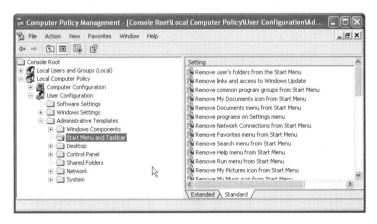

Figure 6-2   Configuring user settings in the local security policy

6

9. Implement the following Start Menu and Taskbar policies.

   a. Prevent students from making changes to Taskbar and Start Menu Settings:

      ■ Double-click **Prevent changes to Taskbar and Start Menu Settings**.

      ■ Click the **Enabled** option button, and then click **OK**.

   b. Remove the Run command from the Start Menu:

      ■ Double-click **Remove Run Menu from the Start Menu**.

      ■ Click the **Enabled** option button, and then click **OK**.

   c. Add a Log off option to the Start Menu:

      ■ Double-click **Add Logoff to the Start Menu**.

      ■ Click the **Enabled** option button, and then click **OK**.

10. Click the **Desktop** policy, and implement the following policies.

    a. Prohibit students from changing the default My Documents path:

       ■ Double-click **Prohibit user from changing My Documents path**.

       ■ Click the **Enabled** option button, and then click **OK**.

    b. Prevent the students from saving settings at exit:

       ■ Double-click **Don't save settings at exit**.

       ■ Click the **Enabled** option button, and then click **OK**.

11. Click the **Control Panel** policy to implement the following policies.

    a. Prevent students from adding or removing programs:

       ■ Open the **Add/Remove Programs** folder.

       ■ Double-click **Remove Add/Remove programs**.

       ■ Click the **Enabled** option button, and click **OK**.

    b. Prevent students from changing the display configuration from Control Panel:

       ■ Open the **Display** folder.

       ■ Double-click **Remove Display in Control Panel**.

       ■ Click the **Enabled** button, and click **OK**.

    c. Prevent students from setting a password on screen savers:

       ■ Double-click **Password protect the screen saver**.

       ■ Click the **Disable** option button, and then click **OK**.

12. Click the **System** policy, and disable use of the command prompt. Record the policy and option button you use on your Student Answer Sheet.

13. Close the Computer Management console. Click **Yes** to save the console. The policy settings you've changed should take effect immediately.

14. Test the effects of the User Configuration Policy on the Administrator user.

    a. Right-click anywhere on the **Taskbar**, and click the **Properties** option. Record the message you receive on the Student Answer Sheet.

b. Click the **Start** button. On your Student Answer Sheet, record new or removed options.

c. Create a folder named **Documents** on the root of your Windows XP drive. Click **Start**, right-click **My Documents**, and click **Properties**. On your Student Answer Sheet, record the results of changing the target path to the Documents folder.

d. Open Control Panel, and double-click **Add or Remove Programs**. Record the message you receive on your Student Answer Sheet.

e. Double-click the **Display** icon. Record the message you receive on your Student Answer Sheet.

f. Click **Start**, **All Programs**, **Accessories**, **Command Prompt**. Record the message you receive on your Student Answer Sheet.

15. Verify that the restrictions apply to all users as follows:

a. Log off as the administrator.

b. Log on as another user.

c. Try to change the taskbar and open a command prompt. Record the results on your Student Answer Sheet.

d. Log off.

16. Follow the steps below to remove the User Configuration restrictions.

a. Log on as administrator, and start the **Computer Policy Management** console.

b. Expand the **User Configuration** folder.

c. Use the **Start Menu and Taskbar** policy (under Administrative Templates) to do the following:

- Double-click **Prevent changes to taskbar and Start menu settings**, click the **Not Configured** option button, and click **OK**.

- Double-click **Remove Run Menu from Start Menu**, click the **Not Configured** option button, and click **OK**.

d. Use the **Desktop** policy to perform the following:

- Double-click **Prohibit user from changing My Documents path**, click the **Not Configured** option button, and click **OK**.

- Double-click **Don't save settings at exit**, click the **Not Configured** option button, and click **OK**.

e. Use the **Control Panel** policy to perform the following actions.

- Enable the Add/Remove programs icon.

- Enable access to the display settings.

- Enable the password protection option on screen savers.

f. Use the **System** policy to enable the command prompt.

g. Exit the Computer Policy Management console.

6

17. Verify that you can now open a command prompt window, access the Run command from the Start menu, change the taskbar, access the Add/Remove programs option, and change display settings.

18. Close all windows and log off.

Lab 6.3 Customizing the Logon Process

Objective

Melendres and Associates is concerned about the legal ramifications of prosecuting an intruder for unauthorized access to their computer system. According to Mr. Melendres, legally an intruder should be warned, prior to attempting to log on, that unauthorized access is prohibited. In addition, Mr. Melendres thinks that displaying the last user's name on the logon window makes it easier for an intruder to attempt to log on. Therefore, he wants the user name field to be blank by default at logon. He is also concerned that, at present, anyone who accesses the logon screen can shut down the shared Windows XP system without logging on. He wants only himself and the administrator to have the right to shut down the system. After completing this lab, you will be able to:

➤ Remove the name of the last user who logged on from the Windows XP logon window

➤ Display a warning message about illegal logons prior to the logon prompt

➤ Disable the Shut Down button from the logon window

➤ Provide a user with the right to shut down the system

Estimated completion time: 15–20 minutes

Activity

1. If necessary, start your computer with Windows XP, and log on as an administrator.

2. Start your **Computer Policy Management** console.

3. If necessary, create the following users.
   - Logon name: **SMelendres**, Full Name: **Sebastian Melendres**.
   - Logon name: **MRodregus**, Full Name: **Meme Rodregus**.

4. Modify the computer configuration policy to remove the name of the last user from the logon screen as follows.
   a. Expand the **Computer Configuration** policy tree.
   b. Browse the **Windows Settings** tree until you find the **Interactive Logon: Do not display last user name** policy. On your Lab 6.3 Student Answer Sheet, record the path to the policy.

c. Double-click the **Interactive Logon: Do not display last user name** policy, and click the **Enabled** option button.

d. Click **OK** to return to the Computer Policy Management console.

5. Require the Ctrl+Alt+Del key combination to be pressed to log on.

a. Double-click the **Interactive Logon: Do not require CTRL+ALT+DEL** policy as shown in Figure 6-3. On your Student Answer Sheet, record the local policy setting you select to require the user to press the Ctrl+Alt+Del keys to log on.

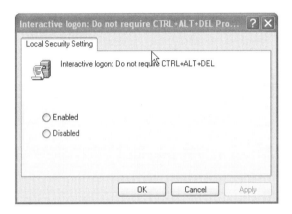

Figure 6-3   Configuring a local security policy option

6. A legal warning message is often required to appear prior to logging on. To enable a legal message box that appears just before the log on window, use the following two policies.

a. Double-click the **Interactive Logon: Message title for users attempting to Logon** policy, and enter: **Unauthorized access to this system is illegal** in the Local policy setting text box. Click **OK** to save your changes.

b. Double-click the **Interactive Logon: Message text for users attempting to Logon** policy, and in the Local policy setting text box enter: **The information on this computer is the property of the Melendres and Associates law firm and is protected by intellectual property law. You must have legitimate access to an assigned account on this computer to access any information. Your activities may be monitored, and any unauthorized access will be punished to the full extent of the law.** Click **OK** to save your changes.

7. To prevent the network from being shut down by users, you can disable the Shutdown button from the logon window. On your Student Answer Sheet, record the policy along with the setting you would use to prevent shutdown prior to logging on.

6

8. Provide the Melendres user with rights to shut down the system.

   a. Click the **User Rights Assignment** policy folder.

   b. Double-click the **Shut down the system** right, and, on your Student Answer Sheet, record default groups to which this right is assigned.

   c. Click **Users**, and then click **Remove** to remove the users group.

   d. Click the **Add** button, and type **Melendres** in the dialog box.

   e. Click **OK** to return to the Local Security Policy Setting window.

   f. Verify that your Melendres user has been added, and then click **OK** to return to the Computer Policy Management console.

   g. Close the Computer Policy Management console and log off.

9. Test the policies you have enabled by logging on as the Rodregus user and attempting to shut down the system from the logon screen.

   a. Log on as the Rodregus user.

   b. On your Student Answer Sheet, record the logon information requested.

   c. Attempt to shut down the computer system using the **Start** menu, **Shut Down** option, and record the results on your Student Answer Sheet.

   d. Log off.

10. Log on as the Melendres user, and attempt to shut down the system.

   a. Log on as the Melendres user.

   b. Attempt to shut down the computer system, and, on your Student Answer Sheet, record the results.

LAB 6.4 WORKING WITH ENCRYPTION

Objective

Mr. Melendres wants to have a shared public folder in which users can store sensitive files in an encrypted format that only they or other selected users can access. Windows XP allows this level of security through file and folder encryption. After completing this lab, you will be able to:

➤ Create a folder to store encyrpted files

➤ Create files in the encrypted folder

➤ Copy files to the encrypted folder

➤ Move files to the encrypted folder

➤ Use the CIPHER command to encrypt, decrypt, or view encryption status information

Estimated completion time: **20–25 minutes**

ACTIVITY

1. If necessary, start your computer with Windows XP, and log on as Mr. Melendres.

2. If necessary, create a folder named **Public** from the root of your Windows XP drive.

3. Launch **WordPad** from the **Start**, **All Programs**, **Accessories** menu, and create a document file that describes the following options of the CIPHER command.
   CIPHER command options:
   /E – Encrypt files
   /D – Decrypt files
   /F – Force encryption on all files, even if already encrypted
   /S – Encrypt files in all subfolders

4. Save the document in the My Documents folder with the name **CIPHER**.

5. Use WordPad to create a second document named **Suspects** that contains a description of two suspected criminals in one of Mr. Melendres' cases (you provide the description). Save the document in the My Documents folder.

6. Exit WordPad.

7. Click **Start**, **My Documents**, and use the **File**, **New** menu to create a sub-folder named **Secured**.

8. Encrypt the Secured folder.
   a. Right-click the **Secured** folder, and click the **Properties** option to display the General properties tab.
   b. Click the **Advanced** button to display the Advanced Attribute window, as shown in Figure 6-4. List the advanced attributes on your Lab 6.4 Student Answer Sheet.

Figure 6-4   Configuring file encryption

c. Click the **Encrypt contents to secure data** check box, and then click **OK** to return to the General tab.

d. Click **OK** to save your changes, and return to the My Documents window.

9. Create a file named **Witness** in the Secured folder.

a. Double-click the **Secured** folder to open it.

b. From the **File** menu, click the **New** option, and click **Text Document**.

c. Enter the name **Witness** for the file, and press **Enter**.

d. Double-click the **Witness** file to start the Notepad application.

e. Enter the names and phone numbers of three fictitious witnesses.

f. Save the document, and exit Notepad.

10. Check the encryption status of the newly created text file.

a. Right-click the **Witness** file, and click the **Properties** option.

b. On the **General** tab, click the **Advanced** button.

c. On your Student Answer Sheet, record all attributes that are set.

d. Click **Cancel** twice to return to the Secured folder window.

e. Double-click the **Witness** file. Notice that the file appears the same as if it were not encryrpted.

f. Close Notepad, and click the **Up** button to return to the My Documents window.

11. Copy the Suspects file to the Secured folder.

a. Right-click the **Suspects** file, and click the **Copy** option.

b. Double-click the **Secured** folder, and from the **Edit** menu, click **Paste**.

c. Right-click the **Suspects** file, and click the **Properties** option.

d. Click the **Advanced** button from the **General** tab, and, on your Student Answer Sheet, record the encryption status of a file copied to an encrypted folder.

e. Click the **Cancel** button twice to return to the Secured folder window.

f. Click the **Up** button to return to the My Documents window.

12. Move the Cipher file to the Secured folder.

a. Right-click the **Cipher** file, and click the **Cut** option.

b. Double-click the **Secured** folder, and click the **Paste** option from the Edit menu.

c. Right-click the **Cipher** file, and click the **Properties** option.

d. Click the **Advanced** button from the **General** tab, and, on your Student Answer Sheet, record the encryption status of a file moved to an encrypted folder.

e. Click the **Cancel** button twice to return to the Secured folder window.

13. Determine the encryption status of a file copied from the encrypted folder.

a. Click **Start**, **My Computer**, and open a window to your Public folder.

b. Arrange and size your windows so you can see both the Public and Secured folders.

c. Hold down the **Ctrl** key while you click the **Witness** file, drag and drop it into the **Public** folder. Verify that the file is now in both windows.

d. Right-click the **Witness** file from the Public folder, and click the **Properties** button.

e. Click the **Advanced** button from the **General** tab, and, on your Student Answer Sheet, record the encryption status of a file copied from an encrypted folder to a nonencrypted folder.

f. Click **Cancel** twice to return to the desktop.

14. Determine the encryption status of a file moved from the encrypted folder.

a. Click the **Cipher** file, and drag and drop it into the **Public** folder. Verify that the Cipher file is now only in the Public folder window.

b. Right-click the **Cipher** file from the Public folder, and click the **Properties** button.

c. Click the **Advanced** button from the **General** tab, and, on your Student Answer Sheet, record the encryption status of a file moved from an encrypted folder to a nonencrypted folder.

d. Click **Cancel** twice to return to the desktop.

15. Use the CIPHER command to check the encryption status of files.

a. Open a Command Prompt window by clicking **Start**, **All Programs**, **Accessories**, **Command Prompt**.

b. Change to the Public folder by entering the following command:

CD \Public [Enter]

c. Enter the following CIPHER command, and, on your Student Answer Sheet, record the status of all files in the Public folder.

CIPHER *.* [Enter]

d. Enter the following CIPHER command (including quote marks), and, on your Student Answer Sheet, record the encryption status of all files in the Secured folder.

CIPHER "\Documents and Settings\smelendres\ MyDocuments\secured*.*" [Enter]

e. Enter the following CIPHER command to decrypt all files in the Public folder:

CIPHER *.* /D /A [Enter]

f. Enter the following CIPHER command to force encryption on the Witness file in the Public folder:

CIPHER Witness.txt /E /A [Enter]

g. Type **Exit** at the command prompt and log off.

16. Log on as administrator, and attempt to access the files in the Secured folder.

a. Log on as your administrator account.

b. Use **My Computer** to navigate to the **Documents and Settings\Smelendres\My Documents** folder.

c. Double-click a file, and record the results on your Student Answer Sheet.

d. Navigate to the **Secured** folder.

e. Double-click the **Suspects** file, and record the results on your Student Answer Sheet.

f. Navigate to the **Public** folder, and double-click the **Witness** file. Record the results on your Student Answer Sheet.

g. Log off.

17. Log on as another user, and attempt to access encrypted files in the Public folder.

a. Log on as the Rodregus user.

b. Navigate to the **Public** folder, and double-click the **Witness** file. Record the results on your Student Answer Sheet.

c. Exit the WordPad application.

d. Double-click the **Cipher** file, and record the results on your Student Answer Sheet.

e. Close all windows and log off.

18. Windows XP Professional allows for more then one user to be able to access an encrypted file. This is only possible if user certificates have been issued through the Microsoft Certificate Service or a third-party certificate service. This lab does not have certificates enabled, therefore, the following procedure will only demonstrate where to add this capability.

a. Log on as Mr. Melendres.

b. Open **My Documents**, and navigate to the **Secured** subfolder.

c. Right-click the **Witness** file, and click **Advanced** on the **General** tab.

d. Click **Details** to display the users able to access this file.

e. To add additional users, you would click **Add** and select users with valid certificates.

f. This ends the demonstration. Close all windows and return to the desktop.

Lab 6.5 Automating the Logon System

Objective

Superior Technical College wants to place a Windows XP Professional computer in its learning resource center, and limit the computer to running only Internet Explorer. The learning resource center manager wants you to configure the computer so that it does not require a logon and will start with only Windows NT 3.51 Program Manager, with only the Internet Explorer option on the desktop. After completing this lab, you will be able to:

➤ Provide an automatic logon for public use

➤ Configure Program Manager to display only Internet Explorer on the desktop

Estimated completion time: **15 minutes**

ACTIVITY

1. If necessary, start your computer with Windows XP, and log on as an administrator.

2. Launch the Computer Policy Management console, and create a user named Anyone.
   a. If necessary, expand **Local Users and Groups (Local)** policy.
   b. Click the **Users** folder, and then click the **Action** menu, **New User** option.
   c. Enter **Anyone** in the User name and Full name text boxes. Enter a password of at least six characters (such as **password**) in both the Password and Confirm password text boxes.
   d. Remove the check mark from the **User must change password at next logon** check box.
   e. Click the **User cannot change password** and **Password never expires** check boxes.
   f. Click the **Create** button to add the new user.
   g. Click the **Close** button to return to the Computer Policy Management console.
   h. Exit the Computer Policy Management console.

3. Configure the Program Manager interface so only Internet Explorer is included on the desktop.
   a. Click the **Start** menu, and click **Run**.
   b. Enter the command **Progman.exe**, and click **OK**.
   c. From the **File** menu, click **New**, and click the **Common Program Group** option button.
   d. Click **OK** to create a Common Program Group.
   e. Enter the name **Internet Explorer**, and click **OK** to create the program group window.
   f. From the **File** menu, click **New**, and verify that the **Program Item** option button is selected.
   g. Click **OK** to display the Program Item Properties window.
   h. Enter **Internet Explorer** in the Description text box, and click the **Browse** button.
   i. Navigate to the **Program Files** folder on your Windows XP drive.
   j. Double-click the **Internet Explorer** folder.
   k. Double-click the **IEXPLORE** program.
   l. Click **OK** to save the Internet Explorer icon in your Program Manager window.
   m. From the **File** menu, click **Exit** to exit the Program Manager application.

6

4. Modify the Windows XP Registry to use Progman.exe as the default shell.

   a. Click the **Start** menu, **Run** option.

   b. Enter the command **regedt32** in the Open text box, and click **OK**.

   c. Select the **HKEY_LOCAL_MACHINE\SOFTWARE\Microsoft** key.

   d. Double-click **Microsoft** and navigate down to the **Windows NT\ CurrentVersion** key.

   e. Click the **Winlogon** folder to display the key values shown in Figure 6-5.

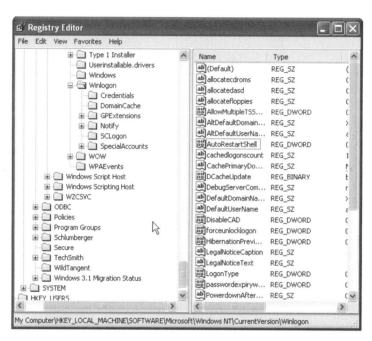

Figure 6-5 Editing the Registry

   f. Double-click the **Shell** value, and, on your Lab 6.5 Student Answer Sheet, record the existing value.

   g. Change the Value data text box to **Progman.exe**.

   h. Click **OK** to save your new setting.

5. Add an AutoAdminLogon registry key to automatically log on the administrator for testing.

   a. From the **Edit** menu, click **New**.

   b. Click **String Value** to create a new key value.

   c. Type **AutoAdminLogon** and press **Enter**.

   d. Double-click the newly created **AutoAdminLogon** value, and enter **1** to enable the auto logon feature.

   e. Click **OK** to save your change.

6. Modify the DefaultUserName registry key to set it to the Anyone account that you created.

   a. Double-click the **DefaultUserName** value, and enter the user name **Anyone** in the key value text box.

   b. Click **OK** to save the key value.

7. Add a DefaultPassword registry key value.

   a. From the **Edit** menu, click **New**.

   b. Click **String Value** to create a new key value.

   c. Type **DefaultPassword**, and press **Enter**.

   d. Double-click the newly created **DefaultPassword** key value, and enter the password for your Administrator in the Value data text box.

   e. Click **OK** to save the new key value.

   f. Exit the Registry editor program.

8. Test the automatic logon.

   a. Perform a Shutdown and Restart function by clicking **Start**, **Shutdown**, **Restart**.

   b. After your machine restarts, describe the results on your Student Answer Sheet.

9. From the **File** menu, click **Logoff**, and click **OK**.

10. Log on as the Administrator.

11. Return the Shell to Windows Explorer.

   a. Click **Run** from the **File** menu.

   b. Enter the command **regedt32** in the Command Line text box, and click **OK**.

   c. Double-click the **Shell** key value, and change Progman.exe back to **explorer.exe**.

   d. Click **OK** to save the key value.

   e. Right-click the **AutoAdminLogon** key value, and click the **Delete** option.

   f. Click **Yes** to confirm the deletion.

   g. Right-click the **DefaultPassword** key value, and click the **Delete** option.

   h. Click **Yes** to confirm the deletion. On your Student Answer Sheet, describe why it is important to remove this key from the Registry.

   i. Close the Registry Editor.

12. Shut down and restart the system to verify that the system is back to manual logon.

   a. From the **File** menu, click **Shutdown**.

   b. Click the **Shutdown and Restart** option button, and then click **OK** to restart your computer.

   c. Log on as Administrator, and verify that the Windows Explorer window is visible.

   d. Log off.

NETWORK PROTOCOLS

Labs included in this chapter

➤ Lab 7.1 Documenting and Removing Network Components

➤ Lab 7.2 Defining an IP Address Scheme

➤ Lab 7.3 Installing and Configuring the TCP/IP Protocol

➤ Lab 7.4 Assigning IP Addresses Automatically

➤ Lab 7.5 Working with IP Protocols

➤ Lab 7.6 Working with Remote Assistance

➤ Lab 7.7 Installing and Configuring Services for Novell

Microsoft MCSE Exam #70-270 Objectives	
Objective	Lab
Install, configure, and troubleshoot the TCP/IP protocol	7.1, 7.2, 7.3, 7.4, 7.5
Using Remote Assistance	7.6
Configuring Support for Novell	7.7

Student Answer Sheets to accompany the labs in this chapter are available for downloading from the Online Companion for this manual at *www.course.com*.

Lab 7.1 Documenting and Removing Network Components

Objective

Prior to changing or adding network components on a computer, it's important to document the existing configuration so that you can return the system to its original state in the event of problems. Because the labs in this chapter require you to change your computer's network configuration, in this first lab you will document your current network settings prior to removing them. After completing this lab, you will be able to:

➤ Use My Network Places to document your current network configuration

➤ Remove existing network protocols and services

Estimated completion time: **10 minutes**

Activity

1. If necessary, start your computer with Windows XP, and log on as an administrator.

2. In this step you document your existing network components so that you can restore them after completing the labs in this chapter. Follow the steps below to record your network configuration.

   a. Click **Start**, and right-click **My Network Places.** Click **Properties** to display the Network Connections window.

   b. Double-click **Local Area Connection**, and, on your Lab 7.1 Student Answer Sheet, record the requested connection information.

   c. Click the **Properties** button to display the Local Area Connection Properties window.

   d. Record the installed network protocols, clients, and services from the Components window on your Student Answer Sheet.

   e. Click each network protocol (such as Internet Protocol (TCP/IP) or NWLink), and then use the **Properties** button to find information about that protocol. On your Student Answer Sheet, record the requested information. Click **OK** after reviewing each protocol to return to the Local Area Connection Properties window.

   f. Click the **Configure** button to display network card configuration properties. Click **Yes** on the Local Area Connection warning message. Use the necessary tabs, and record the network card information requested on your Student Answer Sheet.

   g. Click **Cancel** to return to the Local Area Connection Status window.

   h. Click **Properties** to re-open the Local Area Connection Properties window.

3. To install the necessary protocols and services for the lab projects in this chapter, in this step you first remove any existing protocols (except TCP/IP) and services from your Windows XP Professional computer.

    a. Windows XP requires TCP/IP if a network card or modem is present. If a protocol other than TCP/IP exists, click that protocol and then use the **Uninstall** button to remove it. Click **No** to the restart computer message. You do not need to restart your computer until all components have been removed.

    b. If additional protocols exist, repeat Step 3a to remove them.

    c. Click a service, and use the **Uninstall** button to remove it. Click **No** to the restart computer message.

    d. Repeat Step 3c to remove all services.

    e. Click a client, and use the **Uninstall** button to remove it. Click **No** to the restart computer message.

    f. Repeat Step 3e to remove all clients.

4. Save your changes, and click **Close**.

5. Restart your computer after removing protocols, services, and clients.

LAB 7.2 DEFINING AN IP ADDRESS SCHEME

Objective

The Washington School, a private elementary school, is installing a network consisting of two separate subnets linked together by a Window 2000 server, as shown in Figure 7-1.

The computers attached to the Lab 212 subnet consist of ten Windows XP Professional computers. The office network consists of four networked Windows XP Professional systems used for word processing, desktop publishing, and running specialized school administration software. In addition to accessing shared applications and data files, computers on both networks must be able to access the Internet using proxy server software running on a Windows 2000 server named LabHost. The school has contracted with your company to set up and configure these computers to use only the TCP/IP protocol. Although the school's Internet Service Provider (ISP) has provided the proxy server with an IP address to attach to the Internet, it is up to you to come up with an IP address scheme for computers in the school office and computer lab. After completing this lab, you will be able to:

➤ Define network addresses and subnet masks for a site with multiple subnets

➤ Define IP addresses for all computers on a Class B network

➤ Assign IP addresses to network routers

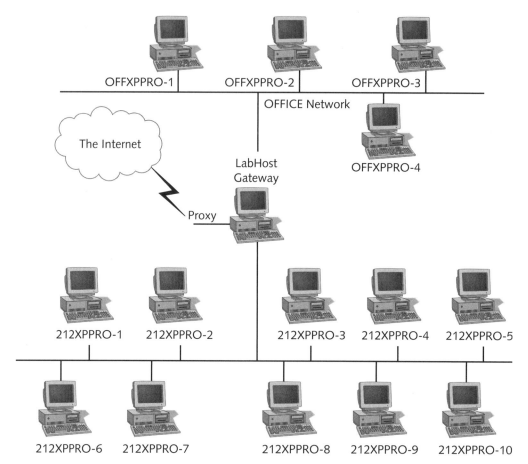

Figure 7-1   Washington School network

Estimated completion time: **15 minutes**

ACTIVITY

The Internet Access Board (IAB) has established three main classes of IP addresses. Class A addresses are intended for very large organizations and provide one octet (or byte) for the network address, and three octets for the host (computer) address. Class B addresses are intended for medium-to-large organizations, and provide two octets or bytes for both network and host addresses. Class C addresses are intended for small-to-medium organizations, and provide three octets to identify the network, and only one octet for the computer. Class A networks have numbers ranging between 1 and 127, Class B networks range from 128 through 191, and Class C networks start in the range of 192 to 226.

Use Figure 7-1 to fill out the Lab 7.2 IP Address Planning Sheet with Class B IP addresses for each computer in the office and in Lab 212.

1. Provide a network address and subnet mask for each subnet.

2. Assign an IP address for each network card in the LabHost server.

3. Assign an IP address and default gateway for each computer.

LAB 7.3 INSTALLING AND CONFIGURING THE TCP/IP PROTOCOL

Objective

Now that you have planned the IP configuration for the Washington School, you will simulate installing and configuring TCP/IP on one of the computers in the school lab. You will use the IP address information identified in the Requirements section below. After completing this lab, you will be able to

➤ Install TCP/IP as the only network protocol

➤ Manually configure an IP address and subnet mask

➤ Configure TCP/IP settings

➤ Identify additional IP protocol options

➤ Configure Internet Explorer to use a proxy server

➤ Install the Microsoft client along with file and print services

Requirements

To perform this lab activity, you or your instructor needs to identify the following computer IP addresses. The Instructor computer will act as the LabHost / DNS / Proxy Server for this exercise.

➤ An IP address for your computer: ...

➤ Subnet mask: ...

➤ IP address of default gateway: ...

➤ IP address of the LabHost Server: ...

➤ IP address of the DNS computer: ...

➤ IP address of Proxy computer: ... Port #: (80)

➤ DNS suffix: (for example, Washington.k12.wi.us)

Estimated completion time: **20–25 minutes**

ACTIVITY 1

After installing network cards and drivers, the next step is to install and configure the TCP/IP protocol. In this activity, you manually install and configure the protocol on one computer; in later labs you will use automatic TCP/IP configuration to speed installation on multiple computers.

1. If necessary, start your computer and log on as an administrator.

2. Configure the TCP/IP protocol.
   a. Click **Start**, right-click **My Network Places**, and click **Properties**.
   b. Double-Click **Local Area Connection**, and click **Properties**.
   c. Click the **Internet Protocol (TCP/IP)** component, and click the **Properties** button to display the Internet Protocol (TCP/IP) Properties window shown in Figure 7-2.

Figure 7-2   Configuring the Internet Protocol (TCP/IP) properties

   d. Click the **Use the following IP address** option button, and enter the IP address and subnet mask for your computer that you identified in the Requirements section.

3. Configure the TCP/IP protocol for default gateway and DNS server. Normally these addresses can be added directly in this window, but you will be using the Advanced window to see additional features.

a. To set the Internet router as the gateway, click the **Advanced** button to display the Advanced TCP/IP Settings windows shown in Figure 7-3.

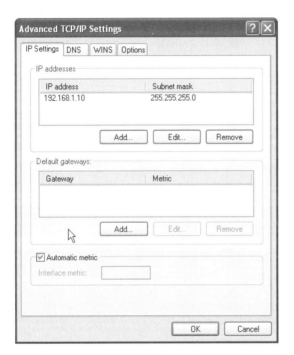

Figure 7-3   Configuring the Advanced TCP/IP settings

b. To configure a default gateway, click the **Add** button in the Default gateways section, and enter the IP address of the gateway you identified in the Requirements section. The Interface metric setting is used to assign a weight to a gateway when multiple gateways are available. The client computer will then use an available gateway with the lowest metric setting.

c. Click **Add** to add the gateway to the Default gateways window.

d. Click the **DNS** tab, and then click the **Add** button to enter the DNS server you identified in the Requirements section.

e. Click the **Options** tab, and use the **Properties** button to record the three types of TCP/IP packet filtering you can apply.

f. Click **Cancel** to return to the Advanced TCP/IP Settings window.

g. Click **OK** to save the gateway settings and return to the Internet Protocol (TCP/IP) Properties window.

h. Click **OK** to return to the Local Area Connection Properties window.

ACTIVITY 2

In this activity you install the Microsoft client and then provide the ability for your computer to share resources by adding File and Print services.

1. To communicate with the school's Windows XP server, you need to install the Microsoft client service on the computer by following the procedure described below.
   a. Click the **Install** button, and, if necessary, click the **Client** component type.
   b. Click the **Add** button, and record the possible client options on your Student Answer Sheet.
   c. Click **Client for Microsoft Networks**, and click **OK** to add the Microsoft client to your Network Components window.

2. Some of the computers in the lab will have printers or folders that need to be shared with other users. To share folders and printers on a Windows XP computer, you need to install the File and Printer Sharing service by following the procedure described below.
   a. Click the **Install** button, and click the **Service** option.
   b. Click the **Add** button, and record the possible services on your Student Answer Sheet.
   c. Double-click the **File and Printer Sharing for Microsoft Networks** option to add this service to the network Components window.

3. Windows XP includes a Quality of Service (QoS) Packet Scheduler. This service optimizes TCP/IP packet size when connecting through different communication types (i.e., modem, LAN, DSL). Install the QoS Packet Scheduler by following the procedure described below.
   a. Click the **Install** button, and click the **Service** option.
   b. Click the **Add** button, and record the possible services on your Student Answer Sheet.
   c. Double-click the **QoS Packet Scheduler** option to add this service to the network Components window.
   d. Click **Close** to save your network component changes and return to the Network Connections window.

4. View the binding order of protocols on your computer.
   a. Click the **Advanced** option from the menu bar, and then click the **Advanced Settings** option.
   b. Verify that the Internet Protocol (TCP/IP) is bound to both the File and Printer Sharing for Microsoft Networks and Client for Microsoft Networks.
   c. Click the **Provider Order** tab, and record the purpose for this tab on your Student Answer Sheet.
   d. Click **Cancel** to return to the Network and Connections window.

e. From the **Advanced** menu, click the **Optional Networking Components** option to display the Windows Optional Networking Components Wizard shown in Figure 7-4.

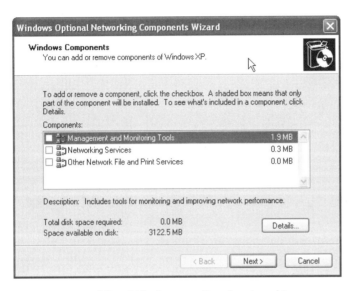

Figure 7-4   Adding Windows optional networking components

f. Click each individual component, and then click the **Details** button. After recording the properties on your Student Answer Sheet, click **Cancel**. When finished, click **Cancel** to return to the Network Connections window.

g. Click **Cancel** to return to the Network Connections window.

h. Close the Network Connections window.

5. Configure Internet Explorer to use LabHost as the proxy server.

a. Click **Start**, and then right-click the **Internet Explorer** icon from your start menu. Click **Internet Properties** to display the Internet Explorer properties window.

b. Click the **Connections** tab, and then click the **LAN Settings** button.

c. Click the **Use a proxy server for your LAN** check box, and enter the IP address of the proxy server you identified in the Requirements section.

d. Enter the port number assigned to your proxy server that you identified in the Requirements section (typically 80).

e. Click the **Advanced** button.

f. On your Student Answer Sheet, record the other TCP/IP services that are assigned to the proxy.

g. Click **Cancel** to return to the Local Area Network (LAN) window.

h. Click the **Bypass proxy server for local address** check box to allow direct access to the Web server attached to the same network as the client.

i. Click **OK** to save the proxy settings.

j. Click **OK** to save the changes to Internet Explorer and return to the desktop.

6. The school administrator is concerned that students or other users will be able to change the TCP/IP configuration. To dispel her concerns, follow the steps below to create a student account, and then verify that the account does not have rights to change the TCP/IP protocol configurations.

a. Create a new limited user named Student (for instructions on creating a new user, see Labs 3.2 and 5.1).

b. Log off.

c. Log on as Student.

d. Click **Start**, **My Network Places**, and click **View network connections** in the Network Tasks section.

e. Double-click **Local Area Connection** to display the Connection Status window, and then click **Properties**.

f. Record the message you receive on your Student Answer Sheet.

g. Click the **Install** button. Record the results on your Student Answer Sheet.

h. Click the **Internet Protocol (TCP/IP)** protocol, and try clicking the **Uninstall** button. Record the results on your Student Answer Sheet.

i. Click the **Internet Protocol (TCP/IP)** property, and click the **Properties** button. Record the results on your Student Answer Sheet.

j. Click **Cancel**, then click **Close** twice to exit.

7. Close the Network Connections window and log off.

ACTIVITY 3

The PING command is often used to test communications between computers. The PING command sends a packet to the destination computer and then waits for a reply. When testing the TCP/IP configuration of your computer, it is often a good idea to use the PING command first to send a packet to your own computer address, and then proceed to PING other computers on your subnet. PINGing a computer on another subnet is a good way to test your gateway configuration. In this activity, you use the PING command to test IP communications between your computer and the Server you identified in the Requirements section of this lab.

1. Log on as an administrator.

2. Use PING to test the IP configuration of your computer.

a. Open a Command Prompt window (**Start | All Programs | Accessories | Command Prompt**).

b. Enter the command: **PING** *ip_address* (where *ip_address* is the IP address of your Windows XP computer), and press **Enter**.

c. Record the results on your Student Answer Sheet.

3. Use PING to test communications between computers.

   a. Enter the command: **PING** *ip_address* (where *ip_address* is the address of the Server computer you identified in the Requirements section), and press **Enter**.

   b. Record the results on your Student Answer Sheet.

4. Type **Exit**, and press **Enter** to close the Command Prompt.

5. Log off.

LAB 7.4 ASSIGNING IP ADDRESSES AUTOMATICALLY

Objective

As a result of your recommendation, the Washington School has decided to implement a DHCP (Dynamic Host Configuration Protocol) server to automatically assign IP addresses to the computers in Lab 212. The DHCP server will have a range of IP addresses called a scope that will be automatically assigned to client computers when they start. A Windows XP Professional computer that is configured to obtain an IP address automatically will go through the following process when it starts:

1. The Windows XP computer broadcasts a request for a DHCP server.

2. Any DHCP server receiving the request sends out an available IP address offer. (By default, broadcast requests for DHCP servers are not passed by routers.)

3. If no DHCP servers respond to the request, the Windows XP Professional computer assigns itself an IP address of 169.254.x.y where x and y represent a unique host number for the subnet.

4. The Windows XP computer sends back an acceptance packet.

5. The DHCP server sends back an acknowledgment and reserves the address for that computer for a default of three days.

6. The Windows XP computer renews the IP address with the DHCP server within the lease period and when it restarts.

To simulate configuring the computers for Lab 212, you need to modify your computer's TCP/IP configuration to obtain IP address information automatically. Using the Windows XP automatic address assignment process allows you to test your network settings without a DHCP server. After completing this lab, you will be able to:

➤ Configure TCP/IP for automatic address assignment

➤ Use IPCONFIG to verify the IP address information assigned automatically by Windows XP when starting without the DHCP server

➤ Use IPCONFIG to release and renew IP address settings

Estimated completion time: **10–15 minutes**

ACTIVITY 1

Configure TCP/IP to obtain IP address information automatically.

1. If necessary, start your computer with Windows XP, and log on as an administrator.

2. Modify the TCP/IP configuration to obtain IP address information automatically.
   a. Click **Start**, right-click **My Network Places**, and click **Properties**.
   b. Double-click **Local Area Connection**, and click the **Properties** button.
   c. Click the **Internet Protocol (TCP/IP)** protocol, and click **Properties**.
   d. Click the **Obtain an IP address automatically** option button.
   e. Click the **Advanced** button, and record the IP address setting on your Lab 7.4 Student Answer Sheet.
   f. Click **OK** two times, and then click **Close** to save your changes and return to the Local Area Connection Status window.
   g. Click **Close** to return to the Network Connections window.
   h. Close all windows, and restart your computer.

3. Record the IP address information automatically assigned by Windows XP.
   a. Log on as the administrator.
   b. Open a Command Prompt (**Start**, **All Programs**, **Accessories**, **Command Prompt**).
   c. Type the command **IPCONFIG**, press **Enter**, and record the IP address information on your Student Answer Sheet. If your IP address is 0.0.0.0, wait a few minutes and then type **IPCONFIG** again.

4. To access computers on other subnets, the computer needs to have a default gateway assigned. While the Windows XP automatic address assignment assigns an IP address and subnet mask, you still need to assign the default gateway and DNS server manually until the DHCP service is operational. Once DHCP is running, your Windows XP Professional computers can obtain their gateway and DNS address automatically. Follow the steps below to configure the default gateway manually for your computer.
   a. Click **Start**, right-click **My Network Places**, and click **Properties**.
   b. Double-click **Local Area Connection**, and click the **Properties** button.
   c. Click the **Internet Protocol (TCP/IP)** protocol, and click **Properties**.
   d. Click the **Advanced** button, and then click the **Add** button in the Default gateways section.
   e. Enter an IP address of **169.254.1.1** for the default gateway, and click **Add**.
   f. Click **OK** two times, and then click **Close** to save your settings and return to the Connection Status window.

g. Click **Close** to return to the Network Connections window.

h. Close the Network Connections window.

i. Open a Command Prompt, type the command **IPCONFIG**, and press **Enter**.

j. On your Student Answer Sheet, record the address of the Default Gateway.

k. Type **Exit**, and press **Enter** to exit the Command Prompt window.

ACTIVITY 2

Once DHCP is operational, the IPCONFIG command can be used to reassign the TCP/IP configuration settings of a Windows XP computer. In this activity you will practice using the IPCONFIG command to verify and reassign the TCP/IP settings. This lab is a simulation and will generate error messages, as a DHCP server is not configured for this course.

1. Reassign TCP/IP settings obtained from a DHCP server.

   a. Open a Command Prompt window.

   b. Enter the command **IPCONFIG /All**, and press **Enter**.

   c. Record the IP Address information on your Student Answer Sheet.

2. The IPCONFIG command also can be used to have the workstation obtain a new address from the DHCP server. This is important if you change IP address settings on the DHCP server and do not want to restart the workstation. In this step, you use the IPCONFIG command to release its current address and get another.

   a. To release the current IP address, enter the following command at the command prompt: **IPCONFIG / Release**, and press **Enter**.

   b. On your Student Answer Sheet, record the message you receive.

   c. To assign a new IP address, enter the command **IPCONFIG /Renew**, and press **Enter**. This will take a few minutes as the system looks for a DHCP server that is not there.

   d. To record the new address settings, enter the command **IPCONFIG /All**, and record the results on your Student Answer Sheet. If a DHCP server were present, any new settings would now be configured.

3. Type **Exit**, and press **Enter** to close the Command Prompt window.

4. Log off.

LAB 7.5 WORKING WITH IP PROTOCOLS

Objective

The Washington School administrator recently informed you that the users on the administration network are unable to access shared resources on computers in Lab 212. You think that this happens because routers do not carry broadcast packets between networks. By default, Microsoft clients find the IP addresses of computer names by broadcasting a request to all computers on the subnet. The computer with the requested name then responds with its IP address. To find the IP address of computers on another subnet, Windows clients need to be configured to use a DNS or WINS server or LMHOSTS file. In a small workgroup environment, where a Windows 2000 server does not exist, creating an LMHOSTS file on each computer that contains the computer names and IP addresses of the computers on the other subnet is often simpler than installing WINS (Windows Internet Service) or DNS (Domain Name Service). After completing this lab, you will be able to:

➤ Use the PING and ARP commands to test and troubleshoot TCP/IP communications

➤ Configure an LMHOSTS file to resolve Windows names to IP addresses

➤ Configure a HOSTS file to resolve Internet names to IP addresses

➤ Use the Telnet protocol to connect to another Windows XP computer

Requirements

For this Lab activity, you need the IP address of your partner's Windows XP computer.

If you do not have access to a Windows XP computer, you can substitute your own Windows XP Professional workstation IP address in this activity.

Estimated completion time: **20–25 minutes**

ACTIVITY

1. If necessary, start your computer, and log on as an administrator.

2. As you learned in Lab 7.4, the IPCONFIG command is useful for checking the IP configuration of a computer. Use the IPCONFIG command as shown in Lab 7.4, Step 3, to record the IP configuration of your computer on your Lab 7.5 Student Answer Sheet.

3. Although IP addresses must be assigned to each computer in order to route packets between networks, the IP address must be converted to a network interface card (NIC) address in order for a packet to be sent between computers attached to the same network cable. The Address Resolution Protocol (ARP) handles the process of converting an IP address to a NIC address. In this step, you use the ARP command to determine the NIC address of your workstation and server.

   a. Open a Command Prompt window.

   b. Type the command **ARP –a**, and press **Enter**.

   c. Record the results of the ARP command on your Student Answer Sheet.

d. Use the PING command to send test packets to your partner's IP address, as shown in Lab 7.3, Activity 2.

e. At the command prompt, type the command **ARP -a**, press **Enter**, and, on your Student Answer Sheet, record the results of the ARP command after PINGing your partner's computer.

f. Type **Exit**, and press **Enter** to exit the Command Prompt window.

4. Using the LMHOSTS file is one way to access Windows computers on other subnets. In this step, you use Notepad to create an LMHOSTS file configured to access the other computer using an alias computer name.

a. Use Windows Explorer to browse to the following folder: WINDOWS\system32\drivers\etc.

b. Double-click the **LMHOSTS.SAM** file, and, if necessary, select **Notepad** as the editing application.

c. Enter the following line at the end of the file. Specify the IP address you identified in the Requirements section of this lab with the alias name MyPartner.

... **MyPartner**

d. Click **File**, **Save As**, and save the file as **LMHOSTS** with NO extension, and then exit Notepad.

5. Although the LMHOSTS file can be used to convert UNC names to IP addresses, the HOSTS file is used by TCP/IP to convert TCP/IP names to IP addresses. In this step, you enter a TCP/IP alias name for your server computer in the HOSTS file, and then PING the server using the TCP/IP alias name.

a. Use **Windows Explorer** to browse to the following folder: **WINDOWS\system32\drivers\etc**.

b. Double-click the **HOSTS** file, and, if necessary, select **Notepad** as the editing application.

c. Enter the following lines at the end of the file, specifying the IP address you identified in the Requirements section with the name TelnetHost, and your IP address identified with the name MyTelnet.

...**TelnetHost**

... **MyTelnet**

d. Save the **HOSTS** file, and exit Notepad.

e. Use the PING command to test the HOSTS file entry by following the steps below:

■ Open a **Command Prompt** window.

■ Use the command **PING** *computer-name* to test each name specified in Step 5c. Record the results on your Student Answer Sheet.

6. The Telnet protocol can be used to access central computers or terminal servers. When using Telnet, your computer becomes a terminal to the other computer. Windows XP allows you to set up a terminal server that accepts Telnet calls from other computers. Windows XP Professional includes a Telnet server that allows clients to access a DOS-like command window on the remote computer. One of the teachers at the Washington School wants to access student computers from her workstation in order to check directory contents and copy files. In this step, you use the Telnet protocol to set up a session with both your own and another Windows XP Professional computer.

a. Start the Telnet service on your Windows XP computer.

- Open the Control Panel by clicking **Start**, **Control Panel**.
- Double-click **Administrative Tools** from the Control Panel window.
- Double-click **Services** and scroll down until you see Telnet service.
- Double-click **Telnet** to display the Telnet Properties window as shown in Figure 7-5.

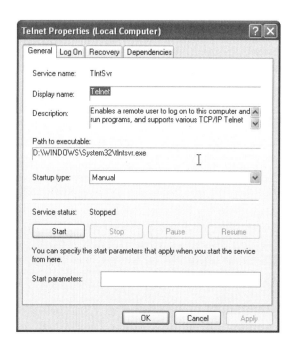

Figure 7-5 Configuring the Telnet properties

- Click **Start** to start the telnet service.
- Close the Telnet Properties window.

b. To test accessing the Telnet service running on your computer, do the following:

- Click **Start**, **Run**, and enter the command **TelNet MyTelnet**. (If necessary, replace the name MyTelnet with the name you assigned to your computer when you modified the HOSTS file in Step 5c.) Log on as the administrator.

- Describe the contents of the Telnet window on your Student Answer Sheet.

- Type **DIR C:**, and press **Enter** to display the contents of your C: drive.

- Browse to your **Public** folder on the Windows XP system drive (D:), and use the **DIR** command to display its contents.

- Type **Exit**, and press **Enter** to exit the Telnet session.

c. If possible, repeat Step 6b to access the Telnet service of another computer from your computer.

d. Stop your Telnet service and log off as follows:

- Open the Telnet Properties Window.

- Click **Stop** to stop the Telnet server.

- Click **OK** to close the Telnet window, and then close all other windows.

- Log off.

7

LAB 7.6 WORKING WITH REMOTE ASSISTANCE

Objective

In order to better provide help desk support to its school office staff, Washington School Division has decided to implement the remote assistance features of XP. Two help desk support staff, located at the school board headquarters, will remotely connect to office computers and provide visual help and troubleshooting of problems. Office staff that need help can request assistance through Windows Messenger or through e-mail. You will be responsible for configuring all systems to allow for remote assistance. The 212 Lab should have all remote assistance features turned off. After completing this lab, you will be able to:

➤ Control Remote Access control of a host computer

➤ Control Remote Access control of a client computer

➤ Establish a remote Assistance session to control another computer

Requirements

To perform this lab activity, you will need to work with a partner running Windows XP. One computer will act as the Help Desk Support system and the other will act as an Office user.

Estimated completion time: **20–25 minutes**

ACTIVITY

For the scenario above, users would have access to Windows Messenger or e-mail. A third method of sending a request for remote assistance is to save the request to a file and then deliver it on a floppy disk, ftp, or network share. To simulate this procedure, the office worker will be saving the assistance request to a shared folder on your help desk computer.

1. Ensure that the office user has access to a share on the help desk computer.
   a. On the computer acting as the office system, log on as an administrator.
   b. Click **Start, My Network Places**, and then click **View workgroup computers** to display a list of the computers in your classroom.
   c. Double-click your partner's computer and open a shared folder. If one is not available, ask your partner to ensure that they have shared a folder with permissions allowing you to create a file.
   d. Close all windows and return to your desktop.

2. Ensure that your computer allows Remote Assistance.
   a. Click **Start, Control Panel**, and then double-click **System.**
   b. Click the **Remote** tab to display the Remote Assistance and Desktop settings.
   c. Record the default setting for Remote Assistance on your Student Answer Sheet. Ensure that the **Allow Remote Assistance invitations to be sent from this computer** box is selected.
   d. Click **Advanced** and record the default setting on your Student Answer Sheet. Ensure that the **Allow this computer to be controlled remotely** box is selected. Note: These settings can only be changed by the administrator or through group policies.
   e. Click **OK** twice to return to Control Panel, and then close all windows.

3. Send an invitation for Remote Assistance.
   a. Click **Start, Help and Support** to display the Help and Support Center.
   b. Click **Invite a friend to connect to your computer with Remote Assistance**. The Remote Assistance help page is displayed.
   c. Click **Invite someone to help you**. You are given three options for contacting your assistant.
   d. At the bottom of the screen, click **Save invitation as a file (Advanced)**.
   e. In the **From** field, type your name to appear on the invitation.
   f. Use the scroll to define an expiration time limit for this invitation as **30 minutes**.
   g. Click **Continue** to display the Save Invitation Page.
   h. Be sure that the **Require the recipient to use a password** checkbox is marked.

i. Provide a password and confirm the password. Record the password on your Student Answer sheet and then provide it to your partner.

j. Click **Save Invitation** to display the Save As window.

k. Using the pull-down menu, select **My Network Places** and navigate to your partner's shared folder. Type your name for the file name and click **Save** to exit. Record the File Name and Path on your Student Answer Sheet.

l. The Help and Support Center returns you to the Remote Assistance page; click **View the status of all my invitations**. A listing of the invitation you've sent appears.

m. Click the radio button beside your invitation, then click **Details**.

n. A dialog box with complete details about the invitation is displayed. Record the details on your Student Answer Sheet. Click **Close**.

o. Close the Help and Support Center.

4. Respond to an invitation for Remote Assistance.

a. On the computer acting as the Help Desk System, navigate to the shared folder where your partner saved the invitation.

b. Double-click the **<partner's name>.msrcincident** file.

c. The Remote Assistant tool launches and prompts you for the password. Note the expiration date to make sure that the invitation has not expired.

d. Type in the password provided by your partner, and then click **Yes.**

e. On the computer acting as the office system computer, a pop-up dialog box appears asking if you want to allow your partner to connect. Click **Yes**.

f. The Remote Assistance control bar appears on the office user's computer. The Remote Assistance desktop access window and control utility appears on the Help Desk computer, as shown in Figure 7-6.

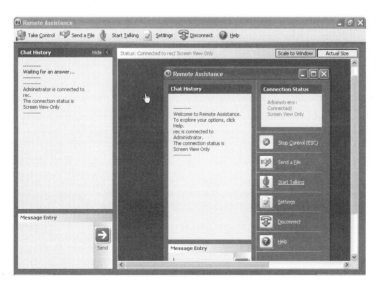

Figure 7-6 The Remote Assistance desktop access window and control utility

g. From either system, type in a short message in the **Message Entry** section, such as **What may I assist you with?**, and then click **Send**.

h. On the Student Answer Sheet, record the features available in Remote Assistance.

i. On the Help Desk computer, click **Take Control** from the top tool bar.

j. On the office computer, a pop-up message will appear as shown in Figure 7-7. Click **Yes** to grant control of the computer.

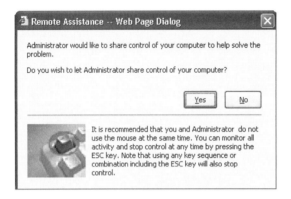

Figure 7-7   Remote Assistance pop-up message

k. On the Help Desk computer, click **OK** when informed that you have taken control.

l. On the Help Desk computer, open and close **My Computer**. Notice that the movements made on the Help Desk computer actually take effect on the Office computer.

m. On the Help Desk computer, click **Disconnect** from the top toolbar.

n. On both computers, click **OK** when informed that Remote Assistance has been disconnected.

o. On both computers, close Remote Assistance and return to the desktop.

p. If time permits, reverse roles and repeat the above steps.

LAB 7.7 INSTALLING AND CONFIGURING SERVICES FOR NOVELL

Objective

The administrator of Washington School has added a Novell 4.0 server to the office that hosts a special grades management program. The program only runs on Novell, so all office systems will need access to the Novell Server. After completing this lab, you will be able to:

➤ Install and configure the NWLink Protocol

➤ Install and configure the Novell Client Service

Requirements

To perform this lab activity, you will need the Windows XP Professional CD-ROM.

Estimated completion time: **20–25 minutes**

ACTIVITY

This lab will simulate the configuration of the Novell Client and Protocol, as a Novell Server has not been configured for this lab.

1. To install NWLink:
    a. If you have not already done so, log on to your Windows XP Professional computer as an administrator.
    b. Click **Start**, right-click **My Network Places**, and then click **Properties**.
    c. Right-click **Local Area Connection**, and then click **Properties**.
    d. In the Local Area Connection Properties dialog box, click **Install**.
    e. Select **Protocol** from the list of available components, and then click **Add**.
    f. Double-click **NWLink IPX/SPX/NetBIOS Compatible Transport Protocol** from the list.
    g. Click **Close** to complete the installation. Click **No** to reboot the computer at this time.
    h. Right-click again on the **Local Area Connection** icon, and select **Properties** to configure NWLink. Note that NWLink NetBIOS has been added to the installed components list.
    i. Select **NWLink IPX/SPX/NetBIOS Compatible Transport Protocol** from the list, and then click **Properties**.
    j. An internal network number for the computer should have been pre-selected by XP. To change it, type up to an 8-digit hexadecimal number, for example, 1FAD or 1999A.
    k. Click the down arrow for the **Frame type** drop-down list and view the frame types. Windows XP will attempt to Auto Detect the frame type used by the Novell server. However, if more than one frame type exists, you will need to specify them. Note that you must specify the network number for the selected frame type. Enter a network number in the space provided.
    l. Select Frame Type as **Auto Detect**. Click **OK**, and then click **Close** to complete the configuration.
    m. Click **No** to reboot the computer at this time.

7

2. To install and configure Client Service for NetWare:

   a. If you have not already done so, log on to your Windows XP Professional computer as an administrator.

   b. Click **Start**, right-click **My Network Places**, and then select **Properties**.

   c. Right-click **Local Area Connection**, and then select **Properties**.

   d. In the Local Area Connection Properties dialog box, click **Install**.

   e. If necessary, select **Client** from the list of available components, and then click **Add**. Note that the only client available to be installed is Client Service for NetWare.

   f. Select **Client Service for NetWare**, and then click **OK**. Click **Yes** to restart your computer when prompted to do so.

   g. After you enter your login information, you will be presented with a Select NetWare Logon window. If a Novell Server is available, either click the Default Tree and Context radio button, and enter the default tree and context for your computer on the network, or provide a name for the preferred server to which the computer will connect (this latter element is selected by default). Click **Cancel**, and then click **Yes** at the NetWare Network message box.

   h. Open the Control Panel by selecting **Start**, **Control Panel**. Note that the CSNW icon appears.

   i. Double-click the **CSNW** icon to open the Client Service for NetWare dialog box. Adjust the Print Options and Login Script Options as desired, and click **OK**.

   j. Note that you receive an information box telling you that the changes will take effect the next time you log in. Click **OK** to continue.

   k. Close all windows and return to the desktop.

3. Uninstall the Novell Client and NWLink protocol.

   a. Click **Start**, right-click **My Network Places**, and then select **Properties**.

   b. Right-click **Local Area Connection**, and then select **Properties**.

   c. In the Local Area Connection Properties dialog box, select **Client Service for NetWare** from the list, and click **Uninstall**.

   d. Click **Yes** to confirm the uninstall, and then click **No** to restart the computer.

   e. Select **IPX/SPX/NetBIOS Compatible Transport Protocol**, and click **Uninstall**.

   f. Click **Yes** to confirm the uninstall.

   g. Click **Yes** to reboot the computer.

CHAPTER EIGHT

REMOTE ACCESS SERVICES

Labs included in this chapter

➤ Lab 8.1 Creating a Connection to a Private Network

➤ Lab 8.2 Creating an Incoming Connection

➤ Lab 8.3 Creating a Virtual Private Network Connection

➤ Lab 8.4 Creating a Dial-up Connection to the Internet

➤ Lab 8.5 Configuring Internet Connection Firewall

➤ Lab 8.6 Installing and Configuring Internet Information Services

➤ Lab 8.7 Sharing an Internet Connection

Microsoft MCSE Exam #70-270 Objectives	
Objective	Lab
Create a dial-up connection to connect to a remote access server	8.1
Create an incoming connection	8.2
Connect to computers by using a virtual private network (VPN) connection	8.3
Connect to the Internet by using dial-up networking	8.4
Configure Internet Connection Firewall	8.5
Configure and troubleshoot Internet Connection Sharing	8.7
Connect to shared resources on a Microsoft network	8.1, 8.3
Manage and troubleshoot Web server resources	8.6

Student Answer Sheets to accompany the labs in this chapter are available for downloading from the Online Companion for this manual at *www.course.com*.

LAB 8.1 CREATING A CONNECTION TO A PRIVATE NETWORK

Objective

Blue Hills Realty is a small realty company owned by Carl Dauer. Currently, the Blue Hills Realty office personnel includes Carl, another real estate agent, and a secretary. Each agent and the secretary are using Windows XP Professional computers in their offices, which are connected to a peer-to-peer network. Carl also acts as an agent for a large real estate company called World Realty. Carl recently purchased a notebook computer (also running Windows XP Professional) and will use it to access the office network from his home, as well as to connect to the Windows 2000 network at World Realty. Most of the time, Carl will be calling into the office from home and a few times while on the road. When he is calling long distance, the system should call him back so that the long distance charges are charged to the company. After completing this lab, you will be able to:

➤ Configure a Windows XP computer to connect to a Private Network (Blue Hills Realty)

➤ Configure a Windows XP computer to connect to a Private Network (World Realty)

➤ Configure dial-up connections to support Callback

Requirements

➤ A Windows XP compatible modem must be installed in your computer. If a modem is not installed, see Step 2 to create a simulated one for this lab.

➤ The following information will be needed for the configuration:

- Blue Hill phone number: 345-5522

- User name: cdauer

- Password: ab1B22CD

- World Realty phone number: 675-5563

- User name: carldauer

- Password: xYtmh88

- Domain: worldrealty.com

Estimated completion time: **10 minutes**

ACTIVITY

1. If necessary, start your computer with Windows XP, and log on as an administrator.

2. Click **Start**, **Control Panel**, and double-click **Phone and Modems Options**. Click the **Modem** tab to display a list of modems installed on your system. If a modem is installed, record the modem type on the Student Answer Sheet, and skip to Step 3. Otherwise, the following steps are necessary to create a simulated modem for this lab.

   a. Click **Add**, and then click the **Don't detect my modem; I will select it from a list** option box.

   b. Click **Next** to display a list of available modems. Select **(Standard Modem Types)** as the Manufacturer and **Standard 56000 bps Modem** as the model. Click **Next.**

   c. Select one of the communication ports listed (COM1 – COM4), and click **Next.**

   d. Click **Finish** to return to the Phone and Modem Options window. Record the modem type on the Student Answer Sheet. Click **OK**, and then close Control Panel.

3. First, you will create a dial-up connection for Blue Hills Realty.

   a. Click **Start**, right-click **My Network Places**, and then click **Properties**.

   b. Click the **Create a new connection** from the Network Tasks list. Click **Next** to display the Network Connection Type window.

   c. If necessary, click the **Connect to the network at my workplace** option button, and click **Next** to start the Network Connection window.

   d. On your Student Answer Sheet, record the two connection types.

   e. Click the **Dial-up connection** option, and click **Next**.

   f. Type **Blue Hills Realty** for the Company Name, and click **Next.**

   g. Type the phone number for Blue Hills, and click **Next.**

   h. Ensure that **Me Only** is selected in the Create this connection for window, and then click **Next**.

   i. Click the **Add a shortcut to this connection to my desktop** option box, and click **Finish** to exit the wizard.

   j. A connection box will automatically appear for Blue Hills Realty. Enter the user name and password, and click the **Save this user name and password for the following users** option box. Ensure that the **Me only** option box is selected.

   k. Click **Properties**, and click the **Options** tab. Clear the **Prompt for name and password, certificate, etc.** option box, as well as the **Prompt for phone number** option box.

   l. Place a check in the **Redial if line is dropped** option box, and click **OK.**

   m. Click **Cancel** to abort the dial attempt.

4. You will now create a connection for World Realty.

   a. Repeat Steps 3a through 3i, substituting the World Realty information from above.

   b. A connection box will appear automatically for World Realty. Click **Properties**, and click the **Options** tab. Place a check in the **Include Windows logon domain option box**, as well as in the **Redial if line is dropped** option box.

   c. Click the **Security** tab to display the security options window. Using the Validate my identity as follows scroll box, select **Required secured password** as the setting. Record the available Validate my identity options on the Student Answer Sheet.

   d. Click **OK**, and then type the user name, password, and domain information from above. Click the **Save this user name and password for the following users** option box. Ensure that the **Me only** option box is selected.

   e. Click **Cancel** to return to the Network Connections window.

   f. Close all windows to return to your desktop. Two new icons should be present for the connections that you create. Double-click each one to test it, and click **Cancel** to abort any dialing attempt.

   g. Close all windows.

5. To configure callback for the dial-up connections, do the following.

   a. Click **Start**, right-click **My Network Places**, and then click **Properties**.

   b. Click **Dial-up Preferences** from the **Advanced** menu item.

   c. Click the **Callback** tab, and ensure that the **Ask me during dialing when the server offers** option box is selected. On the Student Answer Sheet, describe the three callback options.

   d. Click **OK**, and then close the Network Connections window.

LAB 8.2 CREATING AN INCOMING CONNECTION

Objective

Now that you have configured Carl's laptop to call into the office, you will need to configure his desktop to receive calls. As outlined in Lab 8.1, Carl's desktop must support callback when requested. After completing this lab, you will be able to:

➤ Configure a Windows XP system to accept incoming connections

➤ Configure the call back feature of incoming connections

Requirements

➤ A Windows XP compatible modem installed in your computer (See Lab 8.1)

Estimated completion time: **5 minutes**

ACTIVITY

1. If necessary, start your computer with Windows XP, and log on as an administrator.

2. If you have not already done so, create a limited user account for Carl Dauer, using the Blue Hills Realty user information in Lab 8.1.

3. Click **Start**, right-click **My Network Places**, and then click **Properties**.

4. Click the **Create a new connection** from the Network Tasks list. Click **Next** to display the Network Connection Type window.

5. Click the **Set up an Advanced Connection** option button, and click **Next** to display the Advanced Connection Options window.

6. On your Student Answer Sheet, record the two options available.

7. Click the **Accept incoming connections** option, and click **Next** to display the Devices for Incoming connections window.

8. Place a check in the modem box from Lab 8.1, and click **Next** to display the VPN Connection window.

9. Carl's desktop will not be used to support VPN connections through the Internet; therefore, click the **Do not allow virtual private connections** option box. Click **Next** to display the User Permissions window.

10. Scroll down the list and place a check mark in Carl Dauer's box. Click **Properties**, and then click the **Callback** tab to list the callback options. Click **Allow the caller to set the callback number**, and then click **OK** to return to the User Permissions window. Record the callback options on the Student Answer Sheet.

11. Click **Next** to display the Networking Software window. Ensure that Internet Protocol (TCP/IP) is selected, and click **Properties**. For added security, Carl wants to make sure that his computer is the only one available on dial-up. Remove the check mark from **Allow callers to access my local area network**, and click **OK**. On the Student Answer Sheet, briefly describe why disabling this option is a security feature.

12. Click **Next**, and then click **Finish** to close the Incoming Connection wizard. The Incoming Connection icon should now appear on your Network Connections window.

13. Close the Network Connections window to return to the desktop.

8

LAB 8.3 CREATING A VIRTUAL PRIVATE NETWORK CONNECTION

Objective

World Realty has just informed you that it will be implementing a Remote Access Service through the Internet to cut down on long distance costs. You will need to configure a VPN connection on Carl's laptop to gain access to World Realty. You will be using the Point-to-Point Tunneling Protocol (PPTP) to create a Virtual Private Network (VPN). After completing this lab, you will be able to:

➤ Configure Windows XP to use Point-to-Point Tunneling Protocol (PPTP) to establish a Virtual Private Network (VPN) connection

➤ Establish a connection between the computers using PPTP

Requirements

➤ One other Window XP Professional computer must be attached to the network.

➤ You will work with your lab partner to determine which computer will act as the "server" and which computer will be the remote client. The client will be used to make a Virtual Private Network connection to the "server" using your network to simulate the Internet.

Estimated completion time: **20 minutes**

ACTIVITY

1. If necessary, start the computer designated as the World Realty Remote Access Service (RAS) server, and log on as an administrator.

2. Carl Dauer needs a user account so he can access the World Realty network from a remote location. Create a limited user account for Carl using the World Realty User information in Lab 8.1.

3. Modify the Incoming Connections option on the computer identified as the World Realty RAS server computer so access is allowed from the Internet.
   a. Click **Start**, right-click **My Network Places**, and then click **Properties**.
   b. Right-click **Incoming Connections**, and click **Properties** to display the Incoming Connections Properties window, similar to the one shown in Figure 8-1.

Figure 8-1   Configuring the incoming connections properties

    c. If necessary, place a check mark in the **Allow others to make private connections to my computer by tunneling through the Internet or other network** check box by clicking it.

    d. Click the **Users** tab.

    e. Click the check box in front of the user name that you created for Carl Dauer.

    f. Click **OK** to save your changes, and then close the Network connections window.

4. Prior to making a Virtual Private Network connection from the computer designated as the remote client, you need to follow the steps below to determine the IP address of the computer identified as the World Realty RAS server.

    a. Open a Command Prompt window on the World Realty RAS server by clicking **Start**, **All Programs**, **Accessories**, **Command Prompt**.

    b. Type the command **IPCONFIG**, and press **Enter**.

    c. On your Student Answer Sheet, record the IP address of the computer identified as the World Realty RAS server.

    d. Enter the **Exit** command, and press **Enter** to close the Command Prompt window.

5. Create a Virtual Private Network connection option on the computer identified as the remote client.

    a. If necessary, start your client computer and log on as an administrator.

    b. Click **Start**, right-click **My Network Places**, and click the **Properties** option.

c. Double-click the **Create a new connection** from Network Tasks, and click **Next** to display the Network Connection Type window.

d. Click the **Connect to the network at my workplace** option button, and click **Next**.

e. Click the **Virtual Private Network connection** option, and then click **Next**.

f. Type **World Realty VPN** for the Company Name.

g. If you have an Internet Connection configured on your client computer, the Public Network window shown in Figure 8-2, will appear. Click the **Do not dial the initial connection** option button, and click **Next** to display the VPN Server Selection window. If your computer is accessing a shared Internet connection, this step will be skipped, and the VPN Server Selection window will appear.

h. In the Host name or IP address text box, enter the IP address of your World Realty RAS server computer, and click **Next**.

i. Ensure that **Me Only** is selected in the Create this connection for window, and then click **Next**.

j. Click the **Add a shortcut to this connection to my desktop** option box, and click **Finish** to exit the wizard.

k. Click **Cancel** to bypass the Connect World Realty VPN window.

l. Close all windows and return to your desktop.

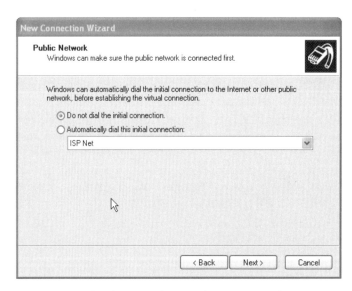

Figure 8-2   Configuring the initial connection for a VPN connection

6. In this step, you test your Virtual Network configuration by simulating a connection from the remote client computer to the World Realty RAS server. You will use your local network as if it were the Internet.

a. If you were accessing the RAS server from a remote client, you would first need to use your Internet Connection option to establish a connection to the Internet. In this step, you will use your Local Area Network to simulate the Internet connection. Therefore, you can assume that a connection to the Internet has already been established.

b. Double-click the **World Realty VPN** icon on your desktop.

c. Enter Carl Dauer's user name and password that you recorded in Step 2.

d. Click **Connect**, and, on your Student Answer Sheet, record the requested Connection Results window information.

7. On the Computer designated as the World Realty RAS server, check the status of incoming users.

a. If necessary, start the computer designated as the World Realty RAS server, and log on as an administrator.

b. Click **Start**, right-click **My Network Places**, and then click **Properties**.

c. A connection for Carl Dauer should be listed as an icon under Incoming as shown in Figure 8-3. Double-click the icon to display Carl's connection status. Click the **Details** tab, and record the connection details on your Student Answer Sheet.

d. Click the **General** tab, and then click **Disconnect** to cancel Carl's connection. Close all windows and return to the desktop.

Figure 8-3   The Network Connection dialog box

8. Remove the World Realty VPN connection from the remote client computer.

a. If necessary, log on to the remote client computer as the administrator.

b. Click **Start**, right-click **My Network Places**, and click **Properties**.

c. Right-click the **World Realty VPN** connection, and click **Delete**.

       d. Click **Yes** to confirm the deletion process.

       e. Close the Network Connections window, and log off.

   9. Remove the Virtual Private Network connection from the server computer.

       a. If necessary, log on to the server computer as the administrator.

       b. Click **Start**, right-click **My Network Places**, and click **Properties**.

       c. Right-click **Incoming Connections**, and click **Properties**.

       d. Click to remove the check mark from the **Allow others to make private connections to my computer** check box.

       e. Click **OK** to save your changes.

       f. Close the Network Connections window, and log off.

  10. If time permits, repeat the lab by reversing the roles of the computers. Make the previous server computer the remote client, and the previous remote client computer the new server.

LAB 8.4 CREATING A DIAL-UP CONNECTION TO THE INTERNET

Objective

Accessing real estate information and advertising on the Internet is becoming an important part of doing business at the Blue Hills Realty office. As a result, each agent and the secretary currently have modems installed in their computers and use them for dial-up access to the Internet. In addition to configuring the dial-up connection to the office network, Carl also wants you to configure a dial-up connection to the Internet from his new notebook Windows XP Professional system. After completing this lab, you will be able to:

➤ Install and configure dial-up access to the Internet

Requirements

➤ The following information will be needed to simulate a connection to a dial-up Internet Service Provider (ISP):

- ISP Name: ISP Net

- ISP phone number: 454-4412

- User name: cdauer

- Password: liku877M

➤ A Windows XP compatible modem installed in your computer (See Lab 8.1)

Estimated completion time: **5 minutes**

ACTIVITY

1. If necessary, start your computer with Windows XP, and log on as an administrator.

2. Click **Start**, right-click **My Network Places**, and then click **Properties**.

3. Click **Create a new connection** from the Network Tasks list. Click **Next** to display the Network Connection Type window.

4. If neccessary, click the **Connect to the Internet** option button, and click **Next** to start the Internet Wizard.

5. On your Student Answer Sheet, record the three options available.

6. Click the **Set up my connection manually** option, and click **Next** to display the Internet connection window. Record the three connection types on your Student Answer sheet.

7. Click **Connect using a dial-up modem**, and click **Next.**

8. Type **ISP Net** for the ISP Name, and click **Next.**

9. Type the phone number for the ISP, and click **Next.**

10. Type in the User name and Password listed above. Take note of the three options at the bottom, and then click **Next.**

11. Click the **Add a shortcut to this connection to my desktop** option box, and click **Finish** to exit the wizard.

12. A connection box will automatically appear for ISP Net. Click the **Save this user name and password for the following users** option box. Ensure that the **Me only** option box is selected.

13. Click **Cancel**, and then close the Network Connections window.

14. Test your Internet connection by performing the following steps. Record the results of the test on your Student Answer Sheet. (*Note*: If you are using a simulated modem, you can still perform this step and verify that the system attempts to dial the phone number you specified in the Requirements section.)

    a. From the desktop, double-click the **ISP Net** icon that you created.

    b. Verify that the User name and Password fields are filled in, and click the **Dial** button.

    c. Observe the dialing and connection process, and record any messages on your Student Answer Sheet.

    d. Close any error messages and windows to return to the desktop.

8

LAB 8.5 CONFIGURING AN INTERNET CONNECTION FIREWALL

Objective

Carl is concerned that Blue Hills computer systems may be vulnerable to unauthorized access during internet connections. Carl wants to have a log of attempted unauthorized access. He also wants to be able to PING the server from his laptop at home in order to troubleshoot network problems. You will use the new Windows XP Internet Connection Firewall service to protect all systems from unauthorized access, as well as log these attempts. After completing this lab, you will be able to:

➤ Configure Internet Connection Firewall on Windows XP

➤ Set up logging for the Firewall

➤ Enable specific types of Internet traffic through the Firewall

Estimated completion time: **5 minutes**

ACTIVITY

1. If necessary, start your computer with Windows XP, and log on as an administrator.

2. Click **Start**, right-click **My Network Places**, and then click **Properties**.

3. Right-click the **ISP Net** connection icon, and click **Properties.**

4. Click the **Advanced** tab to display the Internet firewall settings.

5. Ensure that the **Protect my computer and network by limiting or preventing access to this computer from the Internet** check box is selected. Click the **Learn more about Internet Connection Firewall**, and briefly describe this feature on your Student Answer Sheet. Close the Help window.

6. Click **Settings** to display the Advanced Settings for the Firewall. The services that are checked enable external internet users to access your computer, assuming that you have the appropriate software installed. On your Student Answer Sheet, briefly record what each service is used for. In the next lab (8.6), you will be configuring your computer as a Web server. In order to make this server available to the internet, click **Web Server (HTTP)**. Click **OK** on the Service Settings window.

7. Click the **Security Logging** tab, and then place a check mark in the **Log dropped packets** box. This will log all unsuccessful attempts to access your system. Record the path to the log files on your Student Answer Sheet.

8. Click the **ICMP** tab, and place a check in the **Allow incoming echo request** box. This will allow the use of PING to check the connection to your computer.

9. Click **OK** twice, and then close all windows.

10. This concludes the configuration of Internet Connection Firewall. To update the Firewall software to address the latest security concerns, use the Windows Update feature.

LAB 8.6 INSTALLING AND CONFIGURING INTERNET INFORMATION SERVICES

Objective

Your local Home Town Library has been assigned a permanent Internet address, and wants to set up and manage its Web site. You have volunteered to help install and configure Internet Information Services (IIS) on a Windows XP Professional system in the office of Kristen Nickel. Kristen has been assigned to develop the library's Web page. Prior to installing the IIS software on the library's Windows 2000 Server, she wants to use the Windows XP Professional Internet Information Services on her machine to develop and test the Web page. After completing this lab, you will be able to:

➤ Install Internet Information Services on a Windows XP Professional system

➤ Configure Internet Information Services

Requirements

➤ Access to a copy of the Windows XP Professional CD-ROM

➤ Optionally, another computer on the network to access your Web server

```
Estimated completion time: 30 minutes
```

ACTIVITY

1. If necessary, start your computer with Windows XP, and log on as an administrator.

2. Install Internet Information Services for Windows XP Professional.
   a. Insert the Windows XP Professional CD-ROM, and click **Exit** to close the Windows XP CD window.
   b. Open Control Panel by clicking **Start**, **Control Panel**.
   c. Double-click the **Add or Remove Programs** icon. (If the Add or Remove Programs icon is disabled, follow Step 16 in Lab 6.2 to enable it.)
   d. Click the **Add or Remove Windows Components** icon to start the Windows Components Wizard.
   e. If necessary, click the **Internet Information Services (IIS)** check box, and click **Next** to start the installation. The process to copy files might take several minutes, so this may be a good time for a break.
   f. After all files have been copied, click **Finish** to close the installation wizard, and return to the Add or Remove Programs window.
   g. Close the Add or Remove Programs window.

3. After Internet Information Services has been installed, you can modify Web server parameters such as the path to the Web site files, the default Web page name, and access capabilities. For example, assume Kristen wants to use Index.htm for her opening page. In this step, you document the path to the Web site files, and include Index.htm as one of the default Web page names.

   a. Start the Personal Web Manager application as follows:

- Click **Start**, **Control Panel**.
- Double-click **Administrative Tools**.
- Double-click **Internet Information Services**, and expand **Local Computer**, **Web Sites**, **Default Web Site** to display the default Web Site information as shown in Figure 8-4.

   b. Right-click **Default Web Site**, and Stop the Web service by clicking **Stop**.

   c. Right-click **Default Web Site**, and click **Properties.** Click the **Home Directory** tab.

   d. On your Student Answer Sheet, document the path to the home directory.

   e. Click the **Documents** tab.

   f. Ensure that Index.htm is listed as one of the Default Documents. Use the arrow keys to move Index.htm to the top of the list. This will ensure that Index.htm will be searched for first.

   g. Click **OK** to exit Properties. Click **OK** to close any Inheritance Override messages.

   h. Right-click **Default Web Site**, and Start the Web service by clicking **Start**.

   i. Close all windows to return to the desktop.

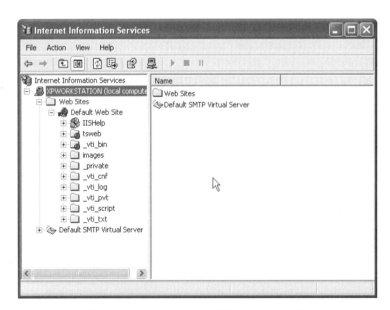

Figure 8-4   Configuring the Internet Information Services

4. Now that she understands how the Web server can be configured, Kristen is ready to do some testing. To test basic Web server operation, you place an HTML file in the default Web site folder, and view the content of the file through Internet Explorer.

   a. Open Notepad (**Start | All Programs | Accessories | Notepad**) and type the following:
   \<html\>
   \<title\>
   Home Town Library
   \</title\>
   \<body\>
   \<P\>\<img src=web.gif\>
   Welcome to the Home Town Library
   \<img src=web.gif\>
   \</body\>
   \</html\>

   b. Click **Save As** from the File menu, and save the document as **Index.htm** in the Default Web Site home directory that you identified in Step 3d on your Student Answer Sheet.

   c. Exit Notepad.

   d. Test the Web page from Internet Explorer as follows:
   - Start Internet Explorer.
   - Click **File**, **Open**, and enter **localhost**.
   - If you receive the "Web page unavailable while offline" message, click the **Connect** button.
   - Your "Welcome to the Home Town Library" page should appear.
   - Close Internet Explorer.

5. A neighboring library in the town of Mikana would like the Home Town Library to host a Web page for their library as well. A Web server can host multiple Web sites by adding virtual directories. In this step, you create a folder for Mikana, and then add a virtual Web site to your Web server configuration.

   a. Use **My Computer** to browse to the **Inetpub** folder located on your Windows XP system drive.

   b. Create a folder named **Mikana** in the Inetpub folder.

   c. Copy the following files from the wwwroot folder you identified in Step 3c into the newly created Mikana folder:
   - Index.htm
   - Web.gif

   d. Rename the Index.htm file as **Default.htm**.

   e. Use Notepad to edit the Default.htm file, and change "Home Town Library" to **Mikana Public Library** in both the \<title\> and \<body\> sections.

   f. Save the Default.htm file, and exit Notepad.

g. Start the Internet Information Service, and right-click **Default Web Site**.

h. Point to **New**, and then click **Virtual Directory** to start the Virtual Directory wizard.

i. Click **Next** to start the wizard, and type **Mikana** as the Alias for the directory. Click **Next** to display the Web Site Content Directory window.

j. Click the **Browse** button, browse to the **Mikana** folder, and click **OK**. Click **Next** to display the Access Permissions window.

k. On your Student Answer Sheet, record the possible access permissions for this directory.

l. Click **Next**, and then **Finish** to close the wizard.

6. In this step, you test the new virtual Web directory for the Mikana library.

a. Clear the Internet Explorer cache as follows:

- Click **Start**, right-click **Internet Explorer**, and click **Internet Properties**.
- Click the **Delete Files** button, and click **OK** to confirm the deletion.
- Click **OK** to exit the Internet Properties window.

b. Start Internet Explorer.

c. Click **File**, **Open**, and enter the following URL: **localhost/Mikana**. Click **OK**.

d. The Welcome to the Mikana Public Library page should be displayed.

e. Click **File**, **Open**, and, to display your Home Town Library page, enter the following URL: **localhost**. Click **OK**.

7. Close Internet Explorer, and log off.

LAB 8.7 SHARING AN INTERNET CONNECTION

Objective

The Blue Hills Realty office is increasing its use of the Internet for accessing land prices and advertising recreational properties. The agency has only one Internet account. When one person is using the Internet, the other users need to wait for that person to disconnect before they can dial in. You recently informed Carl that Windows XP can help solve this problem by sharing an Internet connection. Carl wants you to configure the other computers in his office so that they share the Internet connection on the Windows XP Professional computer in his office. After completing this lab, you will be able to:

➤ Use Windows XP to share an Internet connection

➤ Configure another computer to use the shared Internet connection

To perform this lab, students need to work in teams consisting of at least two computers—where one computer shares its Internet connection with the other computer(s). When sharing an Internet connection, the computer hosting the Internet connection needs to provide IP addresses to the client computer(s). As a result, to perform this lab, the computers sharing an Internet connection need to be isolated from other lab computers that use a separate hub or network cable. Consult your instructor or lab assistant to determine if it is feasible to do these activities in your lab environment.

Requirements

➤ Completion of Lab 8.4

➤ Another Windows XP Professional computer attached to an isolated network hub or cable

➤ Determine which computer will share its Internet connection (referred to as the "server" computer) and which computer will be the "client."

➤ In a classroom environment, you need to obtain permission from the instructor or lab assistant to disconnect both your computer and your lab partner's computer from the main network. You can then connect them using a separate hub or crossover cable to simulate the Blue Hills Realty office network. This is necessary for the computer that you select to host the shared Internet connection and automatically provide IP addresses to only your client computer.

➤ The hub to which your computers are connected cannot have a DHCP server running, because the Internet-sharing computer must be the only one that can give out IP addresses to other computers.

8

Estimated completion time: **25 minutes**

ACTIVITY

1. If working in a classroom environment, you and your lab partner should disconnect your computers from the classroom network, and then connect them using a separate hub or crossover cable.

2. Start the shared Internet connection (server) computer with Windows XP, and log on as an administrator.

3. Share the Internet connection by performing the following procedure on the Internet connection host computer.
   a. Click **Start**, right-click **My Network Places**, and click **Properties**.
   b. Right-click the **ISP Net** icon, and click **Properties**. Click the **Advanced** tab to display the Internet Connection Sharing Properties as shown in Figure 8-5.

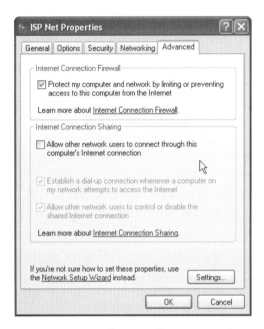

Figure 8-5   Configuring the Internet Connection Firewall

   c. Click the **Allow other network users to connect through this com-puter's Internet connection** check box.

   d. If a warning message regarding user name and password is displayed, take note of the instructions, and click **OK**.

   e. On your Student Answer Sheet, describe the options that are enabled by default when you enable Internet connection sharing.

   f. Click **OK** to save your configuration.

   g. Double-click **Local Area Connection**, and then click **Properties**.

   h. Double-click **Internet Protocol (TCP/IP)**. On the Student Answer Sheet, record how your IP address is assigned and what the new IP address and Subnet mask are.

   i. Click **OK** twice, and then click **Close** to return to the Network Connections window.

   j. Close all windows, and log off.

4. If necessary, start the client computer, and log on as an administrator.

5. Before the client computer can share the Internet connection on your server computer, you first need to configure the client computer's TCP/IP protocol so it obtains IP address information automatically.

   a. Click **Start**, right-click **My Network Places**, and click the **Properties** option.

   b. Right-click the **Local Area Connection** icon, and click **Properties** to display the Components window.

c. Click the **Internet Protocol (TCP/IP)**, and click the **Properties** button.

d. Document the current TCP/IP configuration (manual or automatic IP addressing) on your Student Answer Sheet.

e. If necessary, click the **Obtain an IP address automatically** option button, and click **OK** to return to the Components window. Your client computer now gets its IP address and default gateway from the computer that is sharing its Internet connection. The default gateway for the client will be set to the computer with the Internet connection so that IP packets are routed to the Internet.

f. Click **OK**, and then click **Close** to save your changes and return to the Network Connections window.

6. Close the Network Connections window.

7. Test the shared Internet connection from the client computer.

a. Find and record the client computer's IP address and default gateway by doing the following:

- Open a Command Prompt window.
- Enter the command **IPCONFIG /All**, and record the IP address information on your Student Answer Sheet.
- Enter the command **EXIT**, and press **Enter** to close the Command Prompt window.

b. Click **Start**, right-click **Internet Explorer**, and click **Internet Properties**.

c. Click the **Connections** tab, and then click the **LAN Settings** button.

d. Verify that the **Use a proxy server for your LAN** option is not checked. Click **OK** twice.

e. Close all windows.

f. Start **Internet Explorer**. When Internet Explorer attempts to send a packet to the Internet it will be redirected, using the gateway IP address, to your shared Internet computer. The shared Internet computer should automatically attempt to dial up the ISP and make the connection. Both computers would then be able to share access to the Internet. On your Student Answer Sheet, record what happened on the client and on the server computers.

g. Close all windows on both computers and return to the desktop.

8. After both you and your partner have completed Steps 3 through 7, return the TCP/IP configuration on the client computer back to the settings you recorded in Step 5. Turn off Internet Connection sharing on the server computer, and reset the TCP/IP settings to their original settings.

9. If you are working in a classroom environment, shut down both computers and reattach them to the classroom network.

10. Start both computers and verify that they are operating correctly on the classroom network. Have your instructor or lab assistant confirm system operation and initial your Student Answer Sheet.

8

CHAPTER NINE

PRINTING AND FAXING

Labs included in this chapter

➤ Lab 9.1 Installing and Sharing Printers

➤ Lab 9.2 Configuring and Securing Shared Printers

➤ Lab 9.3 Managing Print Jobs and Printers

➤ Lab 9.4 Setting Up and Accessing Internet Printers

➤ Lab 9.5 Troubleshooting Network Printing

➤ Lab 9.6 Configuring Fax Services

Microsoft MCSE Exam #70-270 Objectives	
Objective	Lab
Connect to local and network print devices	9.1
Manage printers and print jobs	9.2, 9.3
Control access to printers by using permissions	9.2
Connect to an Internet printer	9.4
Monitor, configure, and troubleshoot I/O devices, such as printers...	9.5
Configure and troubleshoot fax support	9.6

Student Answer Sheets to accompany the labs in this chapter are available for downloading from the Online Companion for this manual at *www.course.com*.

Lab 9.1 Installing and Sharing Printers

Objective

The Home Town Library is pleased with your work to help it configure Internet Information Services and set up its Web site (Lab 8.6). Now the library wants you to help set up network printing in its Microlab and office. In addition to the HP LaserJet printer already directly attached to the Microlab network cable, the Library has recently obtained two color ink-jet printers for use in printing graphical information in the Microlab. Both ink-jet printers are to be attached to LPT ports on one of the Windows XP workstations. Rather than have users decide to which color ink-jet printer they should send their output, the head librarian wants the Windows XP operating system to automatically balance the load between the two color ink-jet printers. Then the users have only two printer choices; laser or color ink-jet. This can be accomplished through the Windows XP printer pooling feature, which allows multiple (identical) print devices attached to the print server's LPT ports to share the same printer name and driver. After completing this lab, you will be able to:

> ➤ Install and share a local printer

> ➤ Configure printer pooling to allow one network printer to manage two print devices

> ➤ Install a network printer on a Windows XP Professional workstation

Requirements

> ➤ A Windows XP Professional CD-ROM or other source for printer drivers

> ➤ Optionally, a printer attached to your Windows XP Professional computer

> ➤ Optionally, another Windows XP Professional computer to use as a client (If you are in a classroom lab environment, you can team up with a partner when installing the networked printer.)

Estimated completion time: **20–30 minutes**

Activity

1. Fill out the Lab 9.1 Printer Planning Worksheet that follows this Activity. Include each printer to be used in your networked printer environment. If you have a physical printer device attached to your computer, use that printer device to simulate one of the color ink-jet printers in the lab scenario.

2. If necessary, start your computer with Windows XP, and log on as an administrator.

3. In this step, you simulate setting up the Windows XP computer that will share the two ink-jet printers. If you have a printer attached to your computer, use that printer and associated printer driver to simulate one of the color ink-jet printers. Follow the steps below to create and share a local printer on the LPT1 port.

   a. Click **Start**, **Printers and Faxes** to open the Printers and Faxes window.

   b. Click the **Add a printer** task, and click **Next** to start the Add Printer Wizard.

   c. Verify that the **Local printer attached to this computer option** button is selected, and, if necessary, click to remove the check mark from the **Automatically detect and install my Plug and Play printer** check box. Click **Next** to display the Select a Printer Port window.

   d. List the available printer port options on your Lab 9.1 Student Answer Sheet.

   e. Select **LPT1: (Recommended Printer Port)**, and click **Next**.

   f. Select the correct printer manufacturer and model identified on your Lab 9.1 Printer Planning Worksheet for this printer, and click **Next**. If you have previously installed this printer, a Use Existing Driver message will be displayed. Click **Next** to keep the existing driver.

   g. Enter the Printer name you specified on your Lab 9.1 Printer Planning Worksheet for this printer.

   h. Click **No** to the default printer question.

   i. Click **Next** to display the Printer Sharing window.

   j. Click the **Share name** option button, and record the default name of the printer on your Student Answer Sheet.

   k. Enter the printer name you specified on your Lab 9.1 Printer Planning Worksheet, and click **Next**.

   l. In the Location and Comment window, enter the printer location and comment information you specified on your Lab 9.1 Printer Planning Worksheet, and click **Next**.

   m. If you have a print device attached to your LPT1 port, click **Yes** to print a test page. If you do not have a print device attached to your computer, click **No**.

   n. Click **Next** to view the printer summary information. Verify that the printer information matches what you specified on your Lab 9.1 Printer Planning Worksheet.

   o. Click **Finish** to add the printer to the Printers window. If you selected the option to print a test page, after the test page prints, click **OK** to continue.

4. Configure Printer Pooling to allow the printer attached to the LPT2 port to use the same logical printer as the one you just created.

   a. Right-click the printer you created in Step 3, and click **Properties**.

   b. Click the **Ports** tab to display the window shown in Figure 9-1.

9

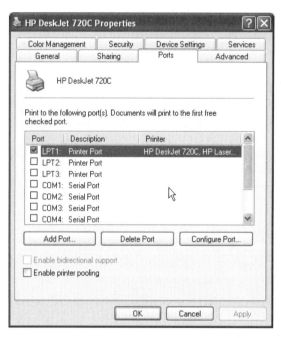

Figure 9-1   Configuring the printer port

    c. Try clicking the port number you specified for the second ink-jet printer, and observe the results.

    d. Click port **LPT1** to re-establish it as the selected printer port.

    e. Click the **Enable printer pooling** check box.

    f. Click the port number you specified for the second ink-jet printer on your Lab 9.1 Printer Planning Worksheet.

    g. On your Student Answer Sheet, record what happens differently when you click this port, as compared with Step 4c.

    h. Click **OK** to save the printer pooling configuration.

    i. On your Student Answer Sheet, briefly describe how enabling printer pooling will make sending output to the ink-jet printers easier for the Microlab users.

5. Install a network printer on the client computer. (*Note*: If you do not have another partner or computer to work with, you can install the network printer on the same computer as your print server.)

    a. If necessary, start the client computer, and log on as administrator. (If working with a lab partner, obtain a copy of their Lab 9.1 Printer Planning Worksheet, and simply use your computer as the client to their shared printer.)

    b. If necessary, click **Start**, **Printers and Faxes** to open the Printers and Faxes window.

    c. Click the **Add a printer** task, and click **Next** to start the Add Printer Wizard.

    d. Click the **A network printer, or a printer attached to another computer** option button, and click **Next** to display the Specify Your Printer window.

e. Click the **Connect to this printer** box, and enter the shared printer name as shown below, replacing *printserver* with the computer identified as the print server computer, and replacing *printer* with the shared name of the printer, as identified on the Lab 9.1 Printer Planning Worksheet.

*printserver**printer*

(If you do not know the shared name of the network printer, you can click the **Next** button, navigate to the shared printer, click to select it, and click **Next**.)

f. If necessary, click the **No** option button to respond to the **Do you want to use this printer as the default printer?** question, and click **Next** to display the summary window.

g. Verify that the location and comment information specified on the Lab 9.1 Printer Planning Worksheet is correct, and click **Finish** to add the network printer to your Printers window. (*Note:* If you are adding the network printer to the print server computer, no additional printer icon is shown, because the computer recognizes the network printer as being the same printer as the existing printer icon.)

h. On your Student Answer Sheet, describe the difference between the local and network printer icons.

i. Close all windows.

6. Test the network printer.

a. Start **WordPad**.

b. Create a sample document describing the difference between the local and network printer icons.

c. Click the **File**, **Print** option, and then click the network printer icon. Record the Status, Location, and Comments information on your Student Answer Sheet.

d. Click the **Print** button.

e. If you have no printer attached to the print server computer, record the error message you receive on your Student Answer Sheet, and click **Cancel**.

f. Pause the print server printer by right-clicking the shared printer, and then clicking the **Pause Printing** option.

g. On the client computer, repeat Steps 6c and 6d, and record the results on your Student Answer Sheet.

h. On the print server computer, double-click your shared printer.

i. Click the document, and then click the **Document** menu, **Properties** option.

j. Record the Owner, Pages, Priority, and Submitted information on your Student Answer Sheet.

k. Click **Cancel** to return to the printer window.

l. Right-click the document, and click the **Cancel** option to remove it from the printer window.

m. Close the printer windows, and log off.

9

Lab 9.1 Printer Planning Worksheet

Name:

Computer ID:

Notes: If you have no physical printer attached to your system, the instructor will provide a list of printers to simulate. For pooled printers, include Print Device, Port, and Location information for each printer.

Print Server ID:

Port:

Print Device Make/Model:

Print Driver:

Printer Name:

Share Name:

Location:

Comment:

Pooled Y or N:

LAB 9.2 CONFIGURING AND SECURING SHARED PRINTERS

Objective

Windows XP allows you to create multiple logical printers that share the same print device. In this lab, you create multiple logical printers to meet the office needs of the Home Town Library. Because its new Lexmark laser printer can operate in either PostScript or standard PCL modes, users should be able to select the appropriate mode as if it were a separate printer.

The laser printer will be attached to Kristen Nickel's Windows XP Professional system, and her computer will act as the print server. Although Kristen will be the operator, three other office staffers, including the head librarian, will be accessing the printer. In addition, the head librarian sometimes needs to print a rush job, and therefore should be able to submit jobs with a high priority. This can be accomplished by creating a separate logical printer for the Lexmark laser that has a higher priority, and is available only to the head librarian.

The library also wants to be able to print large jobs after hours so they do not conflict with other printing needs. This can be accomplished by creating another logical printer for the Lexmark laser whose jobs print only during a specified time. Because the Microlab and office networks are linked together, it is important to ensure that only users on the office network, not the Microlab users, can send output to the Lexmark laser printer. After completing this lab, you will be able to:

➤ Install and share the office laser print device as multiple logical printers with different print configurations, priorities, and times

➤ Secure printers for special user access

➤ Use separator pages when switching a printer between PostScript and PCL modes

Requirements

➤ A Windows XP Professional system that may optionally include an attached printer for testing

➤ A Windows XP CD-ROM or other source for the printer drivers

Estimated completion time: **20–25 minutes**

ACTIVITY

1. Fill out the Lab 9.2 Printer Planning Worksheet that follows this Activity for each of the following logical printers. If you have another print device that is capable of using both PCL and PostScript languages, you may use it rather than the Lexmark Optra Plus printer identified below. If the print device

attached to your computer does not support PCL/PostScript printing, garbled output might result when the PCL or PostScript header page is printed.

- Lexmark Optra Plus printer using the PCL language, available to all office staff
- Lexmark Optra Plus PS printer using the PostScript language, available to all office staff
- A high-priority Lexmark Optra Plus printer using PCL language, available only to the head librarian
- A Lexmark Optra Plus PostScript printer to be used for printing large jobs during off hours

2. If necessary, start your computer with Windows XP, and log on as an administrator.

3. Rather than provide individual users with permissions to use a printer, Microsoft recommends you give the permissions to a group, and then make the users who need to access the printer members of that group. In this step, you create any users or groups you identified on your Lab 9.2 Printer Planning Worksheet (if necessary, review Lab 5.1 on how to create users and groups). Record the user names and passwords, and group names on the Lab 9.2 Student Answer Sheet.

4. Create and share the Lexmark Optra Plus (PCL) printer as a logical printer.
   a. Open the printer window by clicking **Start**, **Printers and Faxes**.
   b. Click **Add a printer**, and click **Next** to start the Add Printer Wizard.
   c. Verify that **Local printer attached to this computer** is selected, and that there is no check mark in the **Automatically detect and install my Plug and Play printer** check box. Click **Next**.
   d. Click the **LPT1** port, and click **Next**.
   e. Select **Lexmark Optra Plus PS**, and click **Next**.
   f. Enter the name you specified for this printer on your Lab 9.2 Printer Planning Worksheet, and click **Next**.
   g. Click the **Share name** option button, enter the shared printer name from the Lab 9.2 Printer Planning Worksheet, and click **Next**.
   h. Enter the Location and Comments specified on your Lab 9.2 Printer Planning Worksheet, and click **Next**.
   i. Click **No** to prevent printing a test page, and click **Next**.
   j. Verify the summary information, and click **Finish** to add the printer to the Printers window. If requested, insert your Windows XP Professional CD-ROM.
   k. With printers that support both PCL and PostScript languages, you can use separator page files located in the WINDOWS\system32 folder to select the printer language for printing a specific job. This saves the operator from having to manually select the language prior to printing the job. To create a separator page that specifies output from a PCL printer, right-click the newly created printer, and click **Properties**.
   l. Click the **Advanced** tab to display the window shown in Figure 9-2.

Figure 9-2   Configuring the printer properties

    m. Click the **Separator Page** button, and click **Browse**.

    n. On your Student Answer Sheet, record the separator page options (files ending with the .sep extension).

    o. Double-click the **pcl.sep** file to send the commands to switch the printer automatically into PCL mode.

    p. Click **OK** to save the separator page selection.

    q. To set security options, click the **Security** tab.

    r. Use the **Advanced** button, and, on your Student Answer Sheet, record the rights given to the creator/owner, the documents to which these rights apply, and any differences between the rights of Administrators and Power Users.

    s. Click **Cancel** to return to the Security tab.

    t. Remove **Everyone** as a user of the printer.

    u. Add the users and groups that you identified on your Lab 9.2 Printer Planning Worksheet as having rights to use this printer.

    v. Click **OK** to save your security changes.

5. Create the Lexmark Optra plus (PostScript) logical printer.

    a. Follow Steps 4b through 4j to create the Lexmark PostScript printer. On the Use Existing Driver window, select the option to **Keep existing driver**.

    b. Right-click the newly created printer, and click **Properties**.

    c. Click the **Advanced** tab.

    d. Click the **Separator Page** button, and click **Browse**.

   e. Double-click the **pscript.sep** file to send the commands to automatically switch the printer into PostScript mode.

   f. Click **OK** to save the separator page selection.

   g. Click the **Security** tab.

   h. Remove **Everyone** as a user of the printer.

   i. Add the users and groups you identified on your Lab 9.2 Printer Planning Worksheet as having rights to use this printer.

   j. Click **OK** to save your security changes.

6. Create the high-priority logical printer for the head librarian.

   a. Follow Steps 4b through 4j to create the Lexmark PostScript printer you identified on your Lab 9.2 Printer Planning Worksheet. On the Use Existing Driver window, select the option to **Keep existing driver**.

   b. Right-click the newly created printer, and click **Properties**.

   c. Click the **Advanced** tab.

   d. Change the Priority to **5**.

   e. Click the **Separator Page** button, browse to the language specified on your Lab 9.2 Printer Planning Worksheet, and click **OK**.

   f. Click the **Security** tab.

   g. Remove **Everyone** as a user of the printer, and add the users and groups you identified on your Lab 9.2 Printer Planning Worksheet.

   h. Click **OK** to save your security changes.

7. Create a NightPrinter logical printer.

   a. Follow Steps 4b through 4j to create the NightPrinter printer.

   b. Right-click the newly created printer, and click **Properties**.

   c. Click the **Advanced** tab.

   d. Click the **Available from** option button, and enter a duration that starts approximately 10 minutes from now and ends approximately 15 minutes from now. (If you were actually setting up the printer for evening printing, you would specify evening hours.)

   e. Click the **Separator Page** button, and select the separator page for the language specified on your Lab 9.2 Printer Planning Worksheet.

   f. Click the **Security** tab.

   g. Remove **Everyone** as a user of the printer.

   h. Add the users and groups that you identified on your Lab 9.2 Printer Planning Worksheet.

   i. Click **OK** to save your security changes.

8. Create network printers on the client computer. If you are working with a lab partner, you may need to wait for your partner to reach this step, and then you must swap computers.

   a. If necessary, create users on the client computer that match the usernames and passwords on your print server computer.

   b. Add the following network printers to your client:
      - Lexmark PCL printer
      - NightPrinter

9. Part of checking out your network printing environment in this lab involves viewing the status of print jobs, and verifying that the night printer does not print until the specified time. To do so, you will pause any printer except the NightPrinter by repeating the following procedure. (*Note:* You will not pause the NightPrinter to verify that the jobs do not start printing until the scheduled time.)

   a. If necessary, open the **Printers and Faxes** window.

   b. Right-click all printers except the NightPrinter, and click **Pause**.

10. Test the printing configuration by sending output from the client to each printer.

11. From the print server computer, check the printers, and verify print job status.

    a. If necessary, wait for your lab partner to reach this step, and then swap back to your print server computer.

    b. On the print server computer, open the Printers window by clicking **Start**, **Printers and Faxes**.

    c. Double-click the **Lexmark PCL** printer, and record the job contents on your Student Answer Sheet.

    d. Double-click the **NightPrinter**, and record the properties of the print job on your Student Answer Sheet.

    e. Wait for the time specified for the NightPrinter, and, on your Student Answer Sheet, record the results you observe when the printer time occurs.

    f. Close all windows and log off.

9

Lab 9.2 Printer Planning Worksheet

Name:

Computer ID:

Notes: In the Printer Group column, identify the name of the group to be given access to this printer. Fill in a Users and Group Planning form (see Chapter 5) to define the members of the group.

Print Server ID:

Port:

Print Device Make/Model:

Print Driver:

Printer Name:Share Name:

Location:

Comment:

Language:

Priority:

Pooled Y or N:

Printer Group:

Operators:

Lab 9.3 Managing Print Jobs and Printers

Objective

The head librarian wants you to write some instructions for the users of the Microlab and office printers. The instructions should note how to perform certain printer management tasks such as pausing and restarting the printer, and holding or canceling print jobs. In addition, because the office laser and Microlab laser printer are the same model, in the event that the office printer is down, the printer operators should have information on how to transfer output to the Microlab laser printer. After completing this lab, you will be able to document how to:

> ➤ Pause and restart the printer

> ➤ View print jobs and printer statistics

> ➤ Cancel and hold print jobs

> ➤ Rearrange print-job sequence, and change priorities

> ➤ Redirect output from one printer to another

Requirements

> ➤ A lab partner with another Windows XP Professional computer, to use for redirecting output from one printer to another

Estimated completion time: **20 minutes**

Activity

1. If necessary, start your computer with Windows XP, and log on as an administrator.

2. Use WordPad or another word-processing application, and design a Printer Procedure form to be used to document the following printing procedures:
   - Pause and resume printing
   - Check print-job size and status
   - Change print-job priority
   - Cancel a print job
   - Redirect output from one printer to another

3. When clearing a paper jam or changing paper or ink cartridges, operators should first pause the printer. After the task has been completed, the printer should be restarted. Follow the steps below to use the Windows XP Help information to find the procedure operators should use to pause and resume printing.

   a. Click **Start**, **Help and Support** to open the Help and Support Center.

   b. In the **Search** dialog box, type in **pause printer** and click the green arrow to start the search.

    c. Click the **Pause or resume printing of a document** topic from the suggested topics list.

    d. Document the process on the Printer Procedure form you created in Step 1. Cut and Paste as necessary.

    e. Test your procedure for pausing and resuming printing to verify that it works as described.

4. Users might want to check the printer status before sending output. Enter **View Documents** in the Search box, and then click the **View documents waiting to print** topic. Use the Printer Procedure form you created in Step 2 to document the process for checking printer status. Test your procedure for viewing the status of documents waiting to print, and verify that it works as described.

5. A user whose print job is waiting in the print queue might want to know the size of the preceding jobs. Enter **Print Queue** in the Search box, and then click **Using the print queue** from the overview topics list. Use the Printer Procedure form you created in Step 2 to document the process you use to view information on the current print queue. Test your procedure to verify that it works as described.

6. When you are finished documenting and testing the procedures in Steps 2 through 5, close the Help and Support Center window.

7. If someone on the office staff needs to quickly print a job on the Microlab ink-jet printer, but there are several jobs in the print queue, the print operator could get the rush job to print next. The staff member does this by changing the print priority of the rush document to be greater than that of the other documents. In this step, you send two jobs to the printer, and then change the second job's priority. Document the procedure you use on your Printer Procedure form.

    a. If you have a print device attached to your workstation, pause that local printer. If you do not have a print device on your workstation, pause the **Lexmark PCL** printer.

    b. Start **WordPad**, and create a document that contains a line that reads **Created first**.

    c. If you have a print device attached to your workstation, print this document to that printer. If you do not have a print device on your workstation, print the document to the Lexmark PCL printer.

    d. Modify the document to read **Created last**.

    e. If you have a print device attached to your workstation, print this document to that printer. If you do not have a print device on your workstation, print the document to the Lexmark PCL printer.

    f. Exit WordPad without saving the document.

    g. Open the **Printers and Faxes** window, and double-click the printer you used.

    h. Double-click the second document, and change its priority to **20**.

    i. Close the printer document list window.

     j. If you have a print device attached to your workstation, restart that printer.

     k. Document the procedure for changing print priority of a document on your Printer Procedure form.

8. Sometimes a user might send the wrong information or document to the printer, and realize it before the output is printed. Use the Windows XP Help information to document on your Printer Procedure form how to pause and cancel a specific print job. Test your procedure for pausing and canceling a document to verify that it works as described.

9. The head librarian wants to be able to redirect output from the library's office Lexmark laser to the Microlab Lexmark laser in the event that the office laser is down. In this step, you practice this process by redirecting output from your Lexmark PCL printer to your lab partner's Lexmark PCL printer.

     a. On your Student Answer Sheet, record your partner's Lexmark PCL printer name, along with a name of a user and password you can use to attach to their computer.

     b. Create a connection to your lab partner's computer as follows:

        ■ Click **Start**, **Run**, and enter *printserver* where *printserver* represents the name of your lab partner's computer.

        ■ If you see an Enter Network Password dialog box, enter the user name and password provided by your partner.

        ■ Close all windows.

     c. Open the Printers and Faxes window by clicking **Start**, **Printers and Faxes**.

     d. Pause your **Lexmark PCL** printer.

     e. Right-click your **Lexmark PCL** printer, and click **Properties**.

     f. Click the **Ports** tab, and then click **Add Port**.

     g. Click the **New Port** button, and enter the UNC name of your partner's printer as follows: *printserver**printer* where *printserver* represents the name of your partner's computer, and *printer* represents the name of their Lexmark PCL printer.

     h. Click **OK** to create the connection.

     i. Click **Close**, and verify that the new printer connection is selected as the port for your Lexmark PCL laser printer.

     j. Close the Printer Properties window.

     k. Start WordPad, and print a job to your Lexmark PCL printer.

     l. From your partner's print server, verify that the job is placed in their printer.

     m. Document the procedure for redirecting output of a document on your Printer Procedure form.

10. Close all windows and log off.

9

LAB 9.4 SETTING UP AND ACCESSING INTERNET PRINTERS

Objective

The Elder Services department at the Maple County Courthouse wants its social workers to be able to print client status reports at the office, whether the social workers are at home or on the road. Mary is one of the social workers who spends a lot of time out of the office. Being able to print to the office's laser printer over the Internet would save her a lot of time. You recently installed a Web server on the office manager's Windows XP Professional workstation, and now you plan to use the Internet Printing Protocol (IPP) to allow Mary to access the Internet to send output to the office laser printer. After completing this lab, you will be able to:

> ➤ Install and download printer drivers using the Internet Printing Protocol

> ➤ Send output over the Internet to a printer attached to a computer running Windows XP Professional Peer Web Services

Requirements

> ➤ Installation of Internet Information Services on your Windows XP Professional computer, as described in Lab 8.6

> ➤ Another Windows XP computer with Internet Explorer 4 or later installed. If working in a lab environment, you can work with a partner to access a printer on their Windows XP Professional system

> ➤ IP address of the print server computer

Estimated completion time: **15 minutes**

ACTIVITY

1. If necessary, start your computer with Windows XP, and log on as an administrator.

2. Create a limited user named **Mary**. On your Lab 9.4 Student Answer Sheet, record the username and password for Mary.

3. Create and share a Lexmark Optra Plus PS printer named **MapleCoPr**. (If necessary, review Lab 9.1, Step 3, on creating and sharing a local printer.) Verify that Mary has rights to use the printer.

4. Use the procedure you documented in Lab 9.3 to pause the **MapleCoPr** printer.

5. Use your intranet to connect to the shared MapleCoPr printer from a client computer. If you are working in a classroom lab, coordinate this step with your lab partner by connecting to their shared MapleCoPr printer.

   a. Open the Printer window by clicking **Start**, **Printers and Faxes**.

   b. Click the **Add a Printer** task, and click **Next** to start the Add Printer Wizard.

   c. If necessary, click the **Network printer** option button, and click **Next**.

   d. Click the **Connect to a printer on the Internet or on a home or office network** option button.

   e. Enter the URL for the intranet printer as follows: ***http://ip_address/printers/MapleCoPr/.printer*** where *ip_address* represents the IP address of the server containing the shared MapleCoPr. Record the URL you enter on your Student Answer Sheet.

   f. Click **Next**, and choose **No** for printing a test page.

   g. Click **Next**, and then click **Finish** to complete the printer installation.

6. Send output to the MapleCoPr intranet printer.

   a. Start **WordPad**.

   b. Create a document named **InternetPrint** that contains your name along with the following line:

   This is a test of Mary's Internet printing.

   c. Click **File**, **Print**, and click the **MapleCoPr** printer in the Select Printer window.

   d. Click **OK**.

   e. From the print server computer, open the **Printers** window, and double-click the **MapleCoPr** printer. Verify that the InternetPrint document is in the print job window.

   f. Close all windows.

7. Use Internet Explorer to manage Internet printers.

   a. Start **Internet Explorer** and enter the following URL: **http://*ip_address*/printers** where *ip_address* is the IP address of the print server computer.

   b. Enter the administrator name and password, and click **OK** to display an All Printers window similar to the one shown in Figure 9-3.

9

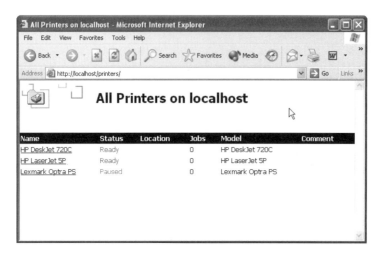

Figure 9-3   Accessing printers through Internet Explorer

    c. Click the **MapleCoPr printer**, and on your Student Answer Sheet, record the Printer and Document actions available.

    d. Close all windows and log off.

LAB 9.5 TROUBLESHOOTING NETWORK PRINTING

Objective

Setting up and managing network printing often involves identifying and fixing problems. There are several techniques that you can use to help you identify and correct common network printing problems. After completing this lab, you will be able to use the following troubleshooting techniques to help resolve network printing problems:

➤ Check for stalled print jobs

➤ Verify that the printer is online (a device setting)

➤ Terminate and re-share the printer on the print server

➤ Re-create the network printer on the client

➤ Reinstall the print driver

➤ Stop and restart the print spooler

Estimated completion time: **15 minutes**

ACTIVITY

1. If necessary, start your computer with Windows XP, and log on as an administrator.

2. Physical print device problems such as a jammed printer, loose cable, or defective print device can cause a document to become stalled in the printer. A stalled document remains in the print queue and will not allow other documents to print after the problem is resolved. It is nearly impossible to simulate a stalled document condition, therefore, the following steps are provided as a guide to when this condition occurs. One or more of these steps may be necessary in order to clear the stalled document.

   a. Restart the document by right-clicking it, and clicking the **Restart** option.

   b. Resume printing by right-clicking the document, and clicking the **Resume** option.

   c. Delete the stalled document by right-clicking it, and clicking **Cancel**.

3. When output from client computers or the local print server does not print, the problem might be that the printer is set for offline printing, as demonstrated by the following procedure.

   a. Open the **Printers and Faxes** window on the print server computer.

   b. Right-click the shared printer, and click **Use Printer Offline**.

   c. From the client computer, print a document to the shared printer.

   d. Double-click the shared printer, and verify that the document is in the print queue.

   e. Click the **Printer** option from the menu bar, and click **Use Printer Offline** to remove the check mark. Record the results on your Student Answer Sheet.

4. The print driver on the client computer might become corrupt or damaged. A corrupt network print driver can most often be fixed by reinstalling just the print driver. Sometimes, reinstalling the entire network printer may be required. In this step, you will first reinstall the print driver, and then delete and reinstall the entire network printer.

   a. On the client computer, right-click the network printer, and click **Properties**.

   b. Click the **Advanced** tab to display the window shown previously in Figure 9-2.

   c. Click the **New Driver** button, and click **Next** to start the New Driver wizard.

   d. Select the printer manufacturer and model, and click **Next**.

   e. Click **Finish**, and, if necessary, insert the Windows XP Professional CD-ROM and click **OK**.

9

     f. To delete the network printer, right-click the printer, and click the **Delete** option.

     g. Click **Yes** to confirm the deletion.

     h. You can now reinstall the network printer by referring back to Lab 9.1, and following Step 3.

5. If multiple client computers are having problems printing, the print spooling service on the print server might be malfunctioning. Stopping and then restarting the print spooler, as demonstrated by performing the following procedure, often can fix this type of problem.

     a. Stop the print spooler service:

- Open **Control Panel**.
- Double-click **Administrative Tools**.
- Double-click **Services** to display a window of services existing on your print server computer.
- Scroll down until you find the Print Spooler service.
- Right-click the **Print Spooler** service, and click **Stop**.

     b. Print a document from WordPad to the shared printer from the client, and, on your Student Answer Sheet, record the message you receive.

     c. Start the Print Spooler service by right-clicking the **Print Spooler** service, and clicking **Start**.

     d. Print a document from the client, and record your results on your Student Answer Sheet.

6. If restarting the print spooler service does not fix the problem, you might need to delete the shared printer and reinstall it. This process can be time-consuming because the client computers also might need to reinstall the network printers associated with the shared printer. In this step, you delete the shared printer from your print server, and then reinstall it.

     a. Click **Start**, **Printers and Faxes** to open the Printers and Faxes window.

     b. Right-click the shared printer to be deleted, and click **Properties**.

     c. On your Student Answer Sheet, record the name and driver information about the printer to be deleted.

     d. Click **Cancel** to close the Properties window.

     e. Right-click the printer, and click **Delete** to delete the shared printer from your print server.

     f. Attempt to print from the client. Record the result on your Student Answer Sheet.

     g. Install a new printer using the same name and driver.

     h. Attempt to print to the network printer from the client. Record the results on your Student Answer Sheet.

   i. If necessary, delete and reinstall the network printer on the client computer.

   j. Close all windows, and log off both computers.

LAB 9.6 CONFIGURING FAX SERVICES

Objective

The fax capability of Windows XP Professional can be very useful for small offices or home users who occasionally need to send and receive faxes. For example, assume you work at home and need to submit an expense report to your manager at Computer Technology Services for some equipment you recently received. Unfortunately, you cannot seem to find the invoice, so you call the vendor who agrees to fax you a copy of the sale information. After completing this lab, you will be able to:

➤ Configure your Windows XP Professional computer to receive a fax through your modem

Requirements

➤ This lab requires a fax-enabled modem to be installed on your computer. If student computers do not have fax-enabled modems available, the instructor may choose to demonstrate this lab to the class.

Estimated completion time: **15 minutes**

ACTIVITY

1. If necessary, start your computer with Windows XP, and log on as an administrator.

2. Create a shared folder named **Faxes** off the root of your Windows XP system drive.

3. Click **Start**, **Printers and Faxes**.

4. If a Fax printer is already listed, right-click it, and click **Delete**. Click **OK** to confirm the deletion.

5. Click the **Install a local fax printer** task.

6. Double-click the new **Fax** icon to display the Fax Console.

7. The Fax Configuration wizard will ride automatically if this is the first time that a Fax Printer has been configured. If it does not, click **Configure Fax** from the Tools menu.

8. Click **Next** to start the wizard.

9. Type in your Sender information, and then click **Next**.

10. Select the modem to be used for faxing, and ensure that the **Enable Send** and **Enable Receive** options are checked.

11. Type **499-4445** as the TSID setting, and click **Next**.

12. Type **499-4445** as the CSID setting, and click **Next**.

13. Click the **Print it on** option box, and select the **Lexmark Optra** printer from the scroll box. Click **Next**.

14. Click **Finish** to close the wizard.

15. Click **Fax Printer Configuration** from the Tools Menu.

16. Click the **Devices** tab, and then click **Properties**. Using the Send and Receive tabs, verify that the options specified above are correct.

17. Click **OK** twice, and close the Fax Console window.

18. Close all windows, and log off.

PERFORMANCE TUNING

Labs included in this chapter

➤ Lab 10.1 Working with Task Manager

➤ Lab 10.2 Establishing a Baseline with Performance Monitor

➤ Lab 10.3 Recognizing Memory Bottlenecks

➤ Lab 10.4 Recognizing Processor Bottlenecks

➤ Lab 10.5 Recognizing Disk Bottlenecks

➤ Lab 10.6 Using Event Viewer

Microsoft MCSE Exam #70-270 Objectives	
Objective	Lab
Optimize and troubleshoot performance of the Windows XP Professional desktop	
Optimize and troubleshoot memory performance	10.1, 10.2, 10.3
Optimize and troubleshoot processor performance	10.1, 10.2, 10.4
Optimize and troubleshoot disk performance	10.2, 10.5
Optimize and troubleshoot processor utilization	10.2
Optimize and troubleshoot network performance	10.2
Install, configure, and troubleshoot network adapters	10.6
Implement, configure, manage, and troubleshoot auditing	10.6

Student Answer Sheets to accompany the labs in this chapter are available for downloading from the Online Companion for this manual at *www.course.com*.

LAB 10.1 WORKING WITH TASK MANAGER

Objective

Dennis Geisler from the Animal Care Center recently called and reported that the Windows XP Professional computer they are using to share their folders and printers seems to be running slower than usual. Dennis explained that the problem seems to get worse later in the day, almost as if the machine is getting tired. When you ask if they have changed anything recently, Dennis reports that they added a few new applications, including a client/server system that has a program that loads on the computer when it starts. Also, the program he occasionally uses to help diagnose animal health problems seems to slow down the system. Dennis wants you to see if you can do anything to speed up the system. After completing this lab, you will be able to:

> ➤ Use Task Manager to view currently running applications

> ➤ Use Task Manager to see which processes are using the most system resources

> ➤ Use Task Manager to terminate a process

> ➤ Use Task Manager to observe processor and memory utilization

Requirements

> ➤ Access to performance utilities found on the Windows XP Professional Resource Kit

> ➤ A copy of the cpustres.exe and leakyapp.exe files from the Windows XP Professional Resource Kit. Copy the files from either the kit or another location specified by your instructor to a folder on your Windows XP system drive. Rename them as follows:

> ■ If necessary, create a folder named Apps on your Windows XP system drive.

> ■ Use My Computer or Windows Explorer to open a window to the Program Files\Resource Pro Kit folder.

> ■ Copy the following files to the Apps folder: **cpustres.exe** and **leakyapp.exe**.

> ■ Rename cpustres.exe to **diagmon.exe**.

> ■ Rename leakyapp.exe to **datamgr.exe**.

Estimated completion time: **20 minutes**

ACTIVITY

1. If necessary, start your computer with Windows XP, and log on as an administrator.

2. To check the processor utilization of the animal diagnosis software that Dennis runs:

   a. Use My Computer or Windows Explorer to open a window to your Apps folder. Simulate starting the diagnostic software by double-clicking the **diagmon.exe** application from the Apps folder.

   b. Start Task Manager by pressing **Ctrl+Alt+Del**, and clicking the **Task Manager** button.

   c. Click the **Performance** tab to display a Performance window similar to the one shown in Figure 10-1.

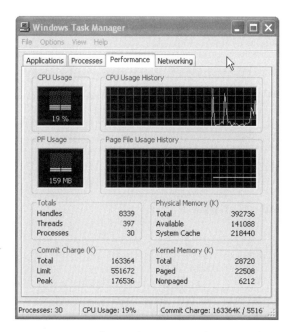

Figure 10-1   The Performance Tab in Windows Task Manager

   d. Record the CPU Usage range on your Lab 10.1 Student Answer Sheet. This CPU Usage range is for one low-activity thread, the Diagmon.exe application.

   e. Switch to the Diagmon.exe application by clicking **CPU Stress** from the Windows XP status bar. In the Thread 1 section, change the Activity setting to **Busy**.

f. Switch to Task Manager by clicking **Windows Task Manager** from the Windows XP status bar, and then record the CPU Usage range on your Student Answer Sheet.

g. To simulate using the Diagmon application, continue to activate all threads at **medium** activity until CPU Usage regularly exceeds 80%. On your Student Answer Sheet, record the number of medium active threads it takes to bring your CPU Usage to above 80%.

h. Click the **Processes** tab. Determine which process is using the most CPU time by clicking the **CPU** column heading to sort the process list by CPU time. On your Student Answer Sheet, record the application using the most CPU time.

i. On your Student Answer Sheet, briefly describe ways that Dennis could improve the performance of his computer when he runs the Diagmon.exe software.

j. Close the Diagmon.exe software.

3. Dennis explained that even when he's not running the Diagmon software, the system seems to get slower as time goes by. You suspect that the client/server database software might be overloading the system. To test the effect of the client/server database software on the Animal Care Center computer, you want to run and test the performance of applications before and after starting the client/server database. Use the following process to test the computer's performance before the client/server database is loaded.

a. Start the following applications from the Start, All Programs, Accessories menu:
- WordPad
- Paint

b. From Paint, open the **Blue Lace 16.bmp** file located in the WINDOWS folder.

c. Open the **Gone Fishing.bmp** file, and observe how long it takes to load the file.

d. Minimize the **Paint** and **WordPad** applications.

4. Start the simulated client/server database software.

a. Use My Computer to browse to the **Apps** folder.

b. From the Apps folder, double-click **datamgr.exe** to simulate Dennis running the database server software.

c. To simulate a faulty program that continues to use up system memory, in the My Leaky App window, click the **Start Leaking** button.

5. Check the system performance with datamgr.exe running.

a. Activate **Paint**, and load the **Blue Lace 16.bmp** graphic file. On your Student Answer Sheet, record any observations regarding the current speed of loading the file, as compared to Step 4.

6. To find out what is slowing down the system, switch to Task Manager by clicking **Windows Task Manager** from the Windows XP status bar. Then do the following:

   a. Click the **Applications** tab, and record the applications and their status on your Student Answer Sheet.

   b. Click the **Performance** tab, and record the CPU Usage range on your Student Answer Sheet. Is this usage range causing the performance problem? Note your response on your Student Answer Sheet.

   c. Click the **Processes** tab, and record the names of the column headings on your Student Answer Sheet.

   d. On your Student Answer Sheet, record the application that is using the most memory.

   e. Add Handle Count columns to the Processes display:
      - Click the **Select Columns** option from the View menu.
      - Click the **Handle Count** check box.
      - Click **OK** to add the selected columns to the Processes tab.

   f. On your Student Answer Sheet, record the process that has the most Handles open.

7. Determine the number of page faults required to open the **Gone Fishing.bmp** file using the Paint application.

   a. Close the Paint application.

   b. Add Page Faults and Virtual Memory Size columns to the Processes display:
      - If necessary, click the **Processes** tab.
      - Click the **Select Columns** option from the View menu.
      - Click the **Page Faults** check box.
      - Click the **Virtual Memory Size** check box.
      - Click **OK** to add the selected columns to the Processes tab.

   c. Start the **Paint** application.

   d. On your Student Answer Sheet, record the number of page faults for the **mspaint.exe** process.

   e. Open the **Gone Fishing.bmp** graphic.

   f. Switch to the **Windows Task Manager** window.

   g. On your Student Answer Sheet, calculate the number of page faults required by MSPAINT to load the Gone Fishing.bmp graphic by subtracting the Initial number of page faults from the number of page faults after loading Gone Fishing.

   h. Close Paint.

8. Exit the datamgr.exe application, and observe how page faults are affected.

   a. Click the **Processes** tab.

   b. Click the **datamgr.exe** process.

   c. Click the **End Process** button.

10

    d. Click **Yes** to terminate the application.

    e. Start the **Paint** application, switch to the **Task Manager** window, and on your Student Answer Sheet, record the number of Initial page faults.

    f. Open the **Gone Fishing.bmp** graphic.

    g. Switch to **Task Manager**, and on your Student Answer Sheet, record the number of page faults for MSPAINT.

    h. On your Student Answer Sheet, calculate the number of page faults required by MSPAINT to load the Gone Fishing graphic.

9. Start **datamgr.exe**, and click the **Start Leaking** button. Look at the Virtual Memory size (VM Size) column, and, on your Student Answer Sheet, record what application is using the most virtual memory. Also record what you observe happening.

10. Close all windows and log off. On your Student Answer Sheet, make a recommendation to Dennis regarding what you believe should be done to fix the client/server database performance problem.

LAB 10.2 ESTABLISHING A BASELINE WITH PERFORMANCE MONITOR

Objective

Dave Mansfield is the Information Systems Manager for the Maple County Courthouse. Maple County recently implemented a Web server, and Dave is concerned about its effect on the performance of computer systems at the courthouse. Dave and his staff are busy implementing new systems. They need your help to set up a network monitoring system and to establish performance baselines. After completing this lab, you will be able to:

➤ Use Performance Monitor to view current system performance

➤ Configure counter logs in Performance Monitor to record system performance

➤ Capture system activity

➤ Use counter logs to create a performance baseline

➤ Configure alerts to notify the administrator when performance counters exceed predefined values

Requirements

➤ Internet Information Services installed on your Windows XP Professional system (Internet Information Services were installed in Lab 8.6)

➤ Optionally, another Windows XP computer to create network activity

➤ In the Apps folder, use Notepad to create a file named **Work.bat**, which contains the following commands that require pressing **Enter** at the end of each line:

Start PING ip_address −n 20

For %%a in (1 2 3 4 5 6 7 8 9 0 a b c d e f) do call Trans.bat

where *ip_address* is the IP address of another computer on your network. If no other computers are available, use your computer's IP address.

➤ In the Apps folder, create a file named **Trans.bat** that contains the following commands:

MD \Labtemp

COPY \WINDOWS \Labtemp

RD /S /Q \Labtemp

> Estimated completion time: **30 minutes**

ACTIVITY

10

1. If necessary, start your computer with Windows XP, and log on as an administrator.

2. Start the **Performance Monitor** tool.

   a. Open **Control Panel**.

   b. Double-click **Administrative Tools**.

   c. Double-click **Performance** to open a Performance Monitor window similar to the one shown in Figure 10-2.

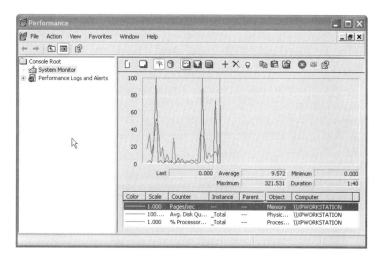

Figure 10-2   The System Monitor

   d. Record the three default counters from the bottom of the Performance window on your Student Answer Sheet.

   e. Clear all counters by clicking **New Counter Set** from the tool bar.

3. Performance Monitor can be used to view current system activity, or to view activity from a log of past activity. In this step, you identify the options available to monitor and view system activity with Performance Monitor.

   a. Counters are used to view the activities of system objects. To add a counter to the graph, click the plus sign (**+**) toolbar icon in the right view pane to display the Add Counters window, as shown in Figure 10-3.

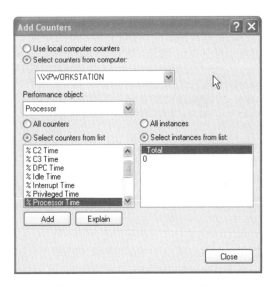

Figure 10-3 Adding counters to System Monitor

   b. Counters can be added for activities on your computer or on other computers on the network. To add counters for activities on your computer, click the **Use local computer counters** option button.

   c. Before selecting the counters, you must identify the performance object you wish to monitor. By default, the **Processor** object is selected first. Each occurrence of the same object is referred to as an instance. Using the Instances options, you can select to include all instances of the object, a specific object instance, or a Total of the object instances. Verify that the **Total** option is selected.

   d. To include all counters for the Processor object, click the **All counters** option button, and click **Add**.

e. To view a specific counter, such as the number of pages/seconds, click the scroll button to the right of the Performance object window, scroll up, and click the **Memory** object.

f. To view just the pages/seconds activity, click the **Select counters from list** option button, and, if necessary, use the scroll bar to scroll down, and then click the **Pages/Sec** counter.

g. Click the **Explain** button to display an explanation of the selected counters. On your Lab 10.2 Student Answer Sheet, describe how Pages/Sec is calculated.

h. Click the **Add** button to add Pages/Sec to the counter list.

i. Click the **Close** button to return to the Performance Monitor graph window.

j. Starting with the left side of the graph window, place your cursor on each toolbar button, and record its description on your Student Answer Sheet.

k. When there are many counters visible, it is difficult to monitor one of the values. The Highlight button allows you to focus on a specific counter. For example, to highlight only the Percent of Processor utilization counter, click the **% Processor Time** counter in the counter window, and then click the **Highlight** button. Wait a moment until the % Processor Time is stable, and then move the mouse around. Observe the effect of placing the mouse on processor utilization.

l. Click the **View Histogram** button to view bars representing the relative system usage of each selected counter.

m. Move your mouse around, and, on your Student Answer Sheet, record the two counters that show the highest activity levels on the histogram.

n. Click the **View Report** button, and move the mouse around. On your Student Answer Sheet, record the counter with the highest value.

o. Click the **View Graph** button to return to Graph view.

p. To clear all counters, click the **New Counter Set** button.

4. In addition to viewing performance statistics, you also can use Performance Monitor to create a log file to help you fill out the Lab 10.2 Baseline Data Worksheet. When creating a baseline, an advantage of a log file is that it allows you to start and stop logging on a predefined schedule. In this step, you use Performance Monitor to add the objects and counters on the Lab 10.2 Baseline Data Worksheet at the end of this activity, to a log file.

a. In the left pane, expand the **Performance Logs and Alerts** option, and then click **Counter Logs** to display the available logs in the right pane.

b. Right-click **Counter Logs**, and click the **New Log Settings** option.

c. Enter **baseline** for your log filename, and click **OK** to display the **baseline** window shown in Figure 10-4.

d. To add individual counters such as Pages/Sec, click the **Add Counters** button, and select the **Memory** object from Performance objects. Scroll down in the Select Counters list, and, if necessary, select **Pages/Sec.** Click **Add** to add the counter, and then click **Close** to return to the baseline window. (The Add Objects button allows you to add all counters for an object at one time.)

10

e. Using Step 4d, add the rest of the counters listed on your Lab 10.2 Baseline Data Worksheet.

Figure 10-4   Configuring performance logging

f. When finished, click **Close** to return to the Baseline properties window.

g. In the Sample Data section, set the interval to every 5 seconds.

h. Click the **Log Files** tab, and record the path to your log file and logfile-name on the Student Answer Sheet.

i. Click the **Schedule** tab, and record the default start time on your Student Answer Sheet.

j. Click **Manually** in the Start log window, and then click **OK** to save the baseline log configuration. A message box will be displayed, indicating that the file does not exist. Click **Yes** to create the file and return to the Performance Logs and Alerts window.

5. Now that you have configured the baseline log counters, the next step in creating a baseline is to log normal usage of the system. In this step, you will manually start the logging process, and then generate system activity using the batch file created in the Requirements section of this lab.

a. To manually start the logging process, right-click your **baseline** log file, and click **Start**.

b. Minimize **Performance Monitor**.

c. Start **Paint**, and load the **Gone Fishing.bmp** file from the \Windows folder.

d. Run the **Work.bat** file created in the Requirements section:

   ■ Click **Start, Run**.

- Click the **Browse** button, and navigate to your Apps folder.
- Double-click the **Work.bat** file.
- Click **OK** to start the program.

e. While the Work.bat file is running, start **WordPad**, and create and save a document file.

f. Run the **Work.bat** file a second time.

g. Wait a few minutes for system activity to settle down.

h. Maximize **Performance Monitor**.

i. Right-click your **baseline** log, and click the **Stop** option.

6. After typical system activity has been logged, you need to view the Baseline performance log, and then record baseline data on your Baseline Data Worksheet. The baseline worksheet can then be used to determine alert values.

a. In the left tree pane, click **System Monitor**.

b. To view logged data, click the **View Log Data** button. Ensure that the Source tab is selected, and click **Log Files.**

c. Click **Add**, and, if necessary, navigate to the **<Drive>\PerfLogs** folder. Double-click the name of the **baseline** file you recorded in Step 4h.

d. Click the **Data** tab, and then click **Add** to display the Add Counters window.

e. Click the scroll button to the right of the Performance Object text box. Notice that, because you are viewing the contents of the log file, only the objects and counters you logged are included in object and counter windows.

f. For any performance object listed, click the **All counters** button, and then click **Add**.

g. After all counters are added to the graph, click the **Close** button, and then click **OK** to close the System Monitor properties window.

h. From the graph window, click each counter, and record the maximum and minimum values on your Lab 10.2 Baseline Data Worksheet.

i. Click the **View Report** button, and record the average value listed for each counter on your Baseline Data Worksheet.

j. On your Lab 10.2 Baseline Data Worksheet, use the average and maximum values to define alert values near the maximums.

7. Now that you have determined alert values, in this step you configure Performance Monitor to use these alert values when monitoring the system.

a. In the left tree pane, right-click **Alerts**, and click the **New Alerts Settings** option.

b. Enter the name **BaseAlerts**, and click **OK** to display the BaseAlerts properties window.

c. Click the **Add** button, and add each object's counter for which you identified an alert.

d. After all alert counters have been added, click the **Close** button to return to the BaseAlerts properties window.

e. On the **General** tab, select each counter, and enter the Alert limit as specified on your Lab 10.2 Baseline Data Worksheet.

10

f. When all limit values have been set, click the **Action** tab, and, on your Student Answer Sheet, record the possible actions, along with the default.

g. Click the **Schedule** tab, and click the **Manually** start scan option.

h. Click **OK** to save the alert settings.

i. Exit Performance Monitor, and close all windows.

j. If you are finished working, log off. In the next lab, you will trigger and evaluate the alerts by inducing additional system activity.

Lab 10.2 Baseline Data Worksheet

Computer ID: **Date:**

CounterMinimum	Maximum	Average	Alert Value

Memory
Available KBytes
Pages/Second
% Committed Bytes in Use

Processor
% Processor Time
Interrupts/sec
% Privileged Time

Network Interface
Current Bandwidth
Bytes Received/sec
Bytes Sent/sec
Packets Received Errors
Packets/sec
Output Queue Length

Physical Disk
Avg Disk Queue Length
% Disk time
Avg Disk Bytes/Read
Avg Disk Bytes/Write
Avg Disk Bytes/Transfer

System
File Data Operations/sec

Thread
% Processor Time

Process
Page Faults/sec
Thread count

LAB 10.3 RECOGNIZING MEMORY BOTTLENECKS

Objective

Dave Mansfield from the Maple County Courthouse recently called regarding an alert message from Performance Monitor. In addition, some of the users have been complaining about the slow response times when accessing the server. Your job is to determine what is causing the alert message, and identify the system performance bottleneck. After completing this lab, you will be able to:

➤ Trigger and view alert messages

➤ Use Event Viewer to view and filter alert messages

➤ Use Performance Monitor to track and identify bottlenecks

Requirements

➤ Completion of Labs 10.1 and 10.2

Estimated completion time: **15 minutes**

10

ACTIVITY

1. If necessary, start your computer with Windows XP, and log on as an administrator.

2. Start **Performance Monitor**, and start the BaseAlerts log.
   a. Open **Control Panel**.
   b. Double-click **Administrative Tools**.
   c. Double-click **Performance** to open a Performance Monitor window.
   d. In the left tree window, expand **Performance Logs and Alerts**, and then click the **Alerts** object.
   e. In the right-side results window, right-click the newly created **BaseAlerts** log, and click **Start**.
   f. Performance Monitor now will begin monitoring system activity.

3. Perform the following procedure to simulate activity at the courthouse.
   a. Start the **datamgr.exe** application, and click the **Start Leaking** button.
   b. Run the **Work.bat** file.
   c. Start **Paint**, and load the **Gone Fishing.bmp** file.
   d. Allow the system to run for a few minutes.

4. Exit the datamgr.exe application.

5. You have just arrived at the courthouse to check the performance of Dave's Windows XP system. In this step, you use Event Viewer to look for any alert messages placed in the application event log.

   a. Open **Control Panel**.

   b. Double-click **Administrative Tools**.

   c. Double-click **Event Viewer**.

   d. In the left tree pane, click **Application**.

   e. Double-click the first **Information message** to display the Event Properties window.

   f. Use the down arrow to scan the event log until you come to an alert message.

   g. Record the date, event ID, type, category, and source information on your Lab 10.3 Student Answer Sheet.

   h. Click **Cancel** to return to the Event Viewer window.

6. You can sort the Event Log window on any of the columns simply by clicking a column heading. For example, click the **Source** column heading to sort by the application that originated the message. On your Student Answer Sheet, record up to five sources of application messages.

7. When you view a log that has events from many sources, it is often beneficial to reduce the messages you see to include messages only from a specified source, event ID, or time. In this step, you filter the application log to view messages only from Performance Monitor.

   a. To filter application messages to view messages only from Performance Monitor, click the **Filter** option on the **View** menu.

   b. In the Event source text box, scroll to locate, and then click the **SysmonLog** event.

   c. Click **OK** to include only Performance Monitor messages.

   d. Click the Event Column to sort the list by event. Scan the Performance Monitor messages and record each different event ID on your Student Answer Sheet.

   e. Use the filter option of Event Viewer (**View**, **Filter**) to count the number of messages for each event ID recorded in Step 7d. Record the number on your Student Answer Sheet.

8. Prior to clearing the log and continuing to troubleshoot the problem, it is often a good idea to archive the log for future use or auditing. In this step, you archive the Application log, and then view the archived log file.

   a. Minimize **Event Viewer**.

   b. Create a folder named **Logs** off the root of the Windows XP system disk.

   c. Maximize **Event Viewer**.

   d. Be sure that the **Application log** is selected in the left tree pane.

   e. Click the **Action** menu and the **Save Log File As** option.

   f. In the **Save in:** text box, browse to the **Logs** folder.

    g. Enter **Alerts** in the File name text box.

    h. Verify that the file type is **Event Log (*.evt)**, and click **Save**.

    i. Clear events from the application log by clicking the **Action** menu and the **Clear all Events** option.

    j. Click **No** to the save Application Log message.

    k. Perform the steps shown below to view the archived application log file:

       ■ Click the **Action** menu and the **Open Log File** option.

       ■ In the Log Type text box, scroll to select the **Application** log.

       ■ Navigate to your **Logs** folder, and double-click the **Alerts.evt** log file.

9. On your Student Answer Sheet, describe the performance bottleneck.

10. You need to save the file in a text format so it can be viewed or edited by other programs. In this step, you save the log in text format, and then view it from Notepad.

    a. Click the **Action** menu and the **Save Log File As** option.

    b. If necessary, use the scroll button to the right of the Save in text box to browse to the **Logs** folder.

    c. Enter the name **Alerts** in the File name text box.

    d. Use the scroll button to the right of the Save as type text box to select the **Text (Tab delimited) (*.txt)** type, and then click the **Save** button.

    e. Minimize **Event Viewer**.

    f. Use **My Computer** or **Windows Explorer** to navigate to the Logs folder.

    g. Double-click the **Alerts.txt** file to open it with Notepad.

    h. On your Student Answer Sheet, identify an advantage and disadvantage of saving log files in text format.

    i. Exit Notepad and close all windows.

10

LAB 10.4 RECOGNIZING PROCESSOR BOTTLENECKS

Objective

Maple County Courthouse is still having performance problems when running certain applications, such as the Drawman.exe graphics design program. Your job is to help determine what is causing the performance bottleneck when running this program. After completing this lab, you will be able to:

➤ Trigger and view alert messages

➤ Use Event Viewer to view and archive messages

➤ Use Performance Monitor to track and identify processor bottlenecks

Requirements

➤ Completion of Lab 10.3

➤ To simulate a graphics design program, use My Computer or Windows Explorer to navigate to your Apps folder, and rename diagmon.exe to **drawman.exe**.

Estimated completion time: **10–15 minutes**

ACTIVITY

1. If necessary, start your computer with Windows XP, and log on as an administrator.

2. Start **Performance Monitor**, and start the **BaseAlerts** log.
   a. Open **Control Panel**.
   b. Double-click **Administrative Tools**.
   c. Double-click **Performance** to open a Performance Monitor window.
   d. In the left tree window, expand **Performance Logs and Alerts**, and then click the **Alerts** object.
   e. In the right-side results pane, right-click the **BaseAlerts** log, and click **Start**. Performance Monitor now begins monitoring system activity.

3. Perform the following procedure to simulate activity at the courthouse.
   a. Use **My Computer** or **Windows Explorer** to navigate to your Apps folder. Start the **drawman.exe** application by double-clicking **Start**.
   b. Set Thread 1 activity level to **Busy**.
   c. Activate Thread 2 and Thread 3 at **Medium** activity levels.
   d. Run the **Work.bat** file.
   c. Allow the system to run for a few minutes.

4. Exit the Drawman.exe application by clicking the **Close** button in the CPU Stress window.

5. Use Event Viewer to look for any alert messages placed in the application event log.
   a. Open **Control Panel**.
   b. Double-click **Administrative Tools**.
   c. Double-click **Event Viewer**.
   d. In the left tree pane, click **Application Log**.
   e. Filter the application log to view messages only from Performance Monitor. Click **View**, **Filter**, and scroll to and click **SysmonLog** in the Event source text box.
   f. Scan the Performance Monitor messages.
   g. On your Lab 10.4 Student Answer Sheet, identify any counters exceeding the alert value.

h. Archive the log by clicking the **Action** menu and the **Save Log File As** option, and entering the name **Processor** in the File name text box. If necessary, browse to the Logs folder you created in the Save in: text box in Lab 10.3, Step 8.

i. Clear the log (**Action, Clear all Events**), and click **No** if you are asked to save a log file. Exit Event Viewer.

6. If necessary, start **Performance Monitor**, and do the following:
   a. Click the **New Counter Set** button to clear any existing counters.
   b. Click the **Add (+)** button, and add the counters you identified in Step 5.
   c. Minimize **Performance Monitor**.

7. Start the **drawman.exe** program, and set the activity of Thread 1 to **Busy**.

8. Use Performance Monitor to monitor the counter(s) you identified in Step 5.
   a. Run the **Work.bat** file, and then maximize **Performance Monitor**.
   b. Observe the Performance Monitor graph, and when the graph is full, click the **Freeze Display** button.
   c. Start **Event Viewer** and check for any Performance Monitor application messages.
   d. Use Event Viewer along with the Performance Monitor graph, and, on your Student Answer Sheet, record the values of any counters that have exceeded their Alert settings.
   e. Archive the Application log, using the name **Processor_x** (replace x with the step number).
   f. Clear the Application log, and exit Event Viewer.
   g. In the Performance Monitor window, click the **Freeze Display** (red **X**) button to reactivate performance scanning.

9. In the **drawman** window, set Thread 2 to **medium** activity, and then repeat Step 8, recording counters exceeding alert values on your Student Answer Sheet.

10. In the **drawman** window, set Thread 3 to **medium** activity, and then repeat Step 8, recording counters exceeding alert values on your Student Answer Sheet.

11. Exit Performance Monitor, and close all windows.

12. Analyze the usage data you collected in Steps 7 through 10, and, on your Student Answer Sheet, identify the thread activity level that caused each counter you identified in Step 5 to exceed its alert value.

10

LAB 10.5 RECOGNIZING DISK BOTTLENECKS

Objective

The disk system can be the cause of performance problems. Disk performance problems usually can be identified when disk-related counters, such as queue length, % Disk Time, or Disk Bytes/Transfer, increase above the baseline. After completing this lab, you will be able to:

➤ Use Performance Monitor to track and identify disk bottlenecks

Requirements

➤ Completion of Lab 10.4

Estimated completion time: **10 minutes**

ACTIVITY

1. If necessary, start your computer with Windows XP, and log on as an administrator.

2. Start **Performance Monitor**, and attempt to add Logical Disk counters.
   a. Open **Control Panel**.
   b. Double-click **Administrative Tools**.
   c. Double-click **Performance** to open a Performance Monitor window.
   d. Click **New Counter Set** button to clear any existing counters.
   e. If necessary, click the **View Current Activity** button.
   f. Click the **Add** button, and add the following PhysicalDisk counters:
      - % Disk Time
      - Current Disk Queue Length
      - Disk Bytes/sec

3. Click **Close** to return to the Performance Monitor graph window.

4. Minimize **Performance Monitor**.

5. Create disk activity by running the following applications:
   a. Start **datamgr.exe**, and click the **Start Leaking** button.
   b. Run the **Work.bat** file.

6. Maximize **Performance Monitor**.

7. After the graph page fills, click the **Freeze Display** button.

8. On your Student Answer Sheet, record each counter's acceptable value range, and its observed range.

9. Exit Performance Monitor.

10. Exit datamgr.exe.

11. Close all windows, and log off.

LAB 10.6 USING EVENT VIEWER

Objective

Sebastian Melendres, from the Melendres and Associates law firm, telephoned to inform you that he can no longer access the network from his Windows XP Professional system. You have been assigned the task of troubleshooting and correcting the problem. After completing this lab, you will be able to:

➤ Use Event Viewer to view system and security messages

➤ Use Event Viewer to view other computer event logs

Requirements

➤ An additional Windows XP Professional computer to use to view a remote computer's event log

10

Estimated completion time: **15 minutes**

ACTIVITY

1. If necessary, start your computer with Windows XP, and log on as an administrator.

2. Perform the following procedure to simulate a network cable problem that Mr. Melendres is having with his computer.

   a. Unplug the network cable from your computer.

   b. Wait a few minutes and then plug the cable back in.

   c. Repeat Steps 2a and 2b two more times.

3. Use Event Viewer to view current System messages.

   a. Start **Event Viewer** by clicking **Start**, **All Programs**, **Administrative Tools**, **Event Viewer**.

   b. Click the **System Log** option.

   c. On your Lab 10.6 Student Answer Sheet, record message information regarding the cable connection.

4. Mr. Melendres is suspicious that someone is attempting to log on to the office network. He wants to be able to check the Security log files on the systems in his office. In this step, you prepare to demonstrate how to monitor security by creating some security audit messages on your computer.

  a. Open **Control Panel**, and double-click **Administrative Tools**.

  b. Double-click **Local Security Policy** to view the Local Security Settings window.

  c. Expand the **Local Policies** object, and click **Audit Policy** to display a window similar to the one shown in Figure 10-5.

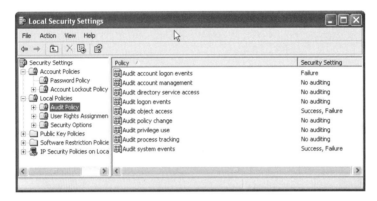

Figure 10-5   Configuring auditing

  d. Double-click **Audit logon events**, and click **Failure** to begin recording failed log on attempts.

  e. Click **OK** to save the audit setting.

  f. Exit the Local Security Settings window and log off.

  g. Attempt to log on as Administrator using an incorrect password.

  h. Attempt to log on again, using an invalid username and password.

  i. Attempt to log on a third time, using a valid username and an incorrect password.

  j. Log on as Administrator (with the correct password), and start **Event Viewer**.

  k. Click **Security Log**, and, on your Student Answer Sheet, record the time, date, and username for each invalid access attempt.

5. In this step, you show Mr. Melendres how to check the Security log on another computer.

  a. If your partner's computer has a different password for the Administrator user, do the following to make a connection to their computer:

    ■ Click **Start**, **Run**, and enter **computername**, replacing *computername* with the name of your partner's computer. (If you do not know your partner's computer name, right-click **My Computer**, click **Properties**, and then click the **Computer Name** tab.)

- Enter the administrator's user name and password in the Enter Network Password window, and click **OK**.
- Close all windows except Event Viewer.

b. In the left tree pane, right-click the **Event Viewer (Local)** object, and then click the **Connect to another computer** option.

c. Enter the name of your partner's computer, or use the **Browse** button to find it.

d. Click **OK** to change to your partner's Event Viewer log.

e. Click **Security Log**, and, on your Student Answer Sheet, record the time, date, and username of each invalid access attempt.

6. Close all windows and log off.

10

WINDOWS XP APPLICATION SUPPORT

Labs included in this chapter

➤ Lab 11.1 Working with DOS Applications

➤ Lab 11.2 Working with 16-bit Windows Applications

➤ Lab 11.3 Working with Win32 Applications

➤ Lab 11.4 Working with Application Compatibility Tools

Microsoft MCSE Exam #70-270 Objectives	
Objective	Lab
Optimize and troubleshoot performance of the Windows XP Professional desktop	
Optimize and troubleshoot application performance	11.1, 11.2, 11.3, 11.4

Student Answer Sheets to accompany the labs in this chapter are available for downloading from the Online Companion for this manual at *www.course.com*.

LAB 11.1 WORKING WITH DOS APPLICATIONS

Objective

The Animal Care Center is considering purchasing a new Windows XP Professional-based system from your company. This new computer will replace one of its older Windows 3.1 computers. One of the requirements for the new system is that it must be able to continue using some older DOS and Windows 3.1 applications, until Win32-based applications replace them. After completing this lab, you will be able to:

➤ Configure AUTOEXEC.NT and CONFIG.NT files for a DOS application

➤ Customize execution parameters for DOS applications

➤ Use Task Manager to view virtual DOS machines (NTVDMs), and change base priorities

Requirements

➤ Optionally, another computer that can be used to test network connections

Estimated completion time: **15 minutes**

ACTIVITY

1. If necessary, start your computer with Windows XP, and log on as an administrator.

2. DOS applications often require certain driver and configuration settings to be made to the system through the CONFIG.SYS and AUTOEXEC.BAT files when the computer starts. Windows XP Professional provides for this need by allowing each virtual DOS machine to process commands from the CONFIG.NT and AUTOEXEC.NT files located in the WINDOWS\SYSTEM32 folder. To demonstrate the use of the AUTOEXEC.NT file in this step, you create a shortcut for the DOS Edit application, modify the AUTOEXEC.NT file, and observe how modifying the file affects starting the Edit application.

   a. Create a shortcut to the Edit application named DOSApp1 (to use as if it were one of the Animal Care Center's DOS applications), as follows:

   ■ Use My Computer or Windows Explorer to open the **WINDOWS\system32** folder.

   ■ Right-click the **edit.com** application, and click the **Create Shortcut** option.

   ■ Drag and drop the **Shortcut to MS-DOS Editor** to your desktop.

   ■ Close the **system32** window.

   ■ Rename the Shortcut to MS-DOS Editor to **DOSApp1**.

    b. Double-click the **DOSApp1** shortcut to load the DOS editor.

    c. Exit the MS-DOS Editor.

    d. Use My Computer to open the **WINDOWS\system32** folder.

    e. Right-click **AUTOEXEC.NT**, and then click **Open**. The NT extension is not a known file type; therefore, an error message requesting which program to use will appear. Click **Select the program from a list**, and then click **OK**.

    f. Select **Notepad** from the Open with window, and then click **OK**. Record all commands except REM on your Lab 11.1 Student Answer Sheet.

    g. Insert the word **REM** in front of the @echo off command at the beginning of the AUTOEXEC.NT file.

    h. Exit Notepad, and save your changes.

    i. Double-click the **DOSApp1** shortcut, and note any changes in the load process on your Student Answer Sheet.

    j. Exit the DOS editor, and close all windows.

3. If a DOS application requires unique startup instructions, you can specify separate AUTOEXEC.NT and CONFIG.NT files for that DOS application by using the execution parameters.

    a. Create another shortcut to the Edit application named DOSApp2 (to simulate another DOS application), as follows:

       ■ Use My Computer or Windows Explorer to open the **WINDOWS\system32** folder.

       ■ Right-click the **edit.com** application, and click the **Create Shortcut** option.

       ■ Drag and drop the **Shortcut to MS-DOS Editor** to your desktop.

       ■ Close the **System32** window.

       ■ Rename the Shortcut to MS-DOS Editor to **DOSApp2**.

    b. Double-click the **DOSApp2** shortcut to load the DOS editor. On your Student Answer Sheet, record whether or not you see the statements from the AUTOEXEC.NT file when starting DOSApp2.

    c. Right-click the **DOSApp2** shortcut icon, and click the **Properties** button to display the Shortcut Properties window.

    d. Click the **Program** tab to display the application execution properties shown in Figure 11-1.

    e. Click the **Advanced** button, and record the existing Autoexec and Config filenames on your Student Answer Sheet.

    f. Change the <PATH>AUTOEXEC.NT filename to **<PATH>AUTO2.NT**.

    g. Click **OK** to save your changes.

    h. Click **OK** to close the Shortcut Properties window.

    i. Use My Computer or Windows Explorer to open the **WINDOWS\system32** folder.

    j. Double-click the **AUTOEXEC.NT** file to open it with Notepad.

11

Figure 11-1 Modifying the properties for a DOS application

  k. Remove the **REM** from in front of the @echo off command.

  l. Save the file as **AUTO2.NT**:

    ■ Click the **File** menu, **Save as** option.

    ■ In the Save as type text box, select **All Files**.

    ■ In the File name text box, enter **AUTO2.NT**.

    ■ Click the **Save** button.

  m. Exit Notepad.

  n. Double-click the **DOSApp2** shortcut to load the DOS editor. On your Student Answer Sheet, record whether or not you see the statements from the AUTOEXEC.NT file.

  o. Try using the DOSApp1 shortcut, and record your observations on your Student Answer Sheet.

  p. Exit both DOS applications, and close all windows.

4. In addition to the CONFIG.NT and AUTOEXEC.NT files, Windows XP allows other DOS application execution parameters to be configured through application properties. In this step, you identify several DOS application configuration parameters.

  a. Right-click **DOSApp1**, and click **Properties**.

b. Click the **Security** tab, and on your Student Answer Sheet, record who is able to run this shortcut, along with their permissions to this file.

c. Click the **Program** tab, and on your Student Answer Sheet, record the Cmd line and Working path.

d. Change the icon to a picture of a computer as follows:
   - Click the **Change Icon** button.
   - Click the computer icon to select it.
   - Click **OK** to return to the Program tab.

e. Remove the check mark from the **Close on exit** check box.

f. Click the **Font** tab, and record the default font size on your Student Answer Sheet.

g. Click the **Memory** tab, and reduce the Conventional memory setting to **400**.

h. Click the **Screen** tab, and change the Usage to **Full-screen**. On your Student Answer Sheet, record the default Performance settings.

i. Click the **Misc** tab, and record the default settings on your Student Answer Sheet.
   - If necessary, disable the screen saver.
   - If necessary, enable mouse exclusive mode.

j. Click **OK** to save the program parameters.

k. Start **DOSApp1** from the shortcut, and, on your Student Answer Sheet, describe the different appearance of the window and what caused this change.

l. Exit DOSApp1, and, on your Student Answer sheet, describe what happens and why.

m. Close all windows.

5. By default, each DOS application runs in its own virtual DOS machine (NTVDM), and all NTVDMs have equal processing priority. In this step, you load multiple DOS applications, and then use Task Manager to modify the base priority of the DOS applications.

a. Start **DOSApp1**.

b. Use the **Alt+Tab** key sequence to rotate to the Windows XP desktop, and start **DOSApp2**.

c. Start **Task Manager** by using the **Ctrl+Alt+Del** key sequence to display the Windows Security window, and then clicking **Task Manager**.

d. Click the **Processes** tab.

e. DOS applications run in NTVDMs. On your Student Answer Sheet, record the CPU Time, Memory Usage, and Handles for each NTVDM application.

f. Right-click the second NTVDM (representing DOSApp2), and record the process options on your Student Answer Sheet.

g. Click **Set Priority**, and record the priority options on your Student Answer Sheet.

h. Click **High** priority, and summarize the warning message on your Student Answer Sheet.

11

     i. Click **Yes** to the change priority class message.

     j. On your Student Answer Sheet, record any changes to the NTVDM parameters you documented in Step 5e.

     k. Right-click the first DOSApp1 NTVDM, and click **End Process**. Click **Yes** to continue.

     l. Close **Task Manager**.

     m.Close **DOSApp2**, and log off.

LAB 11.2 WORKING WITH 16-BIT WINDOWS APPLICATIONS

Objective

In addition to the DOS applications, the original Windows 3.1 computer at the Animal Care Center has two Windows 3.x applications that will need to run on the new Windows XP Professional system. After completing this lab, you will be able to:

➤ Determine the system requirements needed to run multiple Win16 applications in the same NTVDM

➤ Determine the system requirements needed to run multiple Win16 applications in separate NTVDMs

Estimated completion time: **15 minutes**

ACTIVITY

1. If necessary, start your computer with Windows XP, and log on as an administrator.

2. Record system resources in use.

     a. Start **Task Manager**.

     b. Click the **Performance** tab, and record the requested initial system usage statistics on your Lab 11.2 Student Answer Sheet.

3. Copy a Windows 16-bit application to the desktop as follows:

     a. Use My Computer or Windows Explorer to open a window to your **WINDOWS** folder.

     b. Right-click **winhelp.exe**, and click **Copy**.

     c. Right-click your desktop, and click **Paste**.

     d. Rename winhelp.exe to **Win16App1.exe**, to simulate an Animal Care Center Windows 3.1 application.

4. Repeat Step 3 to create another 16-bit application named **Win16App2.exe**. Close My Computer or Windows Explorer.

5. Start **WIN16App1.exe**, and record virtual DOS machine (NTVDM) information.
   a. Double-click the **Win16App1.exe** application.
   b. Switch to **Task Manager**.
   c. Click the **Processes** tab, and, on your Student Answer Sheet, record all applications running in the virtual DOS machine.
   d. Minimize **Task Manager**.

6. Start **WIN16App2**, and record virtual DOS machine (NTVDM) information and performance statistics.
   a. Double-click the **Win16App2** application.
   b. Activate **Task Manager**.
   c. Click the **Processes** tab, and, on your Student Answer Sheet, record all applications running in the virtual DOS machine.
   d. Click the **Performance** tab, and record the requested statistics on your Student Answer Sheet.
   e. Minimize **Task Manager**.
   f. Close Win16App1 and Win16App2.

7. Configure the Win16App2 application to use a separate memory space.
   a. Right-click **Win16App2**, and click **Create Shortcut**.
   b. Right-click **Shortcut to Win16App2**, and click **Properties**.
   c. On the Shortcut tab, click **Advanced** to display a Shortcut window similar to the one shown in Figure 11-2.

11

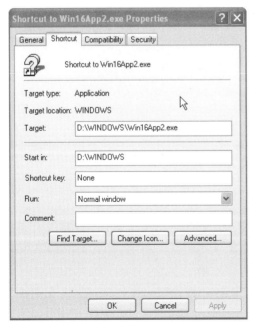

Figure 11-2   Modifying the properties for a 16-bit application

     d. Click the **Run in separate memory space** option, and click **OK** twice to return to the desktop.

8. Start **WIN16App1**.

9. Start **Shortcut to WIN16App2**, and record Task Manager processes and usage statistics.

     a. Double-click the **Shortcut to Win16App2.exe** application.

     b. Activate **Task Manager**.

     c. On your Student Answer Sheet, record all applications running in each virtual DOS machine.

     d. Click the **Performance** tab, and record the requested statistics on your Student Answer Sheet.

     e. Compare usage statistics to those gathered in Step 6. Record any observations on your Student Answer Sheet.

     f. Minimize **Task Manager**.

10. Exit the WinApp1.exe application, and record the Task Manager processes.

     a. Exit WinApp1.exe, and switch to **Task Manager**.

     b. On your Student Answer Sheet, record the number of NTVDMs.

11. Close all applications, and log off.

LAB 11.3 WORKING WITH WIN32 APPLICATIONS

Objective

One of the major considerations when the Animal Care Center purchased its Windows XP Professional-based computers was that it could use a new veterinary software package. The veterinary software package requires that a path be set to the Public folder on the server when a user logs on. One way to establish a path is to use the AUTOEXEC.BAT file to configure Windows XP environment variables. When Windows XP starts, it will check for an AUTOEXEC.BAT file in the system drive, and then scan the AUTOEXEC file for any environment variables or path settings. After completing this lab, you will be able to:

➤ Use AUTOEXEC.BAT to configure path and environmental variables for Win32 applications

➤ Verify path and environmental variable settings

➤ Use Task Manager to view the resources used by Win32 applications

Estimated completion time: **10 minutes**

ACTIVITY

1. If necessary, start your computer with Windows XP, and log on as an administrator.

2. Modify the AUTOEXEC.BAT file to provide a path to the Public folder on your partner's computer.

   a. Use My Computer or Windows Explorer to open a window to the root of your system drive. (Your system drive is the drive that is marked as active, normally the C: drive.)

   b. Right-click the **AUTOEXEC.BAT** file and click **Edit**.

   c. Insert the following commands at the end of the AUTOEXEC.BAT file:

      - **SET VetDrive=P**
      - **SET VetPath=**server_name**\Public** (where server_name is the name of your partner's computer)
      - **SET VetUser=administrator**
      - **PATH=P**

   d. Save **Autoexec.bat**, and exit Notepad.

   e. To implement the new commands you've added to your Autoexec.bat file, you need to restart your computer by clicking **Start**, **Shutdown**, **Restart**.

3. To verify that the environment variables and path settings have been modified, you can use either the Command Prompt or the Registry Editor. In this step, you use the Command Prompt to verify the settings. (In Chapter 13 you will learn how to use a Registry Editor to view or modify Registry values.)

   a. Log on to your computer as the administrator.

   b. Open a Command Prompt window.

   c. To view environment variables, type the command **SET**, and press **Enter**.

4. Dennis is running two Win32 applications on his computer. One of the applications is interactive and needs to run faster than the other application that runs in the background. In this step, you simulate running two applications, and then use Task Manager to view resource usage after changing application priorities.

   a. Right-click the **Drawman** application you renamed in Lab 10.4, and click the **Copy** option.

   b. Right-click the desktop, and click **Paste** to create a copy of the Drawman.exe application.

   c. Rename the copy of Drawman.exe to **Background.exe**.

   d. Start the **Drawman** application.

   e. Activate three threads at **medium** activity level.

   f. Start the **Background** application.

11

    g. Start **Task Manager**, and click the **Processes** tab.

    h. Click the **View** menu, **Select Columns** option.

    i. If necessary, click the **Thread Count** check box.

    j. Click **OK** to return to the Processes window.

    k. On your Student Answer Sheet, record the values from the CPU and Threads columns.

    l. Set the priority of Drawman to Realtime, as follows:

- Right-click the **Drawman** application, and click **Set Priority**.
- Click the **Realtime** priority option. Click **Yes** on the warning window that appears.

    m. Set the priority of the Background application to **Below Normal**:

- Right-click the **Background** application, and click **Set Priority**.
- Click the **Below Normal** priority option. Click **Yes** on the warning window that appears.

    n. From the Task Manager Processes window, record on your Student Answer Sheet any changes to the CPU Usage for the Drawman and Background applications.

    o. From Task Manager, exit the Drawman and Background applications by right-clicking the application, and clicking the **End Process** option.

    p. Exit Task Manager.

    q. Close all windows, and log off.

LAB 11.4 WORKING WITH APPLICATION COMPATIBILITY TOOLS

Objective

After the Animal Care Center upgraded to Windows XP, one application that was used infrequently no longer worked. The application is an add-on application for the veterinary software package, which ran well under Windows 95. One of the veterinarians also brought a custom software package from home that they would like to use, but it does not work. Your task will be to use the built-in compatibility features of Windows XP, as well as the Application Compatibility Tools, to resolve these issues. After completing this lab, you will be able to:

➤ Set compatibility modes for non-compatible applications

➤ Install the Application Compatibility Toolkit

➤ Use Advanced Tools to troubleshoot and fix compatibility issues

Requirements

➤ Access to the Windows XP CD-ROM

Estimated completion time: **20 minutes**

ACTIVITY

1. To install the Applications Compatibility Toolkit (ACT), follow these procedures:

    a. Using My Computer or Windows Explorer, navigate to the **Support / Tools** folder on the Windows XP CD Rom.

    b. Double-click **ACT20.EXE** to start the Application Compatibility Toolkit Install wizard.

    c. Click **Next**, and then click **Install** to start the install procedure and place the toolkit into the **%drive%\program files\Application Compatibility Toolkit** folder.

    d. Click **Finish** to close the install procedure.

    e. Internet Explorer will open and display the default Web page from the ACT folder, similar to the one shown in Figure 11-3.

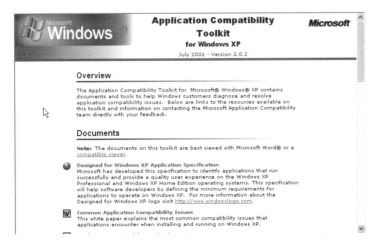

Figure 11-3   Using the Application Compatibility Toolkit

    f. On your Student Answer Sheet, record the key documents, tools, and online resources available to you for resolving compatibility issues.

    g. Close all windows to return to the desktop.

2. Windows XP will automatically resolve issues for thousands of popular applications during the upgrade procedure or during the installation of these applications. Windows XP will also attempt to resolve issues with programs that are not listed in the compatibility database. These programs will also often need manual adjustment. The following procedure will adjust the Veterinary

Add-on package to run as a Windows 95 application. (*Note:* This procedure can also be run as a wizard from the Help and Support Center.)

a. Using My Computer or Windows Explorer, navigate to the **Windows** folder.

b. Locate the **Notepad.exe** application, and create a copy of the program called **VetAddOn.exe.**

c. Right-click **VetAddOn**, **Properties**, and then click the **Compatibility** tab.

d. In the Compatibility mode section, place a check mark in the **Run this application in compatibility mode** box.

e. Click the arrow on the scroll box to list the available compatibility mode. Record these on your Student Answer Sheet. Ensure that **Windows 95** is selected.

f. The add-on application also recommended 256K colors with a screen size of 640 × 480. Place a check mark in the **Run in 256 colors** and **Run in 640 × 480 screen resolution** boxes.

g. Click **OK** to save your settings.

h. Double-click **VetAddOn** to start the application. The screen should flicker and change to 256 colors with a screen size of 640 × 480. Close the program. The screen should return to its original colors and size.

i. Close all windows, and return to the desktop.

3. Compatibility mode for Win95 used in Step 2 automatically selects 51 compatibility fixes. Sometimes an application requires much more specific configuration. In this exercise, you will use the QFixApp utility to test and apply specific fixes for the VetAddOn program.

a. Click **Start**, **All Programs**, **Application Compatibility Toolkit**, and click **QFixApp**.

b. Use the browse button to select **VetAddOn.exe** from the Windows folder, to display a window similar to the one shown in Figure 11-4.

c. Ensure that **Win95** is selected on the layers tab. Then click the **Fixes** tab to view the individual fixes applied by the Win95 preset. Record the number of fixes applied and the total number available on the Student Answer Sheet.

d. Scroll down the list and highlight the **CorrectFilePaths** fix. Record the description of this fix on your Student Answer Sheet. Repeat this for the **EmulatePrinter** and **Win95VersionLie** fixes.

e. Click the **Run** button to test the application. Click **Help**, **About Notepad** from the menu and record the version number on the Student Answer Sheet.

f. Close **VetAddOn**, and click **Win2000** on the Layers pages.

g. Run the program again, and record the version number on your Student Answer Sheet.

h. Close **VetAddOn**, click the **Layers** tab, and select **256Colors**. Then click the **Fixes** tab and take note of the fixes applied. Scroll down and place a check mark on the **Force640×480** box.

i. Click the **Advanced** button, and click the **Create Fix Support** Button.

   j. Record the location of the fix file on your Student Answer Sheet. Click **Yes** to install the fix, and then click **OK**.

   k. Click **Cancel** to exit QFixApp.

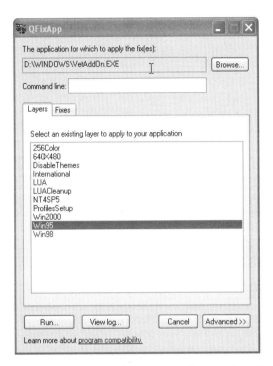

Figure 11-4   Modifying an application's settings using the QFixApp utility

   l. Navigate to the windows folder, and double-click **VetAddOn**. Depending on your video card and monitor, the screen may take a few moments to change mode. Verify that the application starts in 8-bit color in a 640 × 480 screen.

   m. Close all windows, and return to the desktop.

11

CHAPTER TWELVE

WORKING WITH THE WINDOWS XP REGISTRY

Labs included in this chapter

➤ Lab 12.1 Backing Up the Registry

➤ Lab 12.2 Exploring the Registry

➤ Lab 12.3 Changing Registry Data Through Control Panel

➤ Lab 12.4 Backing Up and Restoring Registry Keys

➤ Lab 12.5 Restoring the Registry

➤ Lab 12.6 Using the Reg Command-line Utility

Microsoft MCSE Exam #70-270 Objectives	
Objective	Lab
Recover systems and user data	12.1, 12.4, 12.5, 12.6
Optimize and troubleshoot performance of the Windows XP Professional desktop	12.2, 12.3

Student Answer Sheets to accompany the labs in this chapter are available for downloading from the Online Companion for this manual at *www.course.com*.

Lab 12.1 Backing Up the Registry

Objective

The Windows XP Registry plays a critical role in the operation of your computer by storing hardware and software configuration information. The Registry is a complex information structure that is maintained by the Windows XP operating system, and is usually modified by using Control Panel or through an application's installation process. Occasionally it is necessary for a system administrator to directly access and modify the Registry to correct a problem or modify a setting that is not accessible via Control Panel. To become more familiar with the Registry and how to work with it, in this chapter's labs you are required to access and make changes to Registry values. Because modifying information in the Registry can affect your computer's operation and performance, it is important to make a backup of the Registry data prior to making any changes. Although the Windows XP Backup program is covered in detail in Chapter 15, in this lab you will use the Backup program to make a backup of your computer's Registry. After completing this lab, you will be able to:

➤ Use the Windows XP Backup program to make a backup of the Registry

Requirements

➤ Approximately 400 MB of free space on your hard disk to store the system backup information

Estimated completion time: **10–15 minutes**

Activity

1. If necessary, start your computer with Windows XP, and log on as an administrator.

2. Use My Computer or Windows Explorer to create a folder named **RegBack** on your Windows XP operating system drive.

3. Start the Backup utility by clicking **Start**, **All Programs**, **Accessories**, **System Tools**, **Backup**.

4. Click the **Advanced Mode** link to switch to the Advanced Backup and Restore window.

5. Click the **Backup Wizard (Advanced Button)**, and then click **Next** to start the wizard.

6. Click the **Only backup the System State data** option button, and click **Next**.

7. In the Choose a place to backup your data box, click the **Browse** button, and navigate to the **RegBack** folder you created in Step 2.

8. Type **Registry.bkf** in the File name text box, and click **Save.**

9. Click **Next** to accept your settings, and then click **Finish** to start the Registry backup process. The backup may take 5 to 10 minutes to complete.

10. Record the requested Backup Progress information on your Lab 12.1 Student Answer Sheet.

11. Click **Report**, and check for any error messages. Record the requested report information on your Student Answer Sheet.

12. Exit Notepad, and click **Close** to return to the Backup Utility window.

13. Exit the Backup utility.

LAB 12.2 EXPLORING THE REGISTRY

Objective

You are representing your company, Computer Technology Services, on the Superior Technical College CIS Program Advisory Council. At the last council meeting, you volunteered to give a talk to the council about the Windows XP Registry. Your presentation will consist of two parts. In the first part you will show how Registry data are organized, and then in the second part you will demonstrate how Registry values can be modified using the Control Panel and Registry Editor tools. In this lab, you will prepare for the first part of the presentation by reviewing the Registry key structure using the Regedit program. After completing this lab, you will be able to:

➤ Use the Regedit program to find and view Registry key information

➤ Use Control Panel to modify Registry settings

➤ Identify the relationship between certain Registry keys

12

Estimated completion time: **15 minutes**

ACTIVITY

1. If necessary, start your computer with Windows XP, and log on as an administrator.

2. Create a shortcut for Regedit on your desktop.
   a. Use My Computer or Windows Explorer to open the **WINDOWS** folder.
   b. Right-click the **regedit.exe** program, and click **Copy**.
   c. Right-click your desktop, and click the **Paste Shortcut** option.

3. The Registry contains hardware and software configuration information stored in sections called keys that are arranged in a tree-type structure. In this step, you use the Regedit program to identify the major keys and subkeys that make up the Registry tree.

   a. Double-click the **Regedit shortcut** on your desktop to open the Registry Editor.

   b. Record the five major keys on your Student Answer Sheet.

   c. Expand the **HKEY_LOCAL_MACHINE** key by clicking its plus (+) symbol.

   d. On your Student Answer Sheet, record the five subkeys of HKEY_LOCAL_MACHINE.

4. The HKEY_LOCAL_MACHINE\HARDWARE subkey is automatically loaded with hardware information when Windows XP starts. If there are problems with certain devices, or if you are wondering what devices (such as serial ports) were detected on a computer, you can view the contents of the HARDWARE subkey to determine the system configuration. In this step, you use the HARDWARE subkey to document device settings on your Windows XP system.

   a. Expand HKEY_LOCAL_MACHINE to the **HARDWARE\DESCRIPTION\System** subkey.

   b. Expand the **CentralProcessor** key, and observe the number of processors in your computer (each processor will have a key associated with it).

   c. On your Student Answer Sheet, record the value of the **Identifier** and **Vendor Identifier** for each processor.

   d. Expand the keys until you find the **SerialController** subkey.

   e. On your Student Answer Sheet, record the path to the SerialController key.

   f. Use the SerialController subkey, and, on your Student Answer Sheet, record the port used for each serial controller.

   g. Minimize all HARDWARE subkeys, and exit Regedit.

5. Some Registry keys such as HKEY_LOCAL_MACHINE\HARDWARE are built on the fly when Windows XP boots. However, certain device and security information needs to be stored and then loaded from the WINDOWS\Config folder each time Windows XP starts. In this step, you identify the key information that is stored, and then loaded, each time Windows XP boots.

   a. Use My Computer or Windows Explorer to open the **WINDOWS\ system32\config** folder.

   b. Using the information recorded in Step 3d above, record each subkey of HKEY_LOCAL_MACHINE represented in the Config folder, on your Student Answer Sheet.

   c. Close all windows.

6. The HKEY_LOCAL_MACHINE\SYSTEM subkey contains control set keys that store information, such as device loading sequence, service startup credentials, and startup parameters needed to start Windows XP. In this step, you use

Regedit to identify the control set subkeys on your system, determine which control set is the current control set, and which control set contains the Last Known Good configuration start settings.

a. Start **Regedit** by double-clicking the desktop shortcut.

b. If necessary, select and maximize the **HKEY_LOCAL_MACHINE** window.

c. Expand the **SYSTEM** key by double-clicking it.

d. On your Student Answer Sheet, record the name of each control set key.

e. Click the **Select** key to display values similar to the ones shown in Figure 12-1.

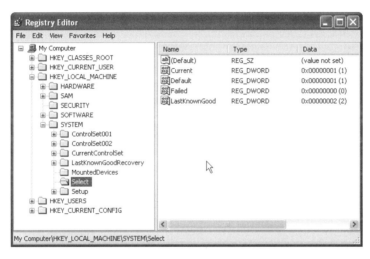

Figure 12-1   Editing the Registry with the Registry Editor

f. The number in the value field of each entry identifies the control set number associated with that configuration. For example, in Figure 12-1 the 0x1 in the Current value entry identifies ControlSet001 as the current control set. On your Student Answer Sheet, identify the control sets to be used for Current, Failed, and Last Known Good configurations.

g. Exit the Registry Editor.

LAB 12.3 CHANGING REGISTRY DATA THROUGH CONTROL PANEL

Objective

The second part of your presentation is to demonstrate how Registry values can be changed using both the Control Panel and Registry Editor tools. During your presentation, you want to make the following points:

➤ Although you can use the Registry Editor tool to change Registry values, this should be done only as a last resort, and only after backing up the Registry as described in Lab 12.1.

➤ For some keys, changing Registry values might be next to impossible, because the values are stored in binary format or are protected by security settings.

➤ Another possible problem when changing Registry values is that certain keys are copies of other subkeys. If you change a copy, it simply will be overwritten when the system restarts.

➤ Whenever possible, Registry values should be changed using Control Panel tools.

In this lab, you will prepare for the second part of your presentation by practicing using Control Panel, along with Regedit, to make changes to Registry values. After completing this lab, you will be able to:

➤ Demonstrate the relationship between the HKEY_CLASSES_ROOT and HKEY_LOCAL _MACHINE keys

➤ Use Control Panel to add an extension to the HKEY_CLASSES_ROOT key

➤ Use Control Panel to modify system and user environmental variables

➤ Use Regedit to find and view environment variables in HKEY_USERS and HKEY_LOCAL_MACHINE keys

➤ Determine the relationship between HKEY_USERS and CURRENT_USER keys

Estimated completion time: **15 minutes**

ACTIVITY

1. If necessary, start your computer with Windows XP, and log on as an administrator.

2. The HKEY_CLASSES_ROOT key contains application associations based on file extension data. The contents of this key are copied from another Registry key, and can be changed by modifying the File Types settings of the Folder Options dialog box. In this step, you modify the contents of the HKEY_CLASSES_ROOT key by using the Folder Options dialog box and determining which other key contains file extensions.

a. Open **Control Panel**, and double-click **Folder Options**.

b. Click the **File Types** tab to display existing file extensions and associated file types.

c. Click the **New** button, and then click **Advanced**.

d. Enter **.let** for the File Extension, and then select **Text Document** for the Associated File Type, as shown in Figure 12-2.

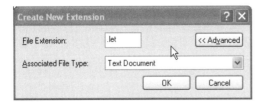

Figure 12-2   Adding a new file extension

    e. Click **OK** to save the entry.

    f. Click **Close** to close the Folder Options window.

    g. Start the **Regedit** application from your shortcut or from the Run window.

    h. In the left Registry Editor pane, highlight **My Computer** by clicking it.

    i. Click **Edit**, **Find**, and enter **.let** in the Find what text box. In the Look at dialog box, click to remove checks from the **Values** and **Data** check boxes.

    j. Click the **Match whole string only** text box, and then click the **Find Next** button.

    k. On your Student Answer Sheet, record the key containing the .let file extension.

    l. Press the **F3** key to continue searching the entire Registry.

    m. On your Student Answer Sheet, record any other keys containing the .let extension. Identify the master key.

    n. Right-click the last **.let** extension you found, and click **Delete**. Click **Yes** to confirm the deletion of the .let extension.

    o. Click **View**, **Refresh** to update the Registry Editor data.

    p. Repeat Steps 2i through 2m and record the results of your search on your Student Answer Sheet.

    q. Exit the Registry Editor, and close all windows.

    r. Open **Control Panel**, and double-click **Folder Options**. Click the **File Types** tab, and use the scroll button to verify that the .let extension has been removed.

3. In this step, you view the results of using Regedit to add another file extension to the HKEY_CLASSES_ROOT key.

    a. Start **Regedit** by double-clicking your desktop shortcut.

    b. Right-click **HKEY_CLASSES_ROOT**, click **New**, and then click **Key**.

    c. Enter **.prg** for the key name, and press **Enter**.

    d. In the right-side results pane, double-click the **Default** entry, and then enter **txtfile** in the Value data text box.

    e. Click **OK** to save your key value.

    f. Collapse the **HKEY_CLASSES_ROOT** key.

    g. Expand the **HKEY_LOCAL_MACHINE** subkey you identified in Step 2.

    h. Scan the subkey value entries to determine if the .prg extension has been added to the master key. Record the results on your Student Answer Sheet.

12

4. Registry keys are also used to contain path and environment variable settings. In this step, you use Control Panel to set user and system environment variables.

   a. Open **Control Panel**, and double-click the **System** icon.

   b. Click the **Advanced** tab, and then click the **Environment Variables** button to display a window similar to the one shown in Figure 12-3.

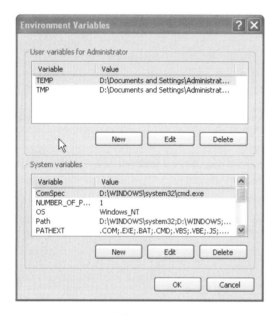

Figure 12-3   Modifying the environment variables

   c. Under the User variables window, click the **New** button and add the following environment variable for the Administrator user:

   ▪ Variable Name: **FirstName**

   ▪ Variable Value: **[Your first name]** (*Note*: Make sure that you use a name that is not already a user or a unique spelling of your name.)

   d. Click **OK** to return to the Environment Variables window. Notice that your first name has been added to the User variables for Administrator window.

   e. Click the **New** button under the System variables window, and enter the following environment variable used by all users:

   ▪ Variable Name: **Organization**

   ▪ Variable Value: **Superior Technical College**

   f. Click **OK** to return to the Environment Variables window.

   g. Click **OK** to close the Environment Variables window.

   h. Click **OK** to close the System Properties window.

   i. Close Control Panel.

5. In this step, you use Registry Editor to find and record the keys used to store user environment variables.

   a. If necessary, start or activate the **RegEdit.exe** Registry editor.

   b. Click **My Computer** in the Registry window.

   c. From the **Edit** menu, click the **Find** option, and enter **[your first name]** in the Find what text box. Make sure there is a check mark in the Data box and that the Match whole string only box is cleared.

   d. Click the **Find Next** button, and, on your Student Answer Sheet, record the key where your name is found.

   e. Click the **Edit** menu, **Find Next** option, and record the next key where your name is found.

   f. Check to see if your first name is found in any other keys. Record your results on your Student Answer Sheet.

   g. Minimize all keys by clicking the **minus (−)** signs.

6. In this step, you use Registry editor to find and record what key(s) are used to store system environment variables.

   a. If necessary, start or activate the **RegEdit.exe** Registry editor.

   b. Click **My Computer** in the Registry window.

   c. From the Edit menu, click the **Find** option, and enter **Superior Technical College** in the Find what text box.

   d. Click the **Find Next** button. On your Student Answer Sheet, record the key where Superior Technical College is found.

   e. Check to see if Superior Technical College is found in any other keys. Record your results on your Student Answer Sheet.

7. Exit Registry Editor, and log off.

12

LAB 12.4 BACKING UP AND RESTORING REGISTRY KEYS

Objective

Mr. Melendres has a new software package named LawManager that he wants you to install on his computer. The software is a 60-day evaluation version that comes with an uninstall program to remove it when the trial period is over. After your experience at the Animal Care Center, you have decided not to trust the uninstall program to clean up its Registry settings. You have decided to create a backup of the Registry prior to installing the software. After completing this lab, you will be able to:

➤ Use Regedit to export and import subkey data

➤ Identify limitations of restoring subkeys with Regedit

Estimated completion time: **15 minutes**

ACTIVITY

1. If necessary, start your computer with Windows XP, and log on as an administrator.

2. Prior to installing new software or editing the Registry, it is a good procedure to back up the entire Registry, as you did in Lab 12.1. You should also make a copy of the particular keys you are working on. In this step, you use Regedit application to save the SOFTWARE subkey, prior to installing the evaluation software for Mr. Melendres.

   a. Use My Computer or Windows Explorer to create a folder named **Keybackup** on your Windows XP system disk.

   b. Close all windows.

   c. Start **Regedit** by double-clicking your desktop shortcut.

   d. Highlight the **HKEY_LOCAL_MACHINE\SOFTWARE** subkey.

   e. Click **Export** from the File menu.

   f. Verify that the **Selected Branch** option button is selected, and that the Software subkey appears in the Selected Branch text box.

   g. Navigate to the **Keybackup** folder.

   h. Enter the name **Software** in the File name text box, and click **Save**.

   i. Minimize all keys, and exit the Registry Editor.

3. In this step, you simulate the changes made to the Software subkey from the installation of the LawManager software package.

   a. If necessary, start **Regedit** by double-clicking the desktop shortcut.

   b. Right-click the **SOFTWARE** key, and create a new subkey named **LawMan**.

   c. Within the Secure subkey, add a string value named **LawUsers** (by right-clicking **News, String Value**), with a value of **c:\program files\LawMan\Users.dat**.

   d. Minimize and expand the **SOFTWARE** subkey to verify the LawMan values.

   e. Delete the **ODBC** software subkey. Click **Yes** to confirm the deletion.

4. In this step, you use the Import Registry option to restore the SOFTWARE key.

   a. Highlight the **HKEY_LOCAL_MACHINE\SOFTWARE** subkey, and click the **File** menu, **Import** option.

   b. Double-click the **Software.reg** file you created in Step 2 to start the restore process.

c. Click **OK** on the completion message.

d. The Regedit import process works by merging key data from the import file into the Registry, and therefore restores missing values, but does not remove existing values. Use Regedit to expand and view your restored SOFTWARE key. On your Student Answer Sheet, record whether importing the Registry removed the LawMan key values and restored the ODBC subkey.

e. On your Student Answer Sheet, briefly describe two methods you could use to return the SOFTWARE key to its condition prior to installing the LawManager software.

5. Exit Regedit to return to the desktop.

LAB 12.5 RESTORING THE REGISTRY

Objective

In Lab 12.4, you learned that it can be difficult to use Regedit to restore Registry keys. Importing a key with Regedit does not remove existing entries. In this lab, you will use the Windows XP Backup utility to simulate restoring the Melendres and Associates computer's Registry to its state prior to installing the LawManager application. After completing this lab, you will be able to:

➤ Use the Windows XP Backup program to restore a Registry backup

Requirements

➤ Your Registry backup from Lab 12.1

➤ Completion of Lab 12.4

Estimated completion time: **10 minutes**

ACTIVITY

1. If necessary, start your computer with Windows XP, and log on as an administrator.

2. Start **Regedit** by double-clicking its desktop icon.

3. Verify that the LawMan subkey you created within the SOFTWARE key in Lab 12.4 is still there. If the LawMan subkey does not exist, repeat Step 3 of Lab 12.4.

4. Exit the Regedit utility.

5. Start the **Backup** utility by clicking **Start**, **All Programs**, **Accessories**, **System Tools**, **Backup**.

12

6. Click **Next** to start the wizard. Click the **Restore Files and Settings** option, and click **Next** to display the What to Restore catalog window.

7. Expand **File** under Items to restore, and then expand **Registry.bfk**. Place a check mark in the **System State** box.

8. Click **Next** to complete your selection.

9. In the Completing the Restore Wizard window, click **Finish** to start the restore process.

10. After the restore process is completed, click the **Report** button, and record the results on your Student Answer Sheet. Compare the results to those you recorded after the backup in Lab 12.1. Note any differences on your Student Answer Sheet.

11. Exit Notepad, and click **Close**.

12. Click **Yes** to restart your computer.

13. Log on as the Administrator.

14. Start **Regedit** by double-clicking its icon.

15. Expand the **Software** key, and check for the LawMan key.

16. Record the results of your findings on your Student Answer Sheet.

17. Exit Regedit, and log off.

LAB 12.6 USING THE REG COMMAND LINE UTILITY

Objective

In addition to the Regedit program, Windows XP provides a command line utility called Reg, to allow Administrators to perform automatic work on the registry. After completing this lab, you will be able to:

➤ Use Reg to backup and restore registry keys

➤ Use Reg to query values in the Registry and send them to a test file

Estimated completion time: **10 minutes**

 ## ACTIVITY

1. If necessary, start your computer with Windows XP, and log on as an administrator.

2. Click **Start**, **All Programs**, **Accessories**, **Command Prompt**.

3. Type **Reg**, and then press enter to display a list of options available for the Reg utility. Record this list on your Student Answer Sheet.

4. To export a portion of the Registry, do the following:
   a. Type **cd \regback**, and press enter to change to the RegBack folder.
   b. Type **Reg Export HKLM\Software softlist**, and press enter to export the HKey_Local_Machine Software Subkey to a file called softlist.
   c. Type **Dir**, and press enter to verify that the softlist file has been created.

5. To import the file into the registry, type **Reg Import softlist** and press enter.

6. To query values from within the registry, such as the Control Sets in Lab 12.2, type **Reg Query HKLM\System\Select**, and press **Enter**.

7. To send the output of the above line to a test file, add a pipe command to the end. Type **Reg Query HKLM\System\Select > mytextfile**, and press enter. Use Notepad to view mytextfile.

8. Close the command prompt window to return to the desktop.

12

BOOTING WINDOWS XP

Labs included in this chapter
➤ Lab 13.1 Working with Startup Options
➤ Lab 13.2 Working with the Boot.ini File
➤ Lab 13.3 Creating a Windows XP Boot Disk

Microsoft MCSE Exam #70-270 Objectives	
Objective	**Lab**
Recover systems and user data	13.1, 13.2, 13.3
Troubleshoot system restoration by using Safe Mode	13.1

Student Answer Sheets to accompany the labs in this chapter are available for downloading from the Online Companion for this manual at *www.course.com*.

LAB 13.1 WORKING WITH STARTUP OPTIONS

Objective

Kristen, head librarian at the Home Town Library, recently called to report that one of the Windows XP computers in the Micro-lab periodically "hangs" when it is first started in the morning. When asked if any new software or hardware had been installed on the system, Kristen reported that a Computer-based Training package had been installed and was working fine on the other systems. Occasionally, incorrect configuration settings, driver incompatibility, or hardware problems can disable normal Windows XP operations, or prevent the system from starting. To make troubleshooting these problems easier, Windows XP provides a number of boot options that can be selected by pressing the F8 key when the boot menu appears. Your job in this lab is to learn how you can use the Windows XP boot options to help you troubleshoot and isolate problems of this sort. After completing this lab, you will be able to:

➤ Boot Windows XP to Safe Mode using command prompt and network options

➤ Enable boot logging and interpret the resulting boot log

➤ Use Last Known Good Configuration to restart a computer

➤ Identify device-loading Registry parameters

In this Lab and the other Labs in this chapter, unless otherwise instructed, select the Microsoft Windows XP Professional operating system and press Enter when starting or restarting your computers.

Estimated completion time: **20 minutes**

ACTIVITY

1. You just started the Home Town Library Windows XP computer in question, and it "hung" during the boot process just after the Microsoft Windows XP Professional banner appeared. Reboot your computer, and, on your Lab 13.1 Student Answer Sheet, record the boot processes that would have completed successfully before the failure.

2. In order to troubleshoot a computer that is "hanging" during the boot process, you need to determine at which step in the loading process the system is halting. One way to do this is to use the startup options to boot the computer, starting with "Safe Mode with Command Prompt" and working up to a Normal boot. In the next few steps, you boot the computer in each of the "Safe" modes, and record the results on your Student Answer Sheet.

   a. Start or reboot your computer and press the **F8** key when you see the boot selection menu. Record the "Safe" boot options on your Student Answer Sheet.

b. Highlight the **Safe Mode with Command Prompt** option and press **Enter**. Highlight **Windows XP Professional**, and press **Enter**. On your Student Answer Sheet, describe the steps that occur after you press the Enter key. Log on as an administrator. When the command prompt appears, record the version and build number on your Student Answer Sheet.

c. One use of the command prompt booting option might be to copy or update system files that have been corrupted or deleted. For example, type the command **cd** and press **Enter**. Then type **Dir ntoskrnl.exe /s** and press **Enter** to search for the Windows XP operating system kernel. On your Student Answer Sheet, record the path to the kernel, along with the creation date.

d. Use Task Manager to check system processes and resource usage as follows:

- Use the **Ctrl+Alt+Del** key combination, and click **Task Manager**.

- On your Student Answer Sheet, record the number of Processes, as well as CPU Usage and the Physical Memory present. Close the task manager window.

e. Type **Exit**, and press **Enter**. After verifying that the system is operating correctly in the Command Prompt mode, the next step in the troubleshooting process is to use the Safe Mode to boot the system without network support. In this step, you boot the computer to Safe Mode and observe system operation:

- Restart your computer by pressing **Ctrl+Alt+Del** and clicking the **Shutdown** button. When you see the boot selection menu, press the **F8** key, highlight the **Safe Mode** option (without networking), and press **Enter**. If necessary, select **Windows XP**, and press **Enter**.

- Log on using your administrator username and password.

- Review the possible causes and suggested action provided in the Desktop Safe Mode message. Click **Yes** to continue.

- One source to check for possible system problems is the Event Viewer System log. To do this, open **Control Panel**, open **Administrative Tools**, and start **Event Viewer**. Click the **System** log, and record any devices that failed to load.

- Close all windows.

f. After the Windows XP kernel loads, it uses the Registry to determine the sequence in which to initialize drivers that were loaded during the boot process. If drivers experience errors as they initialize, the kernel determines what action to take, based on the Error Control Registry entry for that driver. In this step, you use a Registry editor to check the load sequence and error control entries for the disk system on your computer:

- Start **Regedit** from your desktop shortcut.

- Expand the HKEY_LOCAL_MACHINE key to show the \SYSTEM\ControlSet001\Services subkey.

13

- Click the **Alerter** service, and take note of the various values that are in the right pane of the window. Double-click the **ErrorControl** value in the right pane to view the setting in the Value data box. Use the following table to match up the settings.

  Level 0: Ignore.

  Error Level 1: Normal (Message is shown, but boot process continues.)

  Error Level 2: Severe (If Last Known Good Configuration—LKGC—is not in use, restart with LKGC. If LKGC is in use, display message and continue.)

  Error Level 3: Critical (If LKGC is not in use, restart with LKGC. If LKGC is in use, boot process fails.)

g. Use Regedit to search for any service having a Critical or Severe error level:

- Return to the top of the Services selection by clicking on **Services.**
- Click **Edit**, **Find**, and enter **ErrorControl** in the Find what text box.
- If necessary, remove the check marks from the **Keys** and **Data** check boxes, and place a check mark in the Values check box.
- Click **Match whole string only** check box.
- Click the **Find Next** button.
- Press the **F3** key to search for any ErrorControl values greater than 1. Record that service on your Student Answer Sheet.
- Click **Cancel** to close the Edit window.
- On your Student Answer Sheet, use the above table, and record the Error Control and Start levels for each of the **Abiosdsk** and **atapi** services.

h. After searching all Services, click **OK** on the Finished searching message box, and then exit the Registry Editor.

3. Use **My Network Places** to attempt to browse to other computers on your network. Record your results on your Student Answer Sheet.

4. Close all windows.

5. If everything checks out after booting in Safe Mode, the problem could be in the network drivers. In this step, you boot the computer with the Safe Mode with Networking option, and attempt to access computers on the network.

a. Restart your computer.

b. Press **F8** when you see the boot selection menu, and select the **Safe Mode with Networking** option. If necessary, select **Windows XP**, and press **Enter**.

c. Log on as administrator.

d. Use **My Network Places** to browse to the network.

e. On your Student Answer Sheet, record the name of at least one other computer in your workgroup.

6. Because the Safe modes do not load all drivers and services, some problems may only occur in normal boot mode. When this happens, you can use the boot log file to log drivers that load. If the system hangs, reboot in Safe Mode, then read the logged messages to help determine what driver might have caused the problem. In this step, you practice creating and reading a boot log.

a. Restart your computer.

b. Press **F8** when you see the boot selection menu, and select the **Enable Boot Logging** option. Highlight **Windows XP Professional**, and press **Enter**. After Windows XP loads, DO NOT log on.

c. To simulate a system crash, turn off the computer when you see the logon window.

d. Restart the computer in Safe Mode, and log on as the administrator.

- Press **F8** when you see the Windows XP boot selection menu.

- Verify that **Safe Mode** is selected, and press **Enter**. If necessary, select **Windows XP** and press **Enter**.

- Log on as the administrator, and click **OK** to respond to the Windows is running in Safe Mode message.

e. Use **My Computer** or **Windows Explorer** to browse to the **WINDOWS** folder.

f. Double-click the **ntbtlog.txt** file to open it with Notepad.

g. On your Student Answer Sheet, record the information requested.

h. Close Notepad.

i. Restart your computer in Normal boot mode.

- Click **Start**, **Shutdown**, select **Restart**, and then click **OK**.

- Select the Microsoft Windows XP Professional operating system from the boot menu, and press **Enter**.

- Log on as the administrator.

7. Making changes to the system configuration can sometimes cause more problems than it solves. When this happens, you can often correct the problem by booting from the Last Known Good Configuration (LNGC). When you realize that a configuration is bad, it is important not to log on after restarting the system, or the LNGC will be overwritten with the current configuration data. In this step, you simulate using LNGC to correct a screen configuration problem that you create.

a. Right-click any empty space on the desktop, and click **Properties** to display the Display Properties window.

b. Click the **Settings** tab, and record the screen resolution on your Student Answer Sheet.

c. Change your screen resolution, and click **Apply**. Record the revised screen resolution on your Student Answer Sheet.

d. Click **OK** to test your new settings.

e. Click **Yes** to keep the settings.

f. Click **OK** to close the Display Properties window.

13

   g. Restart the computer.

   h. Press the **F8** key when the boot menu appears, and select the Last Known
      Good Configuration option. Highlight **Windows XP Professional**, and
      press **Enter**.

   i. Log on as the administrator.

   j. Right-click any empty space on the desktop, and click **Properties**.

   k. Click the **Setup** tab, and record the restored screen resolution on your
      Student Answer Sheet. Make sure the restored resolution is the same as the
      resolution you recorded in Step 7b.

   l. Close all windows and log off.

LAB 13.2 WORKING WITH THE BOOT.INI FILE

Objective

Superior Technical College has a computer lab in which the student computers need to be
able to boot to multiple operating systems. In addition, because the instructor's station is
used for demonstrations, the college wants to make it easy for presenters to boot the computer to various startup modes without having to use the F8 function key. The Boot.ini file
identifies the location of the Windows XP operating system as well as various startup parameters. Knowing how to modify the Boot.ini file is important when troubleshooting or
configuring Windows XP. After completing this lab, you will be able to:

   ➤ Identify the proper installation sequence for multiple operating systems

   ➤ Use Control Panel to modify the default Boot.ini file parameters

   ➤ Use Notepad to modify the Boot.ini file

   ➤ Add boot options to the Boot.ini file

Estimated completion time: **15–20 minutes**

ACTIVITY

   1. Superior Technical College has contracted with your company to install the
      computer systems in the new Web Page Development lab. In addition to Web
      classes, this lab will be used for teaching DOS and Windows 98. As a result, you
      need to install all three operating systems on the computers. On your Lab 13.2
      Student Answer Sheet, describe the installation sequence you would employ to
      allow all three operating systems to boot through the Windows XP boot selec-
      tion menu.

   2. If necessary, start your computer with Windows XP, and log on as an
      administrator.

3. By default, the boot selection menu provides only a short time for the operator to make a selection before booting from the default operating system. This often does not give users enough time to make a selection. To help prevent booting to the wrong operating system, Superior Technical College wants the computers in the Web lab to wait at least 5 minutes before starting with the default operating system. In this step, you use Control Panel to change the default boot options.

   a. Open **Control Panel**, and double-click the **System** icon.

   b. Click the **Advanced** tab, and then click the **Startup and Recovery Settings** button to display a Startup and Recovery window similar to the one shown in Figure 13-1.

Figure 13-1   Configuring the system Startup settings

   c. On your Student Answer Sheet, record the default operating system, along with the number of seconds given to display the list of operating systems.

   d. Click the down arrow button to the right of the operating system window, and, on your Student Answer Sheet, record the other possible operating system choices.

   e. Change the wait time seconds so the system has to wait for 5 minutes before starting the default operating system. Record the number of seconds you enter on your Student Answer Sheet.

   f. Click **OK** twice to save your changes.

   g. Close Control Panel.

   h. Restart your system and verify that the new wait time is in effect.

4. Because teachers often get interrupted while booting the presentation computer, they want the presentation computer to wait indefinitely for them to
make an operating system selection. This can be done by placing a negative
number (-1) in the time field. In this step, you attempt to use Control Panel to
set the number of seconds to -1.

   a. If necessary, log on as an administrator.
   b. Open **Control Panel**, double-click the **System** icon, and click the
   Advanced tab.
   c. Click the **Startup and Recovery Settings** button, and attempt to change
   the wait time to a negative number. Record the results on your Student
   Answer Sheet.
   d. Click **Cancel** until you exit the System window.
   e. Close Control Panel.

5. As you can see from Steps 2 and 3, only very limited changes can be made to
the boot selection menu from Control Panel. To customize the boot selection
menu, you need to edit the boot.ini file using the edit feature on the Startup
and Recovery window, or a text editor such as Notepad. In this step, you use
the edit feature to open the boot.ini file in order to change the default operating system and set an unlimited wait time.

   a. Return to the Startup and Recovery window as shown in Step 4.
   b. Click **Edit** to open boot.ini with Notepad.
   c. Record the operating system lines on your Student Answer Sheet.
   d. Modify the timeout line to read: **timeout=-1**.
   e. Save the boot.ini file, and exit Notepad.
   f. Click **OK** to exit the Startup and Recovery window.
   g. Click **Settings** to return to Startup and Recovery. Note the timeout value
   on the screen, and then click **Edit.** Notice that the timeout value in the
   boot.ini file reverted back to the value on the screen.
   h. Change the timeout value back to **-1**, and save and exit Notepad. This
   time, click **Cancel** to avoid overwriting the file with the wizard feature.
   i. Close all windows, and restart your computer.
   j. On your Student Answer Sheet, record the result of booting with the wait
   time set to -1.

6. Superior Technical College wants to add the following options to the boot
selection menu:

   ■ Full Hardware Detect (remove /FASTDETECT and add the
   /NOGUIBOOT option)
   ■ Command prompt only (use the /SAFEBOOT:MINIMAL
   (ALTERNATESHELL) option)
   ■ Safe Mode with networking (use the /SAFEBOOT:NETWORK option)

In this step, you use Notepad to add the necessary entries and options to the boot.ini file.

a. Use My Computer or Windows Explorer to open a window for the C: (system) drive.

b. Click **Tools**, **Folder Options**, and click the **View** tab.

c. Verify the following options:

- Show hidden files and folders is selected
- Hide file extensions for known file types is *not* checked
- Hide protected operating system files (Recommended) is *not* checked

d. Click **OK** to return to the LocalDisk (C:) window.

e. Navigate to the root of drive C:, right-click the **boot.ini** file, and click **Properties**.

f. If necessary, remove the check mark in the **Read-only** attribute check box, and click **OK**.

g. Right-click the **boot.ini** file, and click the **Open** option.

h. Using the existing multi()disk()partition() information, add a line to your boot.ini file for each of the above options, to make your boot.ini file similar to the one shown in Figure 13-2. (Your information may differ, depending on your disk configuration.) Record the lines you add on your Student Answer Sheet.

Figure 13-2   Configuring the Boot.ini file

i. Save the boot.ini file, and exit Notepad.

7. In this step, you test each of your boot options.

a. Close all windows, and restart your system.

b. Test each boot option, and, if necessary, make corrections to your boot.ini file.

c. If necessary, record any corrections on your Student Answer Sheet, or attach an updated printout of the boot.ini file.

8. Close all windows, and log off.

LAB 13.3 CREATING A WINDOWS XP BOOT DISK

Objective

Being able to boot from a floppy disk can be important to recovering from corrupted system files or when working with a Windows XP server that has mirrored disk drives. When using mirrored disk drives, if the primary drive fails, the boot floppy can be used to boot the computer from the backup or mirrored drive. For example, the Melendres and Associates law firm recently upgraded to Windows XP Server mirrored disk drives. In this lab, you will learn how to create a Windows XP boot disk that can be used to boot a Windows XP Server or Professional system in the event the primary boot drive or boot sector is damaged. After completing this lab, you will be able to:

➤ Format a Windows XP disk

➤ Copy system files to a disk

➤ Modify the boot.ini file to change the boot partition number

➤ Identify error messages that occur when attempting to boot from a partition that does not contain the Windows XP operating system

➤ Boot your computer from a disk and recover the NTLDR program

Requirements

➤ A blank disk

Estimated completion time: **15 minutes**

ACTIVITY

1. If necessary, start your computer with Windows XP, and log on as an administrator.

2. Format a disk as follows:
   a. Insert a disk in the A drive, and double-click **My Computer**.
   b. Right-click the **(A:)** drive, and click the **Format** option.
   c. Enter **W2KBOOT** in the Volume label text box.
   d. Verify that the Quick Format check box is unchecked. Click **Start** and then **OK to respond** to the warning message to perform a full format. (*Note:* Windows XP does not have a System format option. In the next step, you make a system disk by copying the necessary system files to the formatted disk.)
   e. After the format is complete, click **Close** to exit the Format window.

3. Copy files from the C: (system) drive to your newly formatted disk.

   a. Use **My Computer** to open a window to the C: (system) drive.

   b. Copy the following files to your disk:

   - ntldr
   - ntdetect.com
   - boot.ini

   c. Close all windows.

   d. Write **Windows XP Boot Disk** on the disk label.

4. If you were working with a mirrored drive on a server, the next step would be to modify the boot.ini file on the disk so you can add an option that would load the kernel and other operating system files from the WINDOWS folder of the mirrored drive. In this step, you simulate this process by adding such an option to the boot.ini file on your disk.

   a. Use My Computer or Windows Explorer to open a window for the (A:) drive.

   b. Right-click the **boot.ini** file, and click the **Open with** option.

   c. Double-click **Notepad** to view the boot.ini file.

   d. Add the following line at the end of the [operating system] lines:

   - **multi(0)disk(0)rdisk(1)partition(1)\WINDOWS="Windows XP Mirror Boot"**

If you are using SCSI drives without BIOS support, you need to change the disk numbering to read: SCSI(0)disk(1)rdisk(0).

13

   e. Save the boot.ini file, and exit Notepad.

5. Test your boot disk by restarting your computer with the disk in the drive and selecting the **Normal** boot option. Record the results on your Lab 13.3 Student Answer Sheet.

6. Test your boot disk again by restarting your computer with the disk in the drive and selecting the **Mirrored drive** boot option. Record the error message you receive on your Student Answer Sheet.

7. Remove the disk from drive A:. Restart the computer and log on as the administrator.

8. In this step, you simulate a problem with your hard drive boot partition by changing the partition number in the Boot.ini file of the C: (system) drive. Then you fix the problem by restarting the computer with the Safe Mode option of the boot disk.

   a. Use My Computer or Windows Explorer to open a window to the C: (system) drive.

   b. Right-click the **boot.ini** file, and click the **Open** option.

    c. On your Student Answer Sheet, record the Advanced RISC Computing (ARC) path-name for the Windows XP normal boot option.

    d. Change the Partition number in the Windows XP normal boot option.

    e. Save the **boot.ini** file and exit.

    f. Restart your computer using the modified Windows XP normal boot option.

    g. Record the error message you receive on your Student Answer Sheet.

    h. Insert the Windows XP Boot disk in the drive, and restart your computer.

    i. After Windows XP has booted, log on as the administrator.

    j. Repeat Steps 8a through 8f to change the partition number back to the original correct number you recorded on your Student Answer Sheet for Step 8c.

    k. Remove the Windows XP Boot disk from the drive and restart your computer.

9. In this step, you rename the NTLDR file to simulate a corrupted loader, and then fix the problem by booting in Safe Mode from your Windows XP boot disk.

    a. Use My Computer or Windows Explorer to open a window to the C: (system) drive.

    b. Rename **ntldr** to **ntldr.bak**. Click Yes to respond to the warning message.

    c. Close all windows.

    d. Remove your Windows XP Boot disk from the drive.

    e. Restart your computer, and record the error message on your Student Answer Sheet.

    f. Insert your Windows XP Boot disk, and restart the computer using the Command Prompt mode.

    g. In the Command prompt window, enter the following commands from the root of your boot drive. (In the following commands "drive:\>" represents the command prompt path, and "drive:" is your boot drive. You need to enter only the commands shown in bold.)

    drive:\>**ATTRIB A:\NTLDR –H –S** (Remove Hidden and System Attributes)

    drive:\>**COPY A:\NTLDR C:\NTLDR**

    drive:\>**ATTRIB C:\NTLDR +H +S** (Set Hidden and System Attributes)

    h. Remove the Windows XP Boot disk from the drive, and restart your computer.

    i. Record the result on your Student Answer Sheet.

    j. Close all windows, and log off.

DISASTER RECOVERY AND PROTECTION

Labs included in this chapter

➤ Lab 14.1 Working with File Synchronization and Offline Files

➤ Lab 14.2 Scheduling and Testing Backups and Restores

➤ Lab 14.3 Working with System Restore

➤ Lab 14.4 Protecting the Windows XP Professional System

➤ Lab 14.5 Repairing Windows XP Professional

Microsoft MCSE Exam #70-270 Objectives	
Objective	Lab
Manage and troubleshoot access to and synchronization of Offline Files	14.1
Restore and back up the operating system, system state, and user data	14.2, 14.3, 14.4, 14.5

Student Answer Sheets to accompany the labs in this chapter are available for downloading from the Online Companion for this manual at *www.course.com*.

LAB **14.1** WORKING WITH FILE SYNCHRONIZATION AND OFFLINE FILES

Objective

As the Melendres and Associates law firm's use of the network has expanded, Mr. Melendres has become more concerned about establishing a system to help protect against data loss and restore system operation if a problem or disaster occurs. After meeting with Mr. Melendres, you have agreed to plan and implement a data protection plan that includes four levels. The first level is to synchronize critical case data with the server. Synchronizing the data on the server allows users to maintain a copy of the data on their local computers. In the event that the server is down, users can continue to access case information on their local machines. The second level is to establish a daily backup of the user data on the server. This backup can be used to recover user data in the event of operator error or system disaster. The third level is to reduce the amount of time that it takes to recover workstations in the event of user errors. A quick method of recovering systems to a previous state without having to rebuild the system would be a great time and cost saver. The fourth level is to provide a method to quickly repair problems on the server without having to perform a lengthy reinstall or restore process. In this lab, you will work on the first level by configuring and synchronizing user data. In Labs 14.2 and 14.3, you will continue to set up the data protection plan by implementing levels three and four. In Lab 14.4 and Lab 14.5, you will work on procedures to protect and repair Windows XP. After completing this lab, you will be able to:

➤ Identify the four levels of a data protection plan

➤ Implement and test folder redirection

Requirements

➤ Another Windows XP computer to act as a server for offline files. Decide which computer will act as server and which will act as client.

Estimated completion time: **30 minutes**

ACTIVITY

Currently, the legal assistants move each client's case information to the My Documents folder on their laptop computers to work on it, often away from the network. They then move the file back when finished. The problem with this system is that the case information is not being backed up regularly, and other legal assistants or attorneys cannot access the case files until the files are finished and placed back in the shared Cases folder. If the legal assistants work only on case information stored on the server, they cannot work on the file away from the office. They also would not be able to access the files if the server or network were down. Offline files solve both these problems by allowing data stored on the server to be copied to a laptop and then automatically synchronized when the legal assistant reconnects to the network. The server or network does not need to be available for the legal assistants to work on the files. In this step, you simulate this level of the data protection system by setting up offline files with your partner.

1. On the computer acting as the server:
   a. Open **My Computer** and create a folder on your Windows XP drive called **MA Shared Case Files**.
   b. Right-click the new folder, and click **Properties**. Click the **Sharing** tab, and enable sharing for the folder.
   c. To configure offline files, click **Caching** at the bottom of the window. Offline files are automatically enabled when you share a folder. Record the three available cache settings on your Student Answer Sheet. Indicate which one is the default setting.
   d. Because you do not want the legal assistants to have to manually select which files to make available offline, click **Automatic caching of Documents**.
   e. Click **OK** twice to return to the Control Panel.
   f. Close all windows.

2. On the computer acting as the client:
   a. If necessary, start your computer with Windows XP, and log on as an administrator.
   b. Click **Start**, and **My Computer**.
   c. Click **Folder Options** from the **Tools** menu and then click the **Offline Files** tab.
   d. Place a check mark in the **Enable Offline Files** box. Record the options on your Student Answer Sheet.
   e. Place a check mark in **Create an offline files shortcut on the desktop**.
   f. Click **OK** to return to the My Computer window.
   g. Click **Start**, **My Network Places**, and navigate to the **MA Shared Case Files** folder on your partner's computer.
   h. Create a new file in the folder called **JJHenry.txt**. Type a few lines in the file, and then save and close it.
   i. Close all windows and log off. You should briefly see a File Synchronization box appear.

3. On the computer acting as the server:
   a. Click **Start**, and then right-click **My Network Places**.
   b. Click **Properties**, and then right-click **Local Area Connection**.
   c. Click **Disable** to simulate a network down condition.

4. On the computer acting as the client:
   a. Log in as the administrator.
   b. Click **Shortcut to Offline Files** on your desktop.
   c. Double-click the **JJHenry.txt** file, and add a few more lines of text. Save and close the file.
   d. Close all windows and log off.

14

5. On the computer acting as the server:
   a. Navigate to the **MA Shared Case Files** folder, and open the **JJHenry.txt** file. On your Student Answer Sheet, record the number of lines in the file. Close the file.
   b. Enable your network connection.

6. On the computer acting as the client, log on as administrator.

7. On the computer acting as the server, navigate to the **MA Shared Case Files** folder and re-open the **JJHenry.txt** file. Record the number of lines on your Student Answer Sheet. Close all windows.

8. To better control how files are synchronized or to manually force this process, a Synchronization Manager is available. On the computer acting as the client:
   a. Click **Start**, **All Programs**, **Accessories**, **Synchronize** to list current offline files, as shown in Figure 14-1.

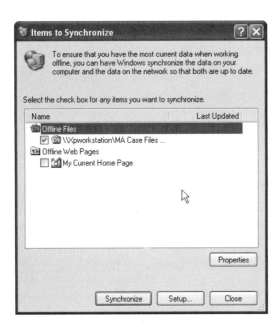

Figure 14-1   Configuring offline folder synchronization settings

   b. Click **Setup**, and, on the Student Answer Sheet, briefly describe the purpose of each of the three tabs. Click **OK** to return to the Synchronization Manager.
   c. To force synchronization, remove the check mark from **My Current Home page**. Then click the **Synchronize** button. (The offline file feature of Windows XP also allows for offline Web Pages.)
   d. Close all windows and return to the desktop.

9. Reverse the roles of client and server computers, and repeat steps 1–8.

10. Close all programs and log off.

LAB 14.2 SCHEDULING AND TESTING BACKUPS AND RESTORES

Objective

A data protection plan is critical to the protection of an organization's data. There are three major daily backup options: Full (also called Normal), Incremental, and Differential. In a Full or Normal backup, the selected files are backed up every day, even if no changes were made. With an Incremental backup, only the files that changed that day are copied to the daily backup. A Differential backup copies all files that have changed since the last Full backup.

After you discuss these backup options with Mr. Melendres, he decides to use a daily Differential backup with Full backup to be made on Mondays. In this lab, you will set up and test the Monday Full backup. You will then set up and test the daily Differential backups. You will also test the integrity of your backup through a verification process as well as test-recovering a series of files. After completing this lab, you will be able to:

➤ Create a Backup Operator user account

➤ Schedule a Monday Full (Normal) backup of selected files

➤ Schedule a Tuesday-to-Friday Differential backup of selected files

➤ Perform and verify the Full (Normal) backup

➤ Perform a restore of selected files

> Estimated completion time: **45 minutes**

ACTIVITY

14

1. If necessary, start your computer with Windows XP, and log on as an administrator.

2. Rather than use the Administrator account to back up the system, Mr. Melendres wants you to create a user account that has only the privilege to back up and restore system and user data. In this step, you create a user named BackOp that has backup and restore privileges.

   a. Open the **Local Users and Groups Management** MCC that you created in Lab 5.1.

   b. Expand **Local Users and Groups**, and right-click **Users**. Click **New User** to display the New User window.

   c. Enter the following user information:
   - User name: **BackOp**
   - Full name: **Backup Operators**
   - Description: **Account used to back up user data**

   d. Enter a password that you can remember, or use **password**, in both Password and Confirm password text boxes.

    e. Clear the **User must change password at next logon**, and then click **Create** to create the new user. Click **Close** to return to the User and Groups Management MCC.

    f. Right-click the new **BackOp** user, and click **Properties**. Click the **Member Of** tab to display the default groups to which this user belongs.

    g. Click **Add** to display the Select Groups window. Type **Backup Operators; Administrators** in the dialog box, and click **OK** to select the groups. Note: Placing the user in the Administrator group is only necessary because of the scheduling feature you will be using. This is not necessary for the BackupOp user to do interactive backups.

    h. Click **OK** to return to User and Groups Management MCC.

    i Close the MCC. Click **Yes** to save the console.

3. To use the Backup utility on your computer in this step, you create a folder named **Backups**.

    a. Use My Computer or Windows Explorer to open a window to the drive containing the Windows XP operating system files.

    b. Create a new folder named **Backups**.

    c. Minimize **My Computer** or **Windows Explorer**.

4. As described earlier, Mr. Melendres wants to perform a Full (Normal) backup every Monday at 11:55 pm. To simulate the Monday backup in this step, you schedule a Full (Normal) backup of the Documents and Settings folder to occur in 5 minutes.

    a. Start the Backup utility by clicking **Start**, **All Programs**, **Accessories**, **System Tools**, and then clicking **Backup**.

    b. Click **Next**, and then insure that **Backup files and settings** is selected. Click **Next** to start the Backup wizard.

    c. On your Lab 14.2 Student Answer Sheet, record the four backup item buttons.

    d. Click the **Let me choose what to backup** option and click **Next** to display the Items to Back Up window.

    e. Select the Documents and Settings folder as follows:

        ■ In the left-side tree pane, click the **+** box to expand **My Computer** and the drive containing the Windows XP operating system.

        ■ Click the check box to the left of the **Documents and Settings** folder.

        ■ Expand the **Documents and Settings** folder, and notice that all subfolders are checked with a blue check mark.

        ■ Click on the **All Users** box. All check marks turn grey and the check mark does not disappear from the All Users folder. The grey marks indicate that this a partial backup of information from the top level of folders; in this case Documents and Settings. Expand **All Users** and take note that none of the folders or files are selected.

        ■ Repeat this procedure for the **Default User** folder.

    f. Click **Next** to display the Backup type, Destination and Name window.

g. Use the **Browse** button to navigate to your **Backups** folder.

h. In the Name field, enter **Monday Normal**, and click **Save**. Click **Next** to display the Completing the Backup or Restore wizard window.

i. To select advanced settings, such as type and schedule for the backup, click the **Advanced** button.

j. Click the scroll button to the right of the Select the type of backup text box, and record the possible backup types on your Student Answer Sheet. Verify that the **Normal** backup type is selected, and click **Next** to display the How to backup options.

k. Identify the three choices on your Student Answer Sheet.

l. Click the **Verify data after backup** option check box, and click **Next** to display the Backup Options window.

m. Click the **Replace the existing backup** option button. For additional security, select the **Allow only the user or administrator access to the backup data...** option, and click **Next** to display the When to Backup window.

n. Click the **Later** button, and type **Monday Full Backup** for the job name. Click the **Set Schedule** button to display the Job Scheduler window. To schedule a weekly backup on Monday, do the following:

- Using the Schedule Task pull-down menu, click the **Weekly** option to display a schedule window similar to the one shown in Figure 14-2.

14

Figure 14-2   Configuring scheduled tasks

- Set the start time to start the backup 5 minutes from the current time shown in the right side of your status bar.
- If necessary, remove the check mark from the Monday check box, and click the check box next to the current day of the week.
- Click the **Settings** tab, and record the options on your Student Answer Sheet. Give an explanation of the three sections listed.
- Click **OK** to return to the When to Backup window.

o. Click **Next**. On the Set Account window, type **<computer name>\BackOp** in the Runs As text box. Enter the password for BackOp in the password and confirm box, and then click **OK**.

p. Click **Finish** to save your Monday scheduled backup, and return to the desktop.

q. Click **Start**, **All Programs**, **Accessories**, **System Tools**, **Scheduled Tasks** tab to display a calendar of scheduled jobs.

r. Double-click the **Monday Full Backup** job to display the properties of the job. Review the setting to be sure that you set it properly. Click **Cancel** to return to the Schedule Task calendar.

s. Close the Schedule Tasks window.

5. Test the Monday Full backup by performing the following procedure.
   a. Start **WordPad**.
   b. Create a new document that contains the statement **This is Monday's case information**.
   c. Save the document as **Case007** in your My Documents folder.
   d. Use the **File**, **Save as** option to save the document a second time with the name **Case008**.
   e. Wait for your Normal backup to execute. A Backup Window will appear and start backing up your files. Take note that, after the backup is complete, a date verification procedure will be carried out on the data backed up.
   f. When the window closes, navigate to the **MyBackup** folder and verify that a backup file has been created.

6. To create a simulated scheduled differential backup for Tuesday, perform the following procedures:
   a. Start the **Backup wizard**, and repeat Steps 4b to 4g above.
   b. In the name file, type **Tuesday Differential**. Using the procedures from Step 4 above, continue through to the Backup Type.
   c. Select **Differential** as the Backup Type. Using the procedures in Step 4, continue to the Schedule window.
   d. Select **Weekly** and set a time 10 minutes from now on today's date.
   e. Complete the necessary steps to close the wizard. Normally you would place a check mark in the Tuesday – Friday boxes to repeat the differential backup on those days.

7. In this step, you simulate weekly activity and backups by changing files in your My Documents folder. You will need to complete this procedure before the 10 minutes you scheduled in Step 6 is up.

   a. Navigate to the **My Documents** folder.

   b. Create a new file called **Case009**, and add a **This is Tuesday's case information** statement.

   c. Open the **Case007** file, and add a **This is Tuesday's case information** statement to the end of the file.

   d. Save the files and exit WordPad.

   e. Wait for your Tuesday Differential backup to occur.

8. No backup is complete until you can verify that the data can successfully be restored. One of the disadvantages of the Differential backup is that when data are lost, you need to restore both the Full backup and the latest Differential backup. In this step, you simulate a Friday morning disaster that deletes all the case files from the My Documents folder of the server computer.

   a. Double-click the **My Documents** desktop icon to open the **My Documents** folder. Delete all the files starting with **Case**.

   b. The first phase in the differential restore process is restoring the Monday Normal backup, and then checking the status of the restored files.

   c. If necessary, start the **Backup** utility, and click **Next**.

   d. Click the **Restore files and settings** button, and click **Next** to display the What to Restore window.

   e. Expand **Monday Normal** backup, and click the check box to the left of the drive letter to restore it and all its subfolders.

   f. Click **Next** to display the Completing Backup and Restore Wizard window.

   g. Click **Advanced** to review the options available for a restore procedure. Record the options of the three windows on your Student Answer Sheet and then return to the Completing Backup and Restore Wizard window.

   h. Click **Finish** to start the Restore procedure.

   i. Click the **Report** button, and scan for any errors.

   j. Click **Close** to return to the Welcome tab.

   k. Double-click **My Documents**, and check to see if all files have been properly restored.

9. In this step, you test the second phase in the differential restore process by restoring the Tuesday backup, and then checking the file status.

   a. If necessary, start the **Backup** utility, and click **Next.**

   b. Click the **Restore files and settings** button, and click **Next** to display the What to Restore window.

   c. Expand the **Tuesday Differential** backup, and click the check box to the left of the drive letter to restore it and all its subfolders.

   d. Click **Next**, and then click **Finish** to start the restore process.

   e. Double-click **My Documents**, and check to see if all files have been properly restored.

14

10. Exit the Backup utility and log off.

LAB 14.3 WORKING WITH SYSTEM RESTORE

Objective

The Backup and Restore procedures that you have implemented work very well for protecting users' data files. Mr. Melendres now wants to know what options are available for recovering Windows XP without having to rebuild the system. This may happen if a user accidentally deletes a program or setting on their local drive. Windows XP monitors changes to your system and creates a backup file prior to any system changes. A backup file is also created on a daily basis at 1:00 a.m. After completing this lab, you will be able to:

➤ View the Restore Points created by XP

➤ Create your own Restore Point

➤ Recover your system to an earlier Restore Point

➤ Undo the Recovery Procedure

Estimated completion time: **15 minutes**

ACTIVITY

1. To view the restore points created by Windows XP, do the following:

   a. Click **Start**, **All Programs**, **Accessories**, **System Tools**, **System Restore**. You can also access System Restore through the Help and Support Center.

   b. Ensure that **Restore my computer to an earlier time** is selected, and click **Next**.

   c. A calendar is displayed with highlighted dates. Click these dates to view the restore points created by Windows XP. On your Student Answer Sheet, record the restore points from the beginning of this course. Distinguish which were daily and which were created by a change in your system.

   d. Click **Cancel** to return to the desktop.

2. To test the capability of System Restore, you will create a Restore Point and then delete a number of files.

   a. Start the **System Restore** program.

   b. Click **Create a restore point**, and click **Next**.

   c. Type **Restore Point prior to file changes**, and click **Create**. There is no facility to change the name or schedule a date for a restore point.

   d. Click **Close** when the procedure is finished.

   e. Open **My Documents**, and delete **Case007** and **Case008**.

   f. Navigate to the **WINDOWS** folder, and create a folder called **Restore Point**. Create a file called **Test Restore** in the new folder.

g. Close all windows.

h. Start the **System Restore** program.

i. Ensure that **Restore my computer to a earlier time** is selected, and click **Next**.

j. Ensure that **Restore Point prior to file changes** is selected, and click **Next**. On the Student Answer Sheet, record the restrictions and procedures of the System Restore process.

k. Click **Next** to start the Restore Procedure. Windows XP will close all programs, and then a System Restore window will appear. Once the procedure is completed, your system will reboot.

l. After logon, a window will open showing final instructions. Click **OK** to return to your desktop.

m. Navigate to the **My Documents** and **WINDOWS** folders, and record the results on the Student Answer Sheet.

n. Close all windows and return to the desktop.

3. If, for whatever reason, the restore procedure did not achieve the desired results, you can undo the Restore procedure using the following steps:

a. Start the **System Restore** program.

b. Click **Undo my last restoration**, and click **Next** to display the Confirm Restoration Undo window.

c. Click **Next** to complete the Undo Restore procedure. Your system will follow the same steps as above.

d. Navigate to the **My Documents** and **WINDOWS** folders, and record the results on the Student Answer Sheet.

e. Close all windows, and return to the desktop.

14

LAB 14.4 PROTECTING THE WINDOWS XP PROFESSIONAL SYSTEM

Objective

Mr. Melendres wants to know what options are available if the Windows XP operating system should become disabled and not boot. Windows XP could be reinstalled and the user data restored from the backup, but reinstalling Windows XP would take quite a bit of time, especially if you need to re-create the users, assign folder permissions, and reinstall printers and application software. For this reason, the fourth level of data protection provides ways that you can recover or repair the Windows XP operating system without having to reinstall it. If the Windows XP operating system is damaged and needs to be reinstalled, you still can save a lot of time by being able to use the Backup utility to restore users, printers, and Registry data. After completing this lab, you will be able to:

➤ Install the Recovery Console

➤ Use the Backup utility to create an Automated System Recovery set (ASR)

Requirements

➤ The Windows XP Professional CD-ROM to install the Recovery Console

Estimated completion time: **15 minutes**

ACTIVITY

1. If necessary, start your computer with Windows XP, and log on as an administrator.

2. Backing up system state data provides a way to recover the Registry, system boot files, and user accounts. Although you probably don't need a daily backup of system state data, it's a good idea to back up the system state data before installing applications, and after creating new users or modifying user account policies. You have done this procedure once in Lab 12.1; however, because of the changes made since then, it needs to be repeated. Refer back to Lab 12.1 now, and repeat the procedure Steps 3 through 9. Then close the Backup utility.

3. If user accounts become damaged or deleted, you can use the system state backup to restore them. In this step, you use the system state backup you made in Step 2 to restore a deleted user account.

   a. Open **Control Panel**, and double-click **Users Accounts**.

   b. Click the **BackOp** user you created in Lab 14.2, and click **Delete the Account**.

   c. Click **Delete Files**, and then click **Delete Account**.

   d. Close all windows.

   e. Start the **Backup** utility, and click **Next**.

   f. Click **Restore files and settings**, and click **Next** to display the What to Restore window.

   g. Expand **File** and your **Registry** backup, and click the check box to the right of the **System State** backup entry.

   h. Click **Next** to display the summary window.

   i. Click **Finish** to start the restore process.

   j. This is a good time to take a break as this process will take a fair amount of time. A time estimate will be shown on the restore window.

   k. Record the requested Restore Progress information on your Student Answer Sheet.

   l. Exit the Backup utility.

   m. Open **Control Panel** and use the **Users Accounts** utility to verify that the BackOp user was restored.

4. Restoring system state information allows you to recover from problems as long as you are able to boot Windows XP. The Recovery Console allows you to troubleshoot and fix certain problems that might prevent Windows XP from fully booting. In this step, you install the Recovery Console so you can select it when booting.

a. Insert your Windows XP CD into your computer's CD-ROM drive.

b. Click **Start**, **Run**.

c. Use the **Browse** button to navigate to the **I386** folder of your CD.

d. Double-click the **WINNT32.EXE** application to insert the WINNT32.EXE command in the Open text box.

e. At the end of the WINNT32.EXE statement, press the spacebar, and then type **/cmdcons**. Your statement should look similar to **E:\I386\WINNT32.EXE /cmdcons**.

f. Click **OK**, and then click **Yes** to install Recovery Console.

g. During the installation, the wizard will attempt to connect to the Microsoft Update Web Service. If you do not have access to the Internet, a Getting Updated Setup Files message window will appear. Click **Skip thus step and continue installing windows**. Click **Next** to continue the installation.

h. When the installation is completed, a Microsoft Windows XP Professional Setup message will appear.

i. On your Student Answer Sheet, record the method given to start the Recovery Console.

j. Click **OK** to close the completion message window.

5. If all else fails, and you are unable to boot the computer to a Safe Mode, a last effort prior to reinstalling Windows XP and restoring the backups is to restore your system using the Automated System Recovery (ASR) disk. In this step, you use the Backup utility to create an ASR set which contains the ASR Disk and a media backup of your system files. This backup does not back up your data files.

a. Start the **Backup** utility, and click **Advanced Mode**.

b. Click the **Automated System Recovery Wizard**, and then click **Next** to display the Backup Destination window.

c. Browse to navigate to the **Backups** folder, and type **ASR backup** for the file name.

d. Click **Next** to display the summary window. DO NOT click Finish. This procedure takes a long time as it backs up all of Windows XP and your settings. After completing the backup of your system, it will also create an ASR floppy disk.

e. Click **Cancel** to abort the ASR Wizard.

f. To use the ASR disk, you would boot from the Windows XP CD. When prompted, you would click F2, and then insert the ASR disk. The system would then rebuild from the CD and backup media. User data would have to be recovered from other backups.

14

LAB **14.5** REPAIRING WINDOWS **XP** PROFESSIONAL

Objective

Recovering from system problems can range from restoring the Registry after uninstalling an application to fixing a system that does not boot. This lab contains problem scenarios from the Melendres and Associates law firm that will give you practice working with the recovery console that you installed in Lab 14.4. After completing this lab, you will be able to:

➤ Use several Recovery Console commands to help restore or troubleshoot the operating system

Requirements

➤ Completion of Lab 14.4

Estimated completion time: **15 minutes**

ACTIVITY

1. If necessary, start your computer with Windows XP, and log on as an administrator.

2. On Monday morning, one of the legal assistants at the Melendres and Associates law firm calls to inform you that the Windows XP computer at their office is not booting. In this step, you use several commands from the Recovery Console to attempt to get the system operating.

    a. Follow the process you recorded on your Lab 14.4 Student Answer sheet for Step 4g to restart the computer in Recovery Console mode.

    b. Enter the number of the Windows XP installation you want to log on to.

    c. Enter the password for the administrator account, and press **Enter**.

    d. Enter the command **listsvc**, and press **Enter** to list all services.

    e. You suspect that the Browser service is causing the system to fail, and decide to disable it. To disable the Browser service, enter the command **disable Browser**, and press **Enter**. Record the original and new start values on your Student Answer Sheet.

    f. To re-enable the Browser service, enter the command **enable Browser**, and press **Enter**. Record the message you receive on your Student Answer Sheet.

    g. Enter the command **enable Browser Service_Auto_Start**, and press **Enter**. Record the message that you receive on your Student Answer Sheet.

    h. Enter the command **diskpart**. Record the partition information on your Student Answer Sheet. Press **ESC** to exit the Disk Partition program.

i. Now you suspect that the problem may be a damaged boot sector. To repair a damaged boot sector, enter the command **fixboot**, and press **Enter**. Record the messages you receive on your Student Answer Sheet.

j. Sometimes booting with a virus-infected disk can corrupt the master boot record. If this happens, Windows XP might not boot or might crash during operation. To repair the master boot record, enter the command **fixmbr**, and press **Enter**. On your Student Answer Sheet, record the message you receive. Enter **N** to skip the repair process.

k. Type **exit**, and press **Enter** to end the Recovery Console mode. Now the system will restart automatically.

14

CHAPTER FIFTEEN

TROUBLESHOOTING WINDOWS XP

Labs included in this chapter

➤ Lab 15.1 Creating a Computer Information File (CIF)

➤ Lab 15.2 Troubleshooting Network Problems

➤ Lab 15.3 Applying Service Packs

Microsoft MCSE Exam #70-270 Objectives	
Objective	Lab
Install, configure, and troubleshoot network adapters	15.1
Configure and troubleshoot the TCP/IP protocol	15.1, 15.2
Implement, manage, and troubleshoot disk devices	15.1
Configure and troubleshoot desktop settings	15.1
Troubleshoot failed installations	15.2
Monitor, configure, and troubleshoot volumes	15.2
Manage and troubleshoot access to shared folders	15.2
Manage printers and print jobs	15.2
Deploy service packs	15.3

LAB 15.1 CREATING A COMPUTER INFORMATION FILE (CIF)

Objective

In the last year, the consulting company you work for, Computer Technology Services, has added several new accounts and hired additional network support specialists and technicians. To better address customer problems and needs, Computer Technology Services wants a computer information file (CIF) created for computers at each customer site. This will allow faster problem resolution and make it easier for new support staff to understand any changes that have been made to the systems. Because of your experience in the field, your manager has asked you to work with the design team and help create forms for the CTS technical support staff to gather information for the computer information files, as well as to document procedures. To do this lab, your instructor may assign you to a student design team. The team should set some design standards and then delegate form designs to various team members. You may wish to use forms found in earlier chapters of this lab manual as samples for your design. At the completion of the project, you might be asked to make a presentation of your forms to your classmates in order to simulate a forms training session to the CTS technical support staff. You will work with other students on your design team to design and create the following:

➤ A form to record system and network information

➤ A form to document backup procedures and schedules

➤ A form to document shared folders and permissions

➤ A form to document problems and solutions

➤ A form to document system changes

➤ A heading page that identifies the printouts and documents to be collected in the CIF

After completing this lab, you will be able to:

➤ Use the Computer Management tools to document system information

➤ Collect necessary printouts and documents for your CIF

Estimated completion time: **30 minutes**

ACTIVITY

1. Work with the other students in your group and use WordPad or your choice of word-processing software to design and create a Computer and Network Information form that includes spaces for the following. (Other information can be added at the discretion of your instructor.)

  ▪ OS name, version, and manufacturer

- System manufacturer, model, type, and name
- Processor type and speed
- BIOS version
- Location of Windows directory (include drive letter, disk number, and partition number)
- Total physical and virtual memory
- Page file space
- Any available ports and expansion capability, such as empty memory slots and disk bays
- Network adapter and driver software
- Protocols in use
- TCP/IP address, subnet mask, and gateway
- Network services and clients loaded

2. Use WordPad or your choice of word-processing software to create a Server Backup form that can be used to document backup procedures. This form should include space for the following:
   - Computer/server name and location
   - Type of backup to be performed each day of the week, along with the name of the user responsible for backup
   - Description of the tape rotation procedure—include any off-site storage sites and disaster recovery plan

3. Use WordPad or your choice of word-processing software to create a Users and Groups form that contains the following information:
   - User full name, logon name, and level of access for each user
   - Group name, purpose, and membership information for each group

4. Use WordPad or your choice of word-processing software to create a Local Folder Security form that can be used to record permissions for each secured folder on the local computer. The form should include space for the following information. (Other information can be added at the discretion of your instructor.)
   - Drive and path to the secured folder
   - Typical and maximum size of shared folder
   - A section to record user and group permissions and inherited permissions in the folder
   - A section to record user and group permissions assigned to the folder

5. Use WordPad or your choice of word-processing software to create a Shared Folder form that can be used to document information about each shared folder. The form should include space for the following information. (Other information can be added at the discretion of your instructor.)
   - Share name of folder
   - Computer hosting the folder
   - Drive and path to the shared folder

15

- Typical and maximum size of shared folder
- User and group shared permissions assigned to folder

6. Use WordPad or your choice of word-processing software to create a Maintenance form that includes the following:
   - Computer identification information
   - Frequency of maintenance
   - Date of maintenance activity
   - Maintenance checklist that includes a minimum of the following items:
     - Display cleaning
     - Fan and mechanical checkout
     - Memory test
     - Disk scanning and defragmentation status
     - Warning messages
     - Network status
   - Space to document any new hardware installations, including device manufacturer, model, and configuration
   - Space to include the date, identification, and location of any service pack or upgrade applied to the system

7. Use WordPad or your choice of word-processing software to create an Application Software form that includes the following:
   - Application name and date of installation
   - License information
   - Location of software files

8. Use WordPad or your choice of word-processing software to create a Service Support Contact form that includes space for the names of support providers, phone numbers, e-mail addresses, Web URLs, and comments.

9. Use WordPad or your choice of word-processing software to create a Problem and Solution form that includes space for the following:
   - Date problem occurred
   - Description of problem
   - Description of each problem resolution attempt, along with results of that attempt

10. Use WordPad or your choice of word-processing software to create a Computer Information File heading page that provides space for the computer's name and location, along with a checklist for all forms and other items such as manuals, software copies, and licenses that are included in the computer's information file.

11. Print out and assemble the forms you've created in Steps 1 through 10. You will be using them to complete the labs in this chapter.

12. To collect information from each computer to be used in a CIF, you will be using the System Information tool.

   a. Click **Start**, **All Programs**, **Accessories**, **System Tools**, **System Information** to open the System Information window as shown in Figure 15-1.

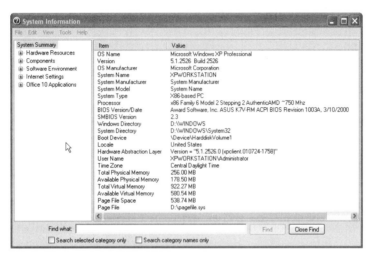

Figure 15-1 Accessing the system information

   b. Expand the four dependents of the **System Summary** entry in the left-side pane—that is, **Hardware Resources**, **Components**, **Software Environment**, and **Internet Settings**—by clicking the boxed plus sign to the left of each unexpanded node.

   c. Take the time to expand and select each item within the resulting node hierarchy. As you view each page of data, consider the value of this data for future troubleshooting and decide whether to print or save the information.

   d. To save the entire database of information, highlight **System Summary** by clicking on it.

   e. Click the **File** menu, and then click **Export** to save the file to your **My Documents** folder. Use **<Computername>-sysinfo.txt** as the File name.

   f. Navigate to your **My Documents** folder, and double-click **<Computername>-sysinfo.txt.** As you can see, a lot of information is present in the file. To selectively export information, highlight the specific area in the Information Tool, such as **Components/Network/Adapter**, and then export this to a file.

   g. Windows XP also keeps a history of changes made to your system. Click the **View** menu, **System History** option.

   h. Export the entire contents to your **My Documents** folder with a file name of **<Computername>-syshist.txt.** Open this file and view the results.

15

    i. The System Information Tool also allows you to remotely view and document other computers. Click the **View** menu, **Remote Computer** option. Click the **Remote Computer on the Network** option, and type in your partner's computer name. Click **OK** to connect to his system. Take a moment to explore that system.

    j. System Information also provides shortcuts to a number of diagnostic tools. Click the **Tools** menu, and review the options presented.

    k. Click **Net Diagnostics**, and then click **Scan your system**. Expand the various results to view that status of your system. Take special note of any failed messages and try to determine their cause. Click the **Save to File** button near the top of the document. Take note of the location of the file, and then close Network Diagnostics.

    l. Close the System Information window to return to the desktop.

LAB 15.2 TROUBLESHOOTING NETWORK PROBLEMS

Objective

In this lab, you will work with a partner to practice using the Computer Information File along with troubleshooting techniques to solve some common network problems. To do this, the lab is broken down into three activities. In Activity 1, you will set up and document a simple network environment for the Wiggerts and Son Heating Company. In Activity 2, you will create a "typical" network problem on your system to simulate the client's problem, and then fill out a Problem and Solution form reporting the trouble. In Activity 3, you will act as the Computer Technology Services support specialist and attempt to solve the problem on your lab partner's computer. After completing this lab, you will be able to:

➤ Set up a simple network environment that includes a shared folder, printer, and several users

➤ Identify common network problems and then "bug" your system by including one of these problems

➤ Using troubleshooting techniques and tools to identify and solve a common network problem

Requirements

➤ To simulate printer problems, you should have access to the Windows XP Professional CD or other source of printer drivers.

➤ A lab partner to work with to troubleshoot network problems

➤ An IP address that you can use to communicate with your partner's computer; If using a manually assigned IP address, record the IP address information here:

IP address: ...

Mask: ...

➤ A second IP address you can use to create an IP address conflict:

Conflicting IP address: ...

Mask: ...

> Estimated completion time: **30 minutes**

ACTIVITY 1

The Wiggerts and Son Heating Company based in Duluth, Minnesota, has been a supplier of specialized furnace parts and accessories since 1982. They have been using a Unix-based central computer system to perform all business-processing needs, but now want to implement a small peer-to-peer Windows XP network in their office located in your city. There are three sales representatives and an administrative assistant who will have Windows XP Professional systems. The three sales representatives need access to shared customer files and price quotations located on the administrative assistant's computer. Although the sales representatives will need to be able to create and modify their own files, they should be able to read only files created by other sales representatives. The administrative assistant will need to have rights to modify or delete any of the shared files. The printer attached to the administrative assistant's computer will be shared by all users, but controlled only by the administrative assistant. In this activity, you will establish the Wiggerts and Son network system, and then use the forms you developed in Lab 15.1 to document the system.

15

1. If necessary, start your computer with Windows XP, and log on as an administrator.

2. Using the techniques you learned in Chapter 5, create the following user accounts by supplying your own user names and passwords. Use the Users and Groups MCC that you created in Lab 5.
   - Create user accounts for the three sales representatives and an administrative assistant.
   - Create a power user account named **PowerMan**.

3. Create a **Customers** folder and **Shared** folder on your NTFS drive. In each folder, create a sub-folder called **Quotes**.

4. According to the scenario, the shared laser printer for the sales office is to be located on the administrative assistant's computer. In this step, use what you learned in Chapter 9 to simulate the shared laser printer by creating and sharing a printer named SalesLaser on your computer.

5. Create the necessary groups, and provide the following NTFS permissions to the groups:
   - Give the Users group Read, Execute, and List folder permissions to Customers and Shared. Be sure that the group named Users inherits these permissions in the Quotes folder.
   - Give the Sales representatives group Modify and Write permissions to both the Quotes and Shared folders.
   - Give the Administrative assistant user Full Control to the Customers and Shared folders.
   - Give the Sales representatives group basic printer permissions to the shared printer.

6. Using what you learned in Chapter 4, share the Shared and Customers folders with the Everyone group that has all shared permissions.

7. Remove the group Everyone from the SalesLaser printer permission, and include the sales representatives group you created in Step 5.

8. Using what you learned in Chapter 7, remove all protocols except TCP/IP. Assign the IP address and Mask information recorded in the Requirements section.

9. Assemble all your forms and any other documents relevant to your computer, and fill in a Computer Information heading sheet for your computer. You will use some of these forms to complete the remaining steps in this lab.

10. Use the Computer Management tools, along with My Computer and My Network Places, to fill in the Computer and Network Information form you created in Lab 15.1.

11. Use the User and Groups form you created in Lab 15.1, and document the users and groups for the Wiggerts and Son network.

12. Use the Shared Folder form to document your shared folders and permissions.

13. Use the Backup Schedule form to document a backup procedure to be used by the administrative assistant.

14. Use the Backup program described in Chapter 14 to backup the system state files. Record the backup activity on your Backup Schedule form.

15. Fill out a Service Support Provider form, showing yourself and Computer Technology Services as service providers.

ACTIVITY 2

One of the most challenging tasks is to simulate computer problems. Often, during an attempt to simulate a problem, you can learn more about the operation of the system than you would by fixing the problem. In this activity, you will select one, or at most, two, of the following "bugs" and then attempt to simulate them in your network system. Although steps are provided to help you implement the problem, you might want to carefully experiment with other ways you can make your computer "misbehave" in the prescribed manner. After you have successfully implemented the problem, you will then fill out a Problem and Solution form describing the symptom(s) of your problem for your partner, who then will act as the computer technician and attempt to fix the problem in Activity 3.

1. Sometimes adding new hardware to a computer or changing hardware configurations can cause an interrupt or memory resource conflict with the LAN card. When this occurs, the LAN connection is removed from My Network Connections window. Follow the steps below to simulate a problem where new hardware added to one of the sales representative's computers causes a conflict of resources with the LAN card.

This procedure may not be possible if the card is integrated into the motherboard or automatically configured by the Plug and Play BIOS.

a. Right-click **My Network Places**, and click **Properties**.
b. Right-click **Local Area Connection**, and click **Properties**.
c. Under the Connect using text box, click the **Configure** button to display the network card driver properties.
d. Click the **Resources** tab, and click to remove the check mark from the **Use automatic setting** check box.
e. Record the existing settings on your Computer and Network Information form.
f. If your network card allows, click either the Interrupt Request or Input/Output range resource, and click the **Change Setting** button.
g. If possible, select a value that shows a conflict with another device.
h. Click **OK**, and click **Yes** to continue using the conflicting resource.
i. Restart your computer, and document the error condition on your Problem and Solution form.

2. When IP addresses are assigned manually, adding a new device to the network with the same IP address as one of the existing computers can disable that computer's communication. The computer's communication can also be disabled if the TCP/IP protocol is accidentally disabled. Follow the steps below to simulate a network problem by either disabling the TCP/IP protocol or changing the IP address to one that conflicts with another computer on the network.

15

    a. To create a conflicting IP address, follow these steps:
- Right-click **My Network Places**, and click **Properties**.
- Right-click **Local Area Connection**, and click **Properties**.
- Click the **Internet Protocol (TCP/IP)** component, and click the **Properties** button.
- Enter the conflicting IP address you identified in the Requirements section.
- Click **OK** twice, and click **OK** to respond to the IP conflict warning message.
- Close the Network Connections window.
- Identify and record the problem on your Problem and Solution form.

    b. Follow these steps to disable the TCP/IP protocol:
- Right-click **My Network Places**, and click **Properties**.
- Right-click **Local Area Connection**, and click **Properties**.
- Click to remove the check mark from the **Internet Protocol (TCP/IP)** component.
- Click **OK**, and respond with **Yes** to the Do you want to disable these components warning.
- Close the Network Connections window.
- Identify and record the problem on your Problem and Solution form.

3. When setting up new computers, or when changing IP configurations, communication between computers can be disrupted either through physical cabling problems or incorrect network addressing. It can sometimes be difficult to distinguish between a cable problem and network address problem because in both cases the computer cannot communicate to other devices. Select one of the following problems to simulate a situation at the Wiggerts and Son network where a newly installed sales representative's computer is unable to communicate on the network.

    a. Follow the steps below to select a different network address or mask:
- Right-click **My Network Places**, and click **Properties**.
- Right-click **Local Area Connection**, and click **Properties**.
- Click the **Internet Protocol (TCP/IP)** component, and click the **Properties** button.
- Record the existing IP address information on your Computer and Network Information form.
- Change either the first number in the IP address, or in the network mask.
- Click **OK** twice, and then close the Network and Connections window.
- Identify and record the problem on your Problem and Solution form.

    b. Disconnect the network cable and restart. Identify and record the problem on your Problem and Solution form.

4. Users will not be able to connect to a network printer and send output if they do not have access permissions, or if the print server is not operating. To simulate a problem where one of the sales representatives is unable to print documents, do one of the following:

  a. Follow the steps below to stop the print server:
    - Open **Control Panel**, and double-click **Administrative Tools**.
    - Double-click **Services**.
    - Scroll down, and right-click the **Print Spooler** service.
    - Click **Stop**.
    - Attempt to access the printer from your computer or your partner's computer, and identify and record the problem on your Problem and Solution form.
    - Using the above steps, restart the Print Spooler.

  b. Follow the steps below to remove the sales rep user from the group you created in Activity 1:
    - Open the **Local Users and Groups Management** MCC.
    - Double-click the **Groups** folder to display all group names in the right-side results pane.
    - In the right-side results pane, double-click the sales representatives group.
    - Click the member to be removed, and then click the **Remove** button.
    - Click **OK**, and close the Local Users and Groups window. Click **No** to save the console.
    - Log on as the sales representative user, and attempt to access the SalesLaser shared printer from your computer or your partner's computer.
    - Identify and record the problem on your Problem and Solution form.

5. Garbled output on a printer can be caused by a defective print device, an incorrect printer language setting, a bad cable, or an incorrect printer driver. In this step, you attempt to generate garbled output on the printer attached to your computer by either changing the printer driver or using the wrong language by sending an incorrect separator page. For example, send a Postscript separator page if you have a PCL print device, or send a PCL separator page to a Postscript print device. Follow the steps below to change either your printer driver or separator page.

  a. Click **Start**, **Printers and Faxes** to open the Printers and Faxes window.

  b. Right-click your **SalesLaser** shared printer, and click **Properties**.

  c. Click the **Advanced** tab.

  d. Follow the steps below to change your printer driver:
    - Click the **New Driver** button, and click **Next** to start the driver wizard.
    - Highlight an incorrect driver by selecting a driver for a different printer of similar type. (You might need to experiment with a few different drivers to obtain the desired garbled output.)
    - Click **Next**, and then click **Finish**.
    - If necessary, insert the CD or provide a path to the selected driver.

15

- After the new driver files are copied to your computer, click **OK** to return to the Printers window.

e. If you have a printer that supports multiple languages, follow the steps below to send an incorrect separator page:

- Click the **Separator Page** button to display the Separator Page dialog box.
- Click the **Browse** button, and, if necessary, navigate to the **WINDOWS\ system32** folder on your Windows XP operating system drive.
- If the printer attached to your computer is set for PCL language, double-click the **pscript.sep** file. If the printer is set for Postscript language, double-click the **pcl.sep** file.
- Click **OK** to save your separator page, and return to the printer properties window.
- Click **OK** to return to the Printers and Faxes window.

f. Close the Printers and Faxes window.

6. Boot errors can often be caused by an incorrect partition number in the boot.ini file, or by missing or corrupt loader or kernel software. Simulate a boot problem that prevents the system from starting by performing one of the following (Step 6a, 6b, or 6c):

a. Follow the steps below to modify the partition number in the boot.ini file:

- Use My Computer or Windows Explorer to open the C: drive window.
- Right-click the **boot.ini** file, and **Open** it with Notepad.
- Follow the instructions from Chapter 13 to increase the partition number of the Windows XP operating system by one.
- Save the file and exit Notepad.
- Restart your computer.
- Identify and record the problem on your Problem and Solution form.

b. Follow the steps below to rename the NTLDR or NTDETECT.COM programs. (Be sure you have an operational Windows XP Professional boot disk such as the one you created in Chapter 13.)

- Use My Computer or Windows Explorer to open a window to the root of your C: drive.
- Right-click either the **NTLDR** or **NTDETECT.COM** program, and rename it using the extension **.BUG**.
- Press **Enter** to save the new name.
- Restart your computer.
- Identify and record the problem on your Problem and Solution form.

c. To simulate a corrupted operating system kernel, follow the steps below to rename the kernel program ntoskrnl.exe.

- Use My Computer or Windows Explorer to open a window to the WINDOWS\system32 folder of your Windows XP operating system drive.
- Locate the ntoskrnl.exe file, and rename it **ntoskrnl.bug**.

- Open the **dllcache** folder.
- Locate the ntoskrnl.exe file, and rename it **ntoskrnl.bug**.
- Close all windows, and restart your computer.
- Identify and record the problem on your Problem and Solution form.

7. Incorrect permissions or conflicting permission assignments are often the cause of users being unable to perform certain network actions. In this step, you prevent one of the sales rep users from accessing files in the Quotes folder by setting up one of the following permission problems.

a. Provide the sales representative group with only the Read shared permissions to the Customers folder.

b. When a group is denied access to a resource, all members of that group also have no access, regardless of what other permissions that group or the members of that group might be assigned. This can sometimes cause a problem if you attempt to secure a resource by denying access to a group. For example, in this step, you simulate an access problem caused when the administrative assistant attempts to increase security by adding the group Everyone to the permissions list of the Customers folder.

c. Another permissions problem can be caused accidentally by preventing a subfolder from inheriting rights from its parent. For example, in this step, you simulate an access problem caused by preventing the Quotes folder from inheriting rights from its parent Customers folder.

- Use My Computer or Windows Explorer to open the **Customers** folder.
- Right-click the **Quotes** folder, and click **Properties**.
- Click the **Security** tab, and record or verify the permission assignments in the inherited permissions section of your Local Folder Security form.
- Click **Advanced**, and then remove the check mark from the **Inherit from parent the permission entries that apply to child objects. Include these with entries explicitly defined here** box.
- Click the **Remove** button to remove the inherited permissions, and keep only the permissions explicitly specified.
- Click **OK**, and then click **Yes** on the Security box. If necessary, modify the assigned permissions section of your Local Folder Security form to only include those users and groups appearing in the Quotes Properties window.
- Click **OK** to save your changes, and return to the Customers folder window.
- Attempt to access the Quotes folder.
- If you made the permission assignments specified in Step 5 of Activity 2, only users in the sales representatives group will be able to access the Quotes folder. All other users, including the administrator, will be denied access.
- Identify and record the problem on your Problem and Solution form.

15

ACTIVITY 3

In this activity you are to move to your partner's computer, and, using only their Problem and Solution form, identify and correct the problem(s) created in Activity 2. After you have solved the problem(s), use the Problem and Solution form to record the solutions.

ACTIVITY 4

Repeat Activities 2 and 3 as time permits.

LAB 15.3 APPLYING SERVICE PACKS

Objective

Obtaining and applying service packs is a necessary part of maintaining operating system software. This can be accomplished using the Windows Update procedure or downloading service packs and installing them manually. After completing this lab, you will be able to:

➤ Use the Windows Update procedure to download and install the latest Windows XP service packs, critical updates, and updated drivers

➤ Manually download and install a service pack or update

Requirements

➤ Access to the Internet to download a Windows XP service pack, or access to a downloaded service pack on your local network; If using an already downloaded service pack, record the network path to the service pack

Estimated completion time:	**40 minutes**

ACTIVITY

1. If necessary, start your computer with Windows XP, and log on as an administrator.

2. Download the service pack using Windows Update.
   a. If necessary, open a connection to the Internet.
   b. Click **Start**, **All Programs**, **Windows Update** to display the Windows Update window. Windows XP will automatically connect to the Microsoft Update Web Site. Note: You may be required to automatically install additional patches prior to or during the following procedures. Click **Yes** to all such requests.
   c. Click **Scan for Updates** to check for new updates. Windows XP will review your system and list critical fixes, updates, and device drivers under the Pick Updates to Install section. Critical updates usually are hot-fixes that have come out after the latest Service Pack. The Service Pack itself will be listed under Windows XP, and any updated drivers that are suggested for you system are under Driver Updates.
   d. Click on the three sections to see what has been found. Click the updates that you want to install, and click **Add.**
   e. Click **Review and Install Updates** to see your selected updates, and then click **Install Now** to begin the installation process.
   f. Click **Accept**, as necessary, to download and install the components you requested.
   g. You may be required to reboot your system after the updates. If not, click **View installation history** to display a history of installed components.
   h. Close the Windows Update window to return to the desktop.

3. Manually download a service pack or update.
   a. If necessary, open a connection to the Internet.
   b. Start **Internet Explorer**.
   c. Go to the ***http://www.microsoft.com/download*** site.
   d. Select **Windows XP Professional** as the product name and **Windows XP** as the operating system. Click **Find It** to display a list of available downloads.
   e. Click the service pack or update that you require. If another Web page is displayed, follow the instructions to open the download dialog box. Click **Save** when prompted, and choose a location to store the file. Click **Save** one more time to download the file.

15

4. Manually install a service pack or update.
   a. Close all applications and windows.
   b. Using My Computer or Windows Explorer, navigate to the folder where you stored the file in step 2.
   c. Double-click the file required (usually **Update.exe** for a service pack).
   d. Follow any prompts that appear.
   e. Restart your computer if instructed.

5. Verify service pack installation.